Democracy Owner's Manual

First Edition

The Voter Outreach and Training Enterprise of the United States of America

Kerry Power
Chairman & Editor in Chief

Bill Bartman
Associate Editor

Jane Power
Copy Editor

Kerry Power
Page Layout & Graphics

Ric Clark
Desktop Publishing Specialist

Patricia Brooks
Pre-Press Specialist

ACKNOWLEDGMENTS:

VOTE USA acknowledges and appreciates the assistance of the following people in the research and preparation of this manual: Special thanks to Gary Ruskin of Public Citizen's Congressional Accountability Project, – Chris McGinn of Public Citizen's-Congresswatch – Jackie Howell of Common Cause – Richard Kimball of the Center for National Independence in Politics – Lisa Davis of the Progressive Policy Institute – Drew Moss of United We Stand, America – Bill Watkins of the American-Center for Law and Justice – Martha Phillips of the Concord Coalition – Hon. Gail Shaffer, NY Secretary of State – Hon. Pauline Kezer, CT Secretary of State – Nicholas Butterworth of Rock the Vote – Rob Nelson of Lead or Leave – most glossary definitions are taken from The American Heritage Dictionary of the English Language, Third Edition (Houghton Mifflin Company) - DC cover photos c/o Photri, Inc. – state house & town hall cover photos by Jim Ferguson – I love USA, Supreme Court justices & Kennedy / Nixon debate photos c/o AP/World Wide Photos - all other photos c/o Photri, Inc.

To order additional publications, or to become a VOTE USA member, contact:
VOTE USA, Inc., 601 Pennsylvania Avenue NW, Suite 900, Washington, DC, 20004
Telephone (202) 626-3800   Fax (202) 626-3801   E-Mail vote@usa.net

The VOTE USA Democracy Owner's Manual
Table of Contents

UNITED WE STAND AMERICA
7616 LBJ Freeway, Suite 727
Dallas, Texas 75251

The VOTE USA Democracy Owner's Manual
Table of Contents

FOREWORD

Martin L. Gross

Author of "The Government Racket," "A Call for Revolution," and "The Tax Racket"

More than anytime in American history, the American voter is confused. He senses that all is not right in Washington, the statehouse, and his local government, but he does not fully understand what. The voter does know that he is dissatisfied, as never before. Polls indicate that while thirty years ago three-fourths of Americans felt Washington, for example, would do the right thing in any given circumstance, that support has now dropped to only twenty five percent of citizens.

There is a sense of unease that the economy — despite occasional rosy statistics — has undergone a structural change for the worse. And they are right. In 1995 The World Bank announced that America has dropped to 7th place in per capita income: $24,750 versus $36,000 for Switzerland and $32,000 for Japan. Our manufacturing wage, once first in the world at today's equivalent of $16 per hour, is now down to $12, some 30% behind Germany's, and dropping.

One Bureau of Labor Statistics fact explains the reason for much of the decline. It is the extraordinary growth of government in America. For the first time in the history of any Western democratic nation, there are more people working in government at all levels than in manufacturing. The numbers are self-explanatory: 19.2 million in government and only 18.4 in manufacturing, a five million shift toward government over the last decade alone.

"Does it make a difference?" we might ask. Yes, all the difference in the world, as government increasingly drains productivity and cash from the private sector to expend it on over a thousand programs, most of which we are ignorant of and do not want. The trend has been near continuous since World War II. In the 1920's, an affluent era, the federal government brought in an enormous surplus. During the Depression we were forced into deficit financing, but the so-called "big government" of FDR spent less than 10% of the GNP while it fed a large portion of the population. And all government in that era — federal, state, and local — cost only 17 cents of each dollar earned in the nation. Government in early postwar America, a period of unrivaled affluence in world history, was equally inexpensive.

Under Harry Truman the nation fought the Korean War, supported Europe through the Marshall Plan, and provided the GI Bill for 14 million returning veterans, the last piece of social legislation for the average American. (One, we might add, that was done without means tests.) Despite all this and a tax structure in which the average American paid only two percent of his income to Washington, Truman brought in a <u>surplus</u> of $16 billion from 1947-52, equal to over $200 billion today. The share of <u>all</u> government then was only 22 cents on the dollar. Contrast that with today, when government takes 40 cents on the dollar and delivers less to the burdened middle class than ever before.

Washington is, of course, the major villain, which is one reason for the ballot box revolution of 1994 that changed the control of Congress. Work to reduce the size of government has begun on both sides of the aisle, but the job may not be completed for more than a decade.

The states and localities have overburdened us as well. Look at just one statistic: the cost of state and local government has risen 350 percent in <u>real</u> dollars just since 1960.

Little wonder Americans are confused, and angry, and frustrated. What can they do? First — and second — and third — they must learn how their democracy works at all levels. By understanding that, they can then learn how it fails them and how to correct it. Only an educated electorate can change what must be changed if America is to survive as the great democracy of the world.

Americans are dissatisfied with the political class, especially Congress, which ranks near the bottom of all professions in opinion polls. Yet they returned over 90 percent of incumbent members to Congress in the last two elections. The problem is the disassociation of our representative system from the needs of the average American. What once worked no longer does. The intervention of enormous campaign chests, lobbyists, and special interests has made Abraham Lincoln's motto "of the people, for the people, and by the people" hollow. In the last presidential election year (1992) over one <u>billion</u> dollars was spent electing just federal officers, prompting the feeling that elections in America today are not won, but bought.

Americans are frustrated by the political class promises of smaller government that have not taken place yet. They see the deficit fall — temporarily — only through ever larger taxes. What was once "for the people" government in America is now for those who have the skill to tap into the federal and state treasuries, whether bureaucrats, businesses, farmers, or unwed mothers. Welfare, which is falsely considered only a small part of our costs, has now exploded, says the Congressional Research Service. In 1995, it will eat up $384 billion a year, three-fourths of which is federal money. The rest is forced onto the shoulders of local government. No wonder property taxes in America have risen 10 percent a year, with no end in sight.

"By the people" is equally hollow. Only 24 states in the Union even have the right of direct democracy — the Initiative — in which voters can place bills on the ballot without yielding to the whims of the political class. Third parties and independents are penalized by election laws designed by the dominant two parties, neither of which is named in the Constitution.

Majority rule in federal elections exists only in one state, Georgia, where runoffs are required if no one truly wins. We are the only nation in the world that permits Presidents to be elected without over 50% of the vote. Our Electoral College System, designed for an earlier era, permits a president to be elected with a 43% vote, or less, along with Governors who lose elections by not receiving a majority, and yet are seated in statehouses.

Americans rightly revere their Constitution, but they do not understand its powers and how to make current government adhere to its dictates. This is especially true of the 10th Amendment of the Bill of Rights, written by Madison to protect us from what he rightly feared could become the "oligarchy" of Washington. Briefly put, it restrains the Federal government from taking total power at the expense of the states and people. Americans must learn how to use that Constitution to maintain their freedom.

Citizens feel not only confused but disenfranchised. To run for office requires a party machine able to raise enormous sums of money and garner an unrealistic number of petitioners. Only Ohio has a law "of the people," requiring only 50 signatures to get one's name placed on the primary ballot for Congress.

Not only is all not well in American government, but those in the political class insist on maintaining power even when the people do not want them. Citizens in 22 states with the Initiative have voted for term limits by a two-thirds majority. Yet politicians continue to fight term limits in the courts; and despite their promises, members of Congress recently defeated a term limits bill in a determined effort to block government "by the people." It seems that they much prefer a system of perks, pork, PAC's, and lobbyists, rather than to answer to the needs of the American voter.

Can it all be changed? Can America return to the primary role in democracy and economics that it has historically had? The answer is <u>Yes if</u> — if the American people learn the intimate details of the operation of our now mismanaged and misguided government, at all levels, and become defenders of our democracy, willing to make the underlying changes needed. It is not a partisan effort for liberals or conservatives, but one for all Americans.

This VOTE USA Democracy Owner's Manual is an excellent first step. It is my opinion that the bulk of this book is supporting material for the first chapter, "American Patriotism Defined," and the last chapter, "The 12 Steps to Political Recovery." For this reason I suggest that these chapters be read first, as they offer an enlightened perspective from which to view the remainder of the book.

Socrates has told us that the worst of all evils is ignorance. If we continue to be unknowing about the most important factor in our future — our government — then we must continue to yield the fate of our lives to others.

No one wants that, and no one need succumb to that easy fatalism. Instead, we must learn, survive, and become masters of our own destiny as Americans.

The choice is ours.

CHAPTER 1

AMERICAN PATRIOTISM DEFINED

by Mr. Kerry Power
Editor in Chief – VOTE USA

GLOSSARY
for American Patriotism Defined

Alienated
1. To cause to become unfriendly or hostile
2. To cause to become withdrawn or unresponsive – isolate or dissociate emotionally

Amuck
1. In a frenzy to do violence or kill..
2. In or into a jumbled or confused state.

Apathetic
1. Feeling or showing a lack of interest or concern, especially regarding matters of general importance or appeal; indifferent.
2. Feeling or showing little or no emotion or feeling; unresponsive.

Aristocracy
1. A hereditary ruling class; nobility.
2. Government by a ruling class.
3. Government by the citizens deemed to be best qualified to lead.
4. A group or class considered superior to others.

Authoritarian
1. Characterized by or favoring absolute obedience to authority, as against individual freedom: an authoritarian regime.
2. Of, relating to, or expecting unquestioning obedience.

Big Brother
1. An omnipresent, seemingly benevolent figure representing the oppressive control over individual lives exerted by an authoritarian government.
2. A character in the novel Nineteen Eighty-Four by George Orwell.

Civil Rights
1. The rights belonging to an individual by virtue of citizenship, especially the fundamental freedoms and privileges guaranteed by the 13th and 14th Amendments to the U.S. Constitution and by subsequent acts of Congress.
2. Of or relating to a political movement, especially during the 1950's and 1960's, devoted to securing equal opportunity and treatment for members of minority groups.

Communism/Communist
1. A system of government in which the state plans and controls the economy and a single, often authoritarian party holds power, claiming to make progress toward a higher social order in which all goods are equally shared by the people.

Complaisence
1. The inclination to comply willingly with the wishes of others.

Coup d'é·tat
1. The sudden overthrow of a government by a usually small group of persons in or previously in positions of authority.

Ethical/Unethical
1. "Ethical" relates to or deals with in accordance with a set of values based on the accepted principles of right and wrong and the moral virtues of hard work and diligence.
2. "Unethical" would be the opposite of "Ethical," often used to describe behavior that takes immediate advantage of any circumstance of possible benefit.

Exploit
1. To selfishly or unethically make use of another person or group.
2. To employ to the greatest possible advantage.

Extraneous
1. Not constituting a vital element or part.
2. Inessential or unrelated to the topic or matter at hand; irrelevant.
3. Coming from the outside

Fascist
1. Relating to a government marked by centralization of authority under a dictator, stringent socioeconomic controls, suppression of the opposition through terror and censorship, and typically a policy of belligerent nationalism and racism.
2. A reactionary or dictatorial person.

Great Depression
1. The severe U.S. economic crisis of the 1930s, supposedly precipitated by the 1929 stock market crash. At the depth (1933) of the Depression, one third of the labor force (16 million people) were unemployed.

Ideology/Ideologies
1. The body of ideas reflecting the social needs and aspirations of an individual, a group, a class, or a culture.
2. A set of doctrines or beliefs that form the basis of a political, economic, or other system.

Malthus, Thomas Robert
1. British economist (1766-1834) who wrote An Essay on the Principle of Population (1798), arguing that population tends to increase faster than food supply, with inevitably disastrous results, unless the increase in population is checked by moral restraints or by war, famine, and disease.

Marx, Karl
1. German philosopher, economist, and revolutionary (1818-1883). Co-wrote The Communist Manifesto (1848) and Das Kapital (1867-1894) with Friedrich Engels.

Orwell, George
1. Pen name of Eric Arthur Blair (1903-1950). British writer whose imaginative fiction attacks totalitarianism and reflects his concern with social justice. His works include Animal Farm (1945) and 1984 (1949).

Parliament
1. A national representative body having supreme legislative powers within the state.
2. Parliament. The national legislature of various countries, especially that of the United Kingdom, made up of the House of Lords and the House of Commons.

Preamble
1. A preliminary statement, especially the introduction to a formal document that serves to explain its purpose.

Proactive
1. Acting in advance to deal with an expected difficulty; anticipatory: not reactive.

this glossary is continued on page 12

AMERICAN PATRIOTISM DEFINED

Kerry Power

Editor in Chief - VOTE USA

"Patriotism is easy to understand in America; it means looking out for yourself by looking out for your country"
— *Calvin Coolidge*

In this chapter I will make my best attempt at fully defining the word patriotism, and the concept of American patriotism. For me, this is a highly challenging and emotional undertaking. Much of what is written in this chapter will reflect my personal opinions and my personal views. It is a composite of my experience in trying to understand, define, and mediate the many different views that make up our highly diverse culture. The predominant problem in American society has often arisen from the different definitions and understandings of words such as patriotism, liberal, conservative, left wing, right wing, etc. These are interesting words, as they often have as many different meanings as people that are asked to define them. Too often, these words are used to denigrate and denounce the opinions of others. People who don't want to be bothered with facts and who are resistant to learning or changing their opinions, will often use these terms to "label" those with opinions different from their own. All too often, when these words are used as labels they will not reflect their true meaning, or they will be used improperly, out of context, to ridicule or insult people, to create divisiveness and disharmony, or to discredit the arguments of others. This behavior, of course, makes for a divided culture that is filled with resentments, prejudices, and separatism. This is hardly an atmosphere that is conducive to a healthy democracy, a healthy society, or any kind of intelligent debate. A formula that I use in conversation as a "rule of thumb" is this; when the name-calling starts, the intelligent debate has ended. Therefore, before people can begin to discuss issues in a meaningful way they must first agree on definitions for the words that will be used in their debates. This will help to create a national atmosphere of mutual understanding, respect, intelligent discourse, and active patriotism. This is my mission in this chapter, in this book, and in my life.

PATRIOTISM

Webster's Dictionary of the English Language defines the word "patriotism" very simply: zealous love of one's country. Webster's also defines the word "patriot" as "a person who loves his native country and will do all he can for it." The famous nineteenth century American author and editor George William Curtis further defines patriotism by writing: "a man's country is not a certain area of land, of mountains, rivers, woods, but it is a principle, and patriotism is loyalty to that principle." This is why the thousands of Americans who have fought and died in foreign wars are referred to as patriots; because they were willing to do all they could do to defend the principles of their country, including leaving their family, risking their life, and even dying if necessary. This, of course, is the most extreme example of patriotic loyalty and national devotion. However, patriotism can be found whenever people gives of themselves to their country, making sacrifices of time and resources, going out of their way to improve their community, their state, or their nation, and is at all times willing to do all that they can do to defend and uphold the country's principles. This is what defines a patriot, and creates the distinction between a patriot and a citizen.

AMERICAN PATRIOTISM

Here in the United States of America, the principles that make our country unique are certainly worth the zealous love, devotion, and loyalty that defines the word "patriot." In the US, it is our principles that originally set us apart from all other forms of government, and caused the US to become the most prosperous, most free, most creative, and most diverse nation in the world. These principles are very clearly and simply defined in the documents that founded this nation.

The Declaration of Independence states that people are entitled to a separate and equal station to which the Laws of Nature and of Nature's God entitle them, and that "We hold these truths to be self evident, that all Men are created equal, that they are endowed by their Creator with certain unalienable rights, that among these are Life, Liberty and the pursuit of Happiness." From these statements, we can derive the principles that one must be devoted to in order to be considered an American Patriot:

1) Equal Opportunity

The "separate and equal station" and "all Men are created equal" statements in the Declaration of Independence define the belief that no person should be considered superior, or granted special status, position, or economic standing, based solely on his or her heredity, beliefs, or affiliations.

2) Rights to a Free and Happy Life

The "unalienable rights" of "Life, Liberty and the pursuit of Happiness" statement in the Declaration of Independence defines the belief that people are entitled to, by divine rights, a happy life of their own choosing. Webster's defines the word "Life" (used in this context) as "a way or manner of existence." Webster's defines "Liberty" as "the condition of being free to choose, esp. as between ways of acting or living, with an implication of wisdom and voluntary restraint / the right to do as one pleases." Webster's defines "Happiness" as "feelings of joy and pleasure mingled in varying degree."

These are the basic principles that make up the foundations of our nation. They form the basis of the belief system that defines an American patriot. Therefore, every American citizen who wishes to be an American Patriot, must love his or her country and the principles that make it unique, and do everything possible to ensure that everyone in these United States has an equal opportunity to live a free and happy life.

BECOMING AN AMERICAN PATRIOT

People who are born in the United States are automatically entitled to all of the rights of citizenship, regardless of whether they love their country or not. Citizens don't need to know anything about the founding principles of the country to enjoy the benefits of citizenship. They are not required by any law to personally ensure that everyone in their sight has an equal opportunity to live a free and happy life. The rights of Freedom and Liberty provide US citizens the right to be ignorant, or apathetic, or selfish, or greedy, or hateful, or all of the above, and they are still entitled to all the social benefits that are granted to every other citizen (these rights, of course, are limited when they interfere with the rights of others). The founding fathers of this country believed that true patriotism could not be mandated, it had to be voluntary. They believed that the basic goodness of mankind would be naturally drawn to patriotic behavior, and that the people of good moral character and conscience would always greatly outnumber the society's parasites. They felt sure that the majority of people would become knowledgeable about the workings of their government, get involved with the actions of their elected representatives, and assist in the progress of their fellow countrymen. By doing so, any American citizen can rise to the highly respected stature of an American Patriot.

To help those who seek to be American Patriots, the founding fathers outlined a system that would make the utopian ideals of the Declaration of Independence possible. They outlined this system in language that could be easily understood by any citizen, in simple terms, so the basic meanings could not be misinterpreted or misconstrued. This set of instructions became the Constitution of the United States. The preamble to the US Constitution outlined a more complete set of principles for the American Patriots to adhere to in their everyday lives. The preamble declares that: "We the People of the United States, in Order to form a more perfect Union, establish Justice, insure domestic Tranquillity, provide for the common defence, promote the general Welfare, and secure the Blessings of Liberty to ourselves and our Posterity, do ordain and establish this Constitution of the United States of America." By dissecting this preamble, with the help of Webster's Dictionary of the English Language, we define the principles that made the United States the envy of the world:

1) Form a More Perfect Union

Webster's defines the word Form, in this context, as "molding by instruction or discipline." Webster's defines the word Perfect, in this context, as "complete or correct in every way, conforming to a standard or ideal with no omissions, errors, flaws or extraneous elements." Webster's defines the word Union, in this context, as "a grouping of states, political groups, etc. for some specific purpose / unity and harmony."

Therefore, the American Patriot strives for perfection in promoting unity and harmony during the continued formation of the United States of America, conforming to the instructions set forth by its Constitution, with no omissions or extraneous elements, until it is complete in every way without errors or flaws.

2) Establish Justice

Webster's defines the word Justice, in this context, as "behavior to oneself or to another which is strictly in accord with currently accepted ethical law or as decreed by legal authority."

Therefore, the American Patriot will make sure that the rights of citizens to do as they please are not abused, and that no interference is caused with others' rights to live in freedom, harmony and happiness.

3) Promote the General Welfare

Webster's defines the word General, in this context, as "pertaining to a whole or to most of its parts, not particular, not local / prevalent, widespread." Webster's defines the word Welfare, in this context, as "a state of being healthy, happy, and free from want / organized work to promote this state in the members of a community who need to be helped."

Therefore, the American Patriot will make certain that most, if not all, of the United States' citizens are healthy, happy, and free from want, and will participate in organized work to promote this state in the members of any community who need to be helped.

4) Provide for the Common Defence

Webster's defines the word Common, in this context, as "belonging or relating to the public and owned or shared by all members of a group (in this case, all the states of the union)." Webster's defines the word Defence (modern spelling: Defense), in this context, as "the act of resisting attack / preparation to meet attack / something which defends."

Therefore, the American Patriot will make certain that the United States is prepared to resist an attack from abroad or from within, by means that are owned and shared by the public.

5) Insure Domestic Tranquillity

Webster's defines the word Insure, in this context, as "to make certain of getting or achieving." Webster's defines the word Domestic, in this context, as "one's own country, not foreign." Webster's defines the word Tranquillity, in this context, as "peaceful and free from agitation (a disturbance, mental or physical, esp. worry / public disturbance on a large scale, or the process of creating it)."

Therefore, the American Patriot will focus on the United States first and foremost, to make certain that it is peaceful and free from any public disturbance on a large scale, and is free from any mental or physical worry.

6) Secure the Blessings of Liberty to Ourselves and our Posterity

Webster's defines the word Secure, in this context, as "to make completely safe against injury or loss." Webster's defines the word Blessings, in this context, as "good fortune or to be enriched." Webster's defines the word Liberty, in this context, as "the condition of being free to choose, esp. as between ways of acting or living, with an implication of wisdom and voluntary restraint / the right to do as one pleases." Webster's defines the word Posterity, in this context, as "generations not yet born."

Therefore, the American Patriot will always make sure that the good fortune with which we are now enriched as a result of our freedom of choice, is made completely safe so it will not be lost by us or be impaired for the generations not yet born.

BEING AN AMERICAN PATRIOT

By sincerely committing one's self to support, defend, and practice the principles outlined in the Constitution's preamble, one becomes an American Patriot. This seems simple enough until you start applying these principles to our modern American society. Using these principles as a baseline, it would seem that many of our elected representatives, and most of our citizenry, would do well to review our nation's founding document. Some will find the contrast between our principles and our current practices disturbing; others will argue that all is as it should be, and many will question whether changing our current system and pursuing the nation's founding ideals is realistic in our modern age. I merely ask that you read this chapter and the rest of this book, and determine for yourself which current trends and philosophies are patriotic and which are not. The patriots of 1776 were faced with the same questions when Thomas Jefferson

wrote, in the Declaration of Independence, "...all experience hath shown, that mankind are more disposed to suffer, while evils are sufferable, than to right themselves by abolishing the forms to which they are accustomed." The remainder of this chapter is devoted to comparing our nation's founding principles with our current national policies and practices. It is broken into six sections representing the six basic principles of the US Constitution. This should help you to better define the Patriot's role in today's modern society.

THE FOUNDING PRINCIPLES OF THE UNITED STATES OF AMERICA

1) Form a More Perfect Union

The American Patriot strives for perfection in promoting unity and harmony during the continued formation of the United States of America, conforming to the instructions set forth by its Constitution, with no omissions or extraneous elements, until it is complete in every way, without errors or flaws.

2) Establish Justice

The American Patriot will make sure that the rights of citizens to do as they please are not abused, and that no interference is caused with other's rights to live in freedom, harmony and happiness.

3) Promote the General Welfare

The American Patriot will make certain that most, if not all, of the United States' citizens are healthy, happy and free from want, and will participate in organized work to promote this state in the members of any community who need to be helped.

4) Provide for the Common Defence

The American Patriot will make certain that the United States is prepared to resist an attack from abroad, or from within, by means that are owned and shared by the public.

5) Insure Domestic Tranquillity

The American Patriot will focus on the United States, first and foremost, to make certain that it is peaceful and free from any public disturbance on a large scale, and is free from any mental or physical worry.

6) Secure the Blessings of Liberty to Ourselves and our Posterity

The American Patriot will always make sure that the good fortune that we are now enriched with, as a result of our freedom of choice, is made completely safe so it will not be lost by us, or be impaired for the generations not yet born.

FORM A MORE PERFECT UNION

Upon close examination you may find that many of today's social and economic problems are caused by the failure of the government, and the US citizenry, to follow the principles of the Constitution. Many Americans have never read it, don't realize the powers it offers to the public, and have allowed situations to develop that are against the founding principles of this nation. Upholding these principles is imperative to the proper functioning of our democracy. The United States of America was formed in 1776 as the greatest social experiment in history. That was the year that Thomas Jefferson's "Declaration of Independence" called for a government system that derives its power from the consent of the governed, and Adam Smith's "Wealth of Nations" called for a self-regulated "free market" economy. The British loyalists of America considered these concepts to be mad, ludicrous philosophies that could never work. But the free market produced technology and systems that offered an alternative to the drudgery of primitive life. The new government overcame the nation's most severe social imperfections such as slavery, genocide, anarchy, and discrimination. Through the years, the concept of a perfect society where all citizens have an equal opportunity to live a free and happy life has come closer and closer to becoming a reality. Yet even after all of America's monumental advances, there are still people who cling to the negative attitudes of the 18th century British Loyalists. They will defend the concept of a privileged ruling class, recite dozens of reasons why it is impossible to have a perfect society, and explain how we should make concessions that will help us to accept the flaws in our system. Ask yourself: how many of your fellow citizens strive to continuously perfect our society, and how many sheepishly accept its imperfections? How many of today's citizens accept our staggering crime rate, permanent poverty class, and progressive cultural decay as social norms, as not important enough to move them from their daily routine?

The founding fathers of our nation knew that a nation with lofty goals would excel far beyond those that don't have them. This concept is as ancient as mankind itself. Second-century Roman philosopher, Marcus Aurelius, once stated: "Our life is what our thoughts make it." William Shakespeare once wrote: "Our doubts are traitors, and make us lose the good we oft would win, by fearing to attempt." Albert Einstein once wrote: "Imagination is greater than knowledge." And a Yale university study proved the concept. By asking the members of the Yale class of '53 if they had a clear and specific set of goals written down, the researchers learned that only 3% of the class had such goals. Twenty years later, researchers followed-up with the Class of '53. To their amazement they found that the 3% who had specific goals, had achieved a financial worth that was greater than the rest of their graduating class combined. They also exhibited greater feelings of fulfillment, joy and happiness. This study serves as the most striking example of the impact that goal setting and optimism can have. History is full of sideline nay-sayers who proclaimed that America could never win against the British, that slavery would never be abolished, that man would never fly, that no one could run a mile in under four minutes, that polio and smallpox could never be cured, that man would never walk on the moon, and that the US will never achieve its goal of social perfection. My response to these naysayers is best summarized by the famous 19th century American poet John Greenleaf Whittier, who wrote; "For all sad words of tongue and pen, the saddest are these, 'it might have been'"

The primary founding principle of this nation calls for the continued pursuit of a perfect society until it is achieved. This is the principle that has historically made the US the most progressive, modern, innovative, and respected nation in the world.

ESTABLISH JUSTICE

There has been lot of debate regarding the government's role in the protection of people's rights to live in freedom, harmony, and happiness. Government systems used for insuring social justice include our criminal justice system, the regulation of industry, taxation of the privileged classes, and welfare programs for the disadvantaged classes. All of these systems were put into place to uphold the rights granted to citizens by the US Constitution. Yet 15% of our population lives in poverty, with no solution in sight, and violent crime has doubled over the past twenty years. The facts are clear: the system isn't working, and the Constitutional principle of establishing justice is not being met. Many people are frightened by the prospect of becoming the next crime statistic. Many inner city residents are frightened to leave their homes after dark, many women are frightened to travel alone, and our police are becoming so cautious and aggressive that they sometimes intimidate the citizens they are sworn to protect. The "punishment versus rehabilitation" debate makes for interesting conversation, but talk won't solve our crime problem. Most of those who "serve time" in our "correctional facilities" commit new crimes shortly after being released. The problem isn't that we don't punish severely enough or that we don't nurture and coddle our prisoners enough: the problem is that we live in an unjust society. Any social system that rewards criminal behavior *invites* criminal behavior. Any society that celebrates the successes of America's wild-west outlaws and urban gangsters invites criminal behavior. Any society that allows crooked politicians to fear only insignificant censures and pardons, while they profit from their violations, invites criminal behavior. Any society that allows stock market swindlers, tax cheats, and corrupt business people to receive short sentences, or maybe just a fine, while they profit from their crimes against the common people, invites criminal behavior. Any society that defends the privilege of wealthy industrialists to use their economic power to exploit the working classes invites criminal behavior. Most Americans are quite aware of these issues. They know that these scenarios are unjust and wrong. Some may joke about it, quipping that "I'd spend a year in jail if I knew I'd have a million dollars when I got out." Others will argue that "the whole system is crooked, right up to the President, and you just have to take what you can get, anyway you can get it." This insidious mind-set grows in a society like a cancer, until everyone loses faith in the system and in each other. Many turn to crime and unethical behavior, taking their cues from our national institutions and "taking what they can get, any way they can get it." Knowledge of criminal

6

activities in our nation's institutions help people to justify their welfare cheating, petty scams, larcenies, and exploitation of those unable to physically defend themselves.

The famous 18th century English essayist and poet, Joseph Addison, once wrote: "There is no greater sign of general decay of virtue in a nation, than want of zeal in its inhabitants for the good of their country." It is crucially important that "we the people" not only get involved in community watch groups and local police programs, but also get involved in rehabilitating our own behavior, in stamping out injustice at the highest levels, and in creating an environment that breeds mutual respect for our social system. The problem of social decay, and its associated crime, needs to be immediately and effectively addressed by all of our nation's citizens, as it is the most crippling violation of people's rights to live in freedom, harmony, and happiness.

PROMOTE THE GENERAL WELFARE

To make certain that most, if not all, of the United States' citizens are healthy, happy, and free from want, our government has instituted organized work to promote this state in the members of any community who need to be helped. Unfortunately, our current welfare system is not working. Many feel that this system merely consists of government handouts that perpetuate a permanent poverty class in the US. While most agree that handicapped and mentally ill people need such handouts, many feel that able-bodied people who are impoverished would be better served by "Workfare" programs that replace handouts with gainful employment. Conservative supporters of "Workfare" point to the highly successful WPA program (Works Progress Administration) that was implemented during the Great Depression, where people in need of help were put to work rebuilding our nation's infrastructure. Liberal supporters of "Workfare" feel that education, worker training, and child-care provisions,

should be added to any proposed "Workfare" program. Conservatives feel that these additions would add too much cost to the programs. Liberals feel that industry should foot the bill, as they will benefit from the newly trained workers. Conservatives warn that "liberal tax-and-spend policies" reduce jobs and ultimately cause more poverty. Liberals suggest that "conservative trickle-down policies" never reach the lower classes and ultimately cause more poverty. This debate will commonly escalate into shouting matches, including a lot of accusations, finger pointing, name calling, insults, and conflict. Meanwhile, America's welfare system goes unchanged.

The US Constitution's preamble calls for unity among the independent states of the American colonies. It also calls for unity and harmony among America's people. Yet many of today's citizens insist on bickering, arguing, and insulting each other, instead of debating their points intelligently and respectfully. Many people, when confronted with theories with which they don't immediately agree, will resort to name calling to denigrate the other person's point. The most popular names for this purpose are "Liberal" and "Conservative." These names are used to attach some kind of negative label on those who speak against the beliefs of the "name caller." People of either ideology will often accuse the other of "screwing-up a good thing" or "getting in the way of progress." This behavior, of course, makes for a divided culture that is filled with resentments, prejudices, and separatism; a perfect environment for those who would undermine the principles of our Constitution. The irony of this practice is that most of the "name callers" don't fully appreciate that both types of people are necessary for the proper functioning of any kind of advancing society.

Webster's defines a "Liberal" as "a person who holds liberal views" or "of or belonging to the Liberal Party." Webster's defines a "Conservative" as "a person of conservative disposition" or "a member of the Conservative Party."

PHILOSOPHICAL EQUILIBRIUM

Liberal

1. Giving freely, giving more than is necessary or usual.

2. Characterized by progressive attitudes.

3. Not subject to common prejudices or conventions (liberal minded).

4. Involving a general enlarging of the mind beyond the professional or technical (a liberal arts education)

Conservative

1. Tending or desiring to conserve and preserve

2. Moderate, cautious, - considered to involve little risk

3. Desiring to maintain existing institutions, and preferring gradual development to abrupt change

4. Old fashioned and traditional

The chart above offers the official Webster's definitions for the "views" and "dispositions" of the Liberal and the Conservative:

As you can see, the relationship between liberals and conservatives is one of balance. Liberals tend to give freely and excessively, while Conservatives tend to moderate and conserve. Liberals are the progressive part of the society, always eager to pursue change, innovation, and advancement. But not all change is good, and while nearly everyone wishes their society to advance, innovations are best approached cautiously. This is where the Conservatives come in. Their natural inclination to caution and résistance to change put all of the Liberals' new ideas to the test. Conservatives preserve the traditional customs and maintain the institutions of the society. Liberals seek to add new customs to the society and modify the existing institutions. This is the natural balance between Liberals and Conservatives; one pioneers into the wilderness to find new opportunities, and the other "holds down the fort."

What can make the terms confusing is their double meanings. President Harry Truman was socially liberal, favoring progressive social programs, but he was fiscally conservative, as he always demanded a balanced budget from Congress. President Ronald Reagan was socially conservative, favoring regressive economic policies, but he was fiscally liberal, demanding that Congress borrow hundreds of billions of dollars to finance government spending programs. Thus, in some cases, people can be both liberal *and* conservative at the same time.

A greater understanding of these terms can be gained from a historical perspective. The Liberal Party was originally a British political party that developed out of the Whig Party in 1868. The Liberal Party was critical of institutions which tend to restrict individual liberty, often expressing itself in demands for freedom of expression, equality of opportunity, and universal education. European liberalism has its roots in the laissez-faire doctrines of Adam Smith, Malthus and Ricardo. It was replaced by the British Labour Party in 1922. The Conservative Party is a British political party that developed out of the Tory Party in the 1830's, with the maintenance of existing institutions as its policy. It brought about much social legislation between 1874 and 1880 and allied with the Liberal Unionists in 1886 to maintain their control of the government through most of the 20th century.

There is an interesting twist in the way these parties, and these ideologies, have flip-flopped their positions over the years. Originally it was the Liberals who pushed for a deregulated economy, and the Conservatives fought the change, supporting the traditional government institutions that regulated the economy. But following the Great Depression, the Liberals started to think that unregulated industry wasn't such a great idea after all. In keeping with their nature, the liberals sought to change the existing system, this time by *increasing* government regulations. The Conservatives, having grown accustomed to deregulated industry, fought to maintain what had now become the traditional economic norm. If we live long enough we may see regulated industry become the traditional system, and these groups' positions may reverse again, back to where they originally started.

Americans need to learn respect for those of liberal or conservative ideologies. We need to remember our roots as much as we need to advance. Neither is better than the other, and it is extremism in either direction that causes problems. Liberals need to remember that the "Counterculture Revolution" of the 1960's spawned a national drug problem, which caused much human suffering. Conservatives need to remember that the traditional discrimination of minorities spawned several national crises, which caused much human suffering. But together, Liberals and Conservatives can guard against each other's flaws, draw upon each other's qualities, consider the possibilities of progressive new ideas, the virtues of existing institutions, and the benefits of working together.

PROVIDE FOR THE COMMON DEFENCE

Let's face it; the world is still a very violent place. As distressing as it may be, there is still no shortage of evil people in this world who would kill you to plunder what you own, and think nothing of it. Whether it is a gang of looters in a Los Angeles riot, or a nuclear superpower bent on world domination, the United States needs to stay prepared to resist any attack. A strong military establishment, and the assurance that we will use it, provides an effective deterrent to any nation that might otherwise threaten our citizens at home or while they are abroad.

Such a powerful military system would normally cause concern regarding the possibility of a military overthrow of our democratic government; as this has happened in so many other countries. But the founding fathers of this nation were wise enough to assert that the US military, owned and shared by the public, be ultimately controlled by the Congress, which represents the will of the people. A further assurance is provided by the fact that all members of the US Armed Forces are expected to uphold the principles of the US Constitution, first and foremost. Since a military "coup d'état" is clearly in violation of the principles outlined in the US Constitution, which each member of the military is sworn to uphold, it would be quite difficult for a group of renegade Generals to orchestrate such a crime. Here again, we find another important reason why everyone in the US should be intimately aquainted with the US Constitution.

Since the preamble to the US Constitution implies that our military is for defensive purposes only, it is important that we guard against any potential abuses of this massive power. Whether the US had the legal right to invade North Korea or North Vietnam is still a matter of great debate. Some argue that the US had to meet the Communists on these small fields of battle, to stem the tide of communist expansion, and avoid a large-scale world war. Others argue that these conflicts served only to fuel the war-machine economies of the world's superpowers. Since history cannot be reversed, nor can the deaths of over 100,000 US troops and millions of Asian civilians, I assert that the American men and women who served in these "police actions" were patriots who served their country when called, believed in fighting against communist tyranny, and whose sacrifices serve as an ongoing reminder that military power should never be implemented capriciously or abused.

In addition to the loss of life, trillions of our tax dollars were spent on weapons systems that were known to be obsolete, on maneuvers that were known to be unnecessary, on bureaucracies that border the ridiculous, on "secret operations" that cost tens of billions of dollars (not even Congress knows what they were), on $400 hammers, $200 screwdrivers, $50 screws, etc. It has become apparent that "we the people" need to provide for a common defence from the Defense Department's wasteful spending! It seems that "we the people" need to re-examine why our government would spend billions of dollars to support Central-American mercenaries and Kuwaiti dictators when we have so many wars to win here at home. It seems that "we the people" need to ensure that there is no abuse or waste in the great military system that provides for our common defense.

INSURE DOMESTIC TRANQUILLITY

The insuring of domestic tranquillity involves getting all of the people of the United States to get along with each other. This is quite a trick in a nation where people are free to think, say, and do nearly anything that they want. Many arguments will arise between people of differing ideologies, such as the Liberals and Conservatives mentioned before. But, when either of these ideologies becomes extreme, and starts to dictate how others should think and live, domestic tranquillity gives way to public disturbances, mental worry, and even physical harm. Political extremism has proven to be as dangerous and destructive to the US as almost any other threat. The US Civil War was caused by extremists, fought over political ideology, and cost more American lives than any other war. More recently, the social conflict over US involvement in Vietnam caused a social rift in this country that seriously challenged the nation's domestic tranquillity, bringing riots, injury, and death to many innocent Americans. In order to guard against any future threats to our delicate social fabric, it is important to understand the concept of political extremism.

When people are supportive of liberalism, they are often characterized as being a part of society's "Left Wing." Similarly, when people are supportive of conservatism, they are often characterized as being a part of society's "Right Wing." These terms originate from 19th century Britain, where Parliament members with views that differed most from traditional authority or opinion were seated to the left of the presiding officer, and those members who associated themselves with traditional authority or opinion were seated to the right of the presiding officer. Thus, these two groups became the "Left Wing" and "Right Wing" of Parliament.

In modern times, these terms are commonly reserved for political extremists. Left Wing extremists who are supportive of radical social changes, sometimes including Marxist socialism or communism, are commonly referred to as "Leftists." Right Wing extremists who are highly reactionary,

POLITICAL BALANCE

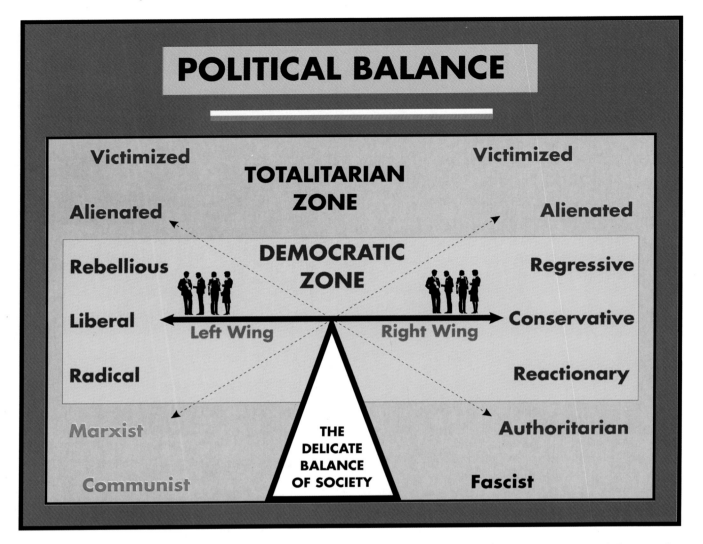

supportive of an authoritarian ruling class, or even fascism, are commonly referred to as "Rightists." What separates the Liberals from the Leftists, and the Conservatives from the Rightists, is the extent of their extremism. The chart above titled "Political Balance" illustrates the political extremes in both directions and the net effect of this extremism.

As you can see, rational people who are willing to debate their ideologies reasonably and draw upon the qualities offered by both liberalism and conservatism, create balance and social tranquillity in their society. But if the society begins to "lean" too far to the left or too far to the right, it runs the risk of falling into a totalitarian state. The most extreme examples of this phenomenon are illustrated by the recent histories of Russia and Germany. The scenarios were quite similar in both countries, where difficult economic conditions caused a public demand for drastic social changes. Russia experienced the *Radical* overthrow of its traditional Czarist monarchy, and drafted a new constitution quite similar to that of the USA. But instead of seeking a new balance in their society, Russia continued to lean to the left, into the policies of *Marxist* socialism, and it wasn't long before the *Communist* Party took complete control of Russia, and began its bloody *Victimization* of anyone that opposed their opinions. A decade later the Nazi Party formed in Germany as a *Reactionary* movement to thwart the spread of communism, and to restore the traditional

German Reich. But instead of seeking a new balance in their society, the Germans continued to lean to the right, into *Authoritarian* rule under Adolph Hitler, and it wasn't long before the *Fascist* Nazi Party took complete control of Germany, and began its bloody *Victimization* of anyone that opposed its opinions.

These are the most striking examples of wing extremism run amuck. But, the United States has never fallen as far into political extremes as many other nations. Here in the US, there has always been more of an "action and reaction" cycle, created from wing extremism. We have had the good fortune of pulling ourselves out of such crises, though rarely without bloodshed. This is where we can study the cause and effect of political extremism, using the "Political Balance" chart as a guide:

Following the American Civil War, the reestablished union accelerated into the Industrial Revolution. *Conservative* investment bankers became *Reactionary* to the prospects that industrialization offered to them. Soon thereafter, they created monopolies, bilked consumers, exploited workers, and by the turn of the century they had effected a return to the traditional system of *Authoritarian* ruling class aristocracy. The Left Wing working class felt exploited and *Alienated*, became *Rebellious*, and massive strikes and violent labor riots ensued. As the *Liberal* labor unions gained power and influence, *Radical* changes in America's political and economic systems were called for.

There was much talk of a **Marxist** takeover of American industry, the **Communist** Party was actively recruiting angry workers, and now it was America's *Right Wing* that became **Alienated**. President Roosevelt's "New Deal" addressed many of the grievances of the working class, and he was able to effect a **Regressive** political movement back to a democratic free market system, by adding **Radical** new changes. The political environment became more **Conservative** during World War II as the **Liberal** President became aware that the US had to assume a more traditional disposition to win the war. Following the war, President Harry Truman became very **Reactionary** about the global communist movement and commissioned American troops to North Korea. Soon thereafter, Senator Joe McCarthy embarked on an anti-Communist crusade that was nearly **Authoritarian**, as his "Committee on Un-American Affairs" publicly persecuted anyone who ever opposed the government's actions, or who spoke publicly about progressive or unusual topics. Thousands of Left Wing Americans, who had never even *considered* communism, became **Alienated** by what was dubbed "McCarthyism."

Ten years later, millions of Left Wing Americans became **Rebellious**, demanding their rights to dress, act, and talk about anything they wanted. They denounced America's military involvement in Vietnam, and demanded **Liberal** programs to help the nation's discriminated minorities and distressed poor. The civil rights and peace movements of the Left Wing soon evolved into a **Radical** "counterculture" movement by the mid 1960's. This movement staged massive protests that challenged all of the nation's traditional institutions. This movement re-introduced **Marxist** preachings, **Alienated** the Right Wing, and even became destructive at times. Riots and bloody conflicts ensued as the Right Wing countered with **Regressive** police actions, reminiscent of the labor riots that occurred five decades earlier. It was not until the Ohio National Guard shot into a crowd of young protesters at Kent State University, killing four and wounding nine, that America began to come to its senses. The murders of unarmed US citizens, by US troops, on American soil, while those citizens were exercising their Constitutional rights, caused even the most ardent members of *both* Wings to reconsider their positions.

Thereafter, it only took a few years for America's rational **Liberals** and **Conservatives** to come to a mutual agreement regarding their differences. They agreed that America's involvement in Vietnam would end, given a reasonable amount of time to withdraw; that Americans can dress, act, and talk any way they want, provided they respect existing institutions; and that both Wings of society will work harder in the future to insure that political extremism never again threatens America's domestic tranquillity.

But the recent murders and bombings that have taken place at various abortion clinics, and the massive tragedy of the Oklahoma City bombing, remind us that this work is not done.

SECURE THE BLESSINGS OF LIBERTY TO OURSELVES AND OUR POSTERITY

The final founding principle of our nation decrees that we will always make sure that the good fortune that we are now enriched with, as a result of our freedom of choice, is made completely safe so it will not be lost by us, or be impaired for the generations not yet born.

This means planning for the future, sacrificing a little of our time, investing a little of our profits, and thinking about what today's actions will translate into tomorrow. In this time of rapid technological and social change, it is more important than ever that we think carefully about our actions. This is no time for apathy, complacence, or laziness. The world is now at a crucial turning point where communication technologies will change our future forever. Just as the human race evolved from the agricultural age to the industrial age, and then to the information age of today, I believe we will grow into what will become "the awareness age." In this era, the billions of pages of research, knowledge, and interpretation, produced by the thousands of research centers from around the globe, will become streamlined, universally understood, and utilized by the general public. This will be the era when humans fully realize the power of their intellect, grow out of their reactive impulses, and become proactive shapers of their mutual destiny.

The "Electronic Information Superhighway" will provide the accessibility to information, with 500 interactive TV stations, and the contents of the Library of Congress being piped into your home. This technology will bring world-wide video conferencing (complete with translation), interactive shopping services, and an inexpensive college education to everyone who wants one, right into our living rooms.

But just as motorized tractors marked the end of the agricultural age and robotics marked the end of the industrial age, the "Electronic Information Superhighway" will mark the end of the information age. The ending of each of these eras required the human race to adapt to the social changes that occurred as a result of ever-advancing technology, whether they liked it or not.

As the year 2000 approaches, I believe it's time to put away our antiquated notions about government and politics. No longer do our government officials need to ride their horse-drawn carriages to Washington, or speak to us from the backs of trains. Likewise, we no longer need to put our nation's future and fate solely in the hands of our elected representatives. By evolving into this new awareness age, we can realize the system of self government that Thomas Jefferson could only dream about. VOTE USA is a first step into this evolution, transforming the mountains of societal data into an easy-to-understand source of social awareness, and providing the means for an average person to take part in "a government of the people, for the people, and by the people."

I believe that VOTE USA personifies the essence of the awareness age. George Orwell's dark vision of a "Big Brother" watching you can be transformed into the most liberating event in human history, with technology allowing "Little Brother" to become an active director of what "Big Brother" does. Never before has such awesome power been available to the populace. Working together with this new power, the American people can easily attain the heightened level of awareness that will make a virtual utopia possible in the United States. Then we can teach the rest of the world how to do the same, right from our living rooms.

Whether this version of the future is "to be, or not to be, that is the question." The answer is up to you; as the future will only be what you make it.

GLOSSARY

for American Patriotism Defined
(continued)

Radical

1. Departing markedly from the usual or customary; extreme.
2. Favoring or effecting fundamental or revolutionary changes in current practices, conditions, or institutions.

Reactionary

1. Characterized by reaction, especially opposition to progress or liberalism; extremely conservative.

Regressive

1. Tending to return or revert or move backward.
2. Characterized by regression or a tendency to return to a previous, usually worse or less developed state.
3. Decreasing proportionately as the amount taxed increases (a regressive tax).

Ricardo, David

1. British economist (1772-1823) whose major work, Principles of Political Economy and Taxation (1817), supported the laws of supply and demand in a free market.

Smith, Adam

1. Scottish political economist and philosopher (1723-1790). His book, Wealth of Nations (1776), laid the foundations of classical free-market economic theory.

Tory Party

1. British political party, founded in 1689, that was the opposition party to the Whigs and has been known as the Conservative Party since about 1832. In the US, the Tory Party favored the British side during the American Revolution (also called Loyalist).
2. Supportive of traditional political and social institutions against the forces of democratization or reform.

Unalienable

1. Not to be separated, given away, or taken away.

Utopia

1. An ideally perfect place, especially in its social, political, and moral aspects.

Whig Party

1. A 18th and 19th century British political party that was opposed to the Tories.
2. A 19th-century American political party formed to oppose the Democratic Party and favoring high tariffs and a loose interpretation of the Constitution.

CHAPTER 2

GOVERNMENT SYSTEMS DEFINED

by Dr. Edwin J. Feulner
President – The Heritage Foundation

GLOSSARY

for Government Systems Defined

Apathetic
1. Feeling or showing a lack of interest or concern, especially regarding matters of general importance or appeal; indifferent.
2. Feeling or showing little or no emotion or feeling; unresponsive.

Bicameral
1. Composed of or based on two legislative chambers or branches: a bicameral legislature.

Enunciates
1. To pronounce; articulate.
2. To state or set forth precisely or systematically

Electoral College
1. A body of electors chosen to elect the President and Vice President of the United States.

Executive
1. A person or group having administrative or managerial authority in an organization.
2. The chief officer of a government, state, or political division.
3. The branch of government charged with putting into effect a country's laws and the administering of its functions.

Fascist
1. An advocate or adherent of a system of government marked by centralization of authority under a dictator, stringent socio-economic controls, suppression of the opposition through terror and censorship, and typically a policy of belligerent nationalism and racism.
2. A reactionary or dictatorial person.

Hobbes, Thomas
1. English political philosopher (1588-1679) who wrote Leviathan (1651), which outlined his philosophy that human beings are fundamentally selfish.

Ideology/Ideologies
1. The body of ideas reflecting the social needs and aspirations of an individual, a group, a class, or a culture.
2. A set of doctrines or beliefs that form the basis of a political, economic, or other system.

Judicial
1. Of, relating to, or proper to courts of law or to the administration of justice: the judicial system.
2. Decreed by or proceeding from a court of justice.
3. Belonging or appropriate to the office of a judge.

Jurisdiction
1. The territorial range of authority or control.
2. Law. The right and power to interpret and apply the law: courts having jurisdiction in this district.
3. a. Authority or control: islands under U.S. jurisdiction.
   b. The extent of authority or control: a family matter beyond the school's jurisdiction.

Legislative/Legislation
1. The act or process of legislating; lawmaking.
2. A proposed or enacted law or group of laws.

Moral
1. Of or concerned with the judgment of the goodness or badness of human action and character: moral scrutiny; a moral quandary.
2. Conforming to standards of what is right or just in behavior; virtuous: a moral life.
3. Arising from conscience or the sense of right and wrong: a moral obligation.

Parliament
1. A national representative body having supreme legislative powers within the state.
2. Parliament. The national legislature of various countries, especially that of the United Kingdom, made up of the House of Lords and the House of Commons.

Party (political)
1. An established political group organized to promote and support its principles and candidates for public office.

Propaganda
1. The systematic propagation of a doctrine or cause or of information reflecting the views and interests of those people advocating such a doctrine or cause.
2. Material disseminated by the advocates of a doctrine or cause

Third World
1. Underdeveloped or developing countries, especially those not allied with Communist countries.
2. Minority groups as a whole within a larger prevailing culture.

Tyranny
1. Absolute power, especially when exercised unjustly or cruelly
2. Use of absolute power: A tyrannical act.

GOVERNMENT SYSTEMS DEFINED

Dr. Edwin J. Feulner
President – The Heritage Foundation

"Man's capacity for justice makes democracy possible, but man's inclination to injustice makes democracy necessary"
— *Reinhold Niebuhr*

THE FUNCTIONS OF GOVERNMENT

Any form of government must perform the following four basic functions:

1. Control dangerous or irresponsible behavior and keep the peace. The government must craft laws that maintain time-honored social standards and create mechanisms for enforcing those laws, including penalties for those who do not obey.

2. Promote the general welfare by establishing standards for trade and economic activity. This usually includes establishment of a monetary system, a uniform system of weights and measures, standard laws between private parties to contracts, and a system of roads.

3. Provide for the common defense. This includes establishment of military forces capable of defending the nation's territorial integrity and of engaging in whatever military actions are necessary to ensure national security.

In order for anyone to understand and appreciate the United States' form of government, they must first understand the concept of government itself, the different forms of government in the world today, and their various economic systems. This information will help you to develop a true appreciation for our own system, as well as an understanding of the foreign governments our nation must interact with daily.

4. Govern relations with foreign nations. This includes negotiation of the rules under which international trade, military cooperation, and international communication will take place.

Most political scientists define good government as government that effectively accomplishes the above objectives, while also allowing those it governs the maximum possible personal, economic, and political freedom. With these considerations in mind, we will consider the several kinds of government in the world today.

THE IMPORTANCE OF GOVERNMENT

Whenever a large group of people must interact, there tends to be a difference of opinion on how certain situations should be handled. Those who find murder and pillage a reasonable means of subsistence must be controlled and disciplined by others who understand that these threaten the survival of society. In such situations, a specific set of rules must be agreed upon by reasonable people, based upon commonly understood moral rules and values. A government is the only socially accepted group that can use force to to ensure that everyone abides by these rules, thus maintaining the society's standards. Otherwise, a state of disorder and confusion would ensue, differences of opinion would necessarily spark violence, opposing groups would clash, and life for most people would be, in the words of political philosopher Thomas Hobbes, "solitary, poor, nasty, brutish and short."

AUTHORITARIAN GOVERNMENT

An authoritarian government uses police and military forces to preserve itself in power, and sometimes to expand the borders of the nation. An elite ruling class usually underlies the authority of the government. Such governments typically allow the general population to exercise some, but not the full range of generally recognized economic and political freedoms. Under authoritarian government, people may be allowed to own businesses or property, to elect local officials, and even, on occasion, to criticize government policies, as long as those activities do not conflict with the authority and decisions of the rulers.

Authoritarian dictators can call themselves dictators, kings, generals, or even presidents or chairmen. Dictators usually come to power through military takeover (such as Muammar Quadhafi who seized power in Libya in 1969 or Manuel Noriega of Panama), or through the overthrow of another dictator.

TOTALITARIAN GOVERNMENT

Totalitarian government goes several steps beyond authoritarianism. A specific group, usually represented by a political party that does not allow opposition parties, imposes an ideological formula over the laws, customs and economic life of a society, usually in the name of a utopian idea of justice. Examples include Nazi Germany, and the communist parties of the former Soviet Union, China, Cuba, Cambodia, Vietnam, and many others.

In practice, the social and moral disruptions such ideological approaches cause are so traumatic that the entire experiment in human engineering must usually be abandoned following a prolonged period of catastrophic suffering and bloodshed.

Under totalitarian systems all authority rests with the party, which purports to represent the peoples' interests. But, in practice, under totalitarian rule, the people have no say in the workings of the government, the economy, or the culture. Often a strong leader, who in truth is a dictator, eventually uses the reigning ideology to justify his own absolute rule over every detail of the peoples' lives. Adolph Hitler was "Der Fuhrer" or "The Leader" of Germany from 1933 to 1945. His rule was distinguished by the systematic murder of more than 6 million Jews, millions of others, and by extreme brutality toward the conquered peoples of Europe.

Adolf Hitler saluting his followers in 1939

Communist rally in the former Soviet Union

Josef Stalin of the Soviet Union, Mao Tse-tung of China, Fidel Castro of Cuba, and Pol Pot of Cambodia are other examples of such dictators. These men would issue their decrees, some for public display, others for private retribution, which the party organization would elevate to the status of absolute truth through propaganda, in an overt and many times frankly conscious effort to supplant religious belief in the hearts and minds of the people.

In authoritarian or totalitarian governments, freedom of speech, of the press, of religion, of assembly, and of political activity are entirely forbidden or greatly restricted. Opposition to the policies of the existing government can result in imprisonment, torture, and many times, death. An authoritarian government will try to gain public support through propaganda campaigns including mass meetings, rallies, and controlled media (newspapers, radio and television). Totalitarian governments will use the same means for purposes of indoctrination in the intricacies of the reigning ideology.

From 1936 until its dissolution, the former Soviet Union claimed to have a "peoples'" democratic government based on a constitution. While the Soviet constitution did mention a democratic system including rights to free speech, press, assembly, etc., the exercise of these rights were redefined in ideological terms, such that only those who agreed with the government were tolerated, and only political candidates chosen by the Communist Party could run for public office. Without opposition, it was easy to achieve the goal of a 95 or 97 percent vote for the party's candidate.

Freed from the checks and balances of democracy, authoritarian or totalitarian governments can reach decisions quickly in times of crisis without considering the wishes of the people. Obviously this is only an "advantage" for those doing the governing. Dictatorial governments need not take time out for debate or legislative votes. While giving the impression of efficiency, however, the societies they control lack the vitality of societies with high degrees of individual freedom. Eventually this lack of vitality causes social and economic development to fall behind, and the ruling regime must ultimately either self-destruct, as in the case of the Soviet Union, or compromise its ideology and adapt to changing circumstances, as have the rulers of China.

DEMOCRATIC GOVERNMENT

The term *democracy* comes from the Greek words *demos* and *kratos*, which mean "people" and "authority." Thus democracy refers to governments in which authority ultimately rests with the people of the nation. There are two types of democratic governments: Direct Democracy and Representative Democracy.

In a direct democracy, the people themselves make laws and implement them, and settle any disputes that arise. This "pure" form of democracy was practiced in some of the ancient Greek city-states such as Athens, and is still practiced, on a limited scale, in New England town meetings, some of the smaller territorial divisions, or "cantons" of Switzerland, and in those states of the United States that permit lawmaking by referendum. In a direct democracy the people are not outside the political system. They *are* the government, and a majority vote of the citizens has the force of law.

This system, as the ancient Greeks discovered, rarely functions efficiently, even in small towns or communities where citizens can reach consensus on the issues at hand. The main problem with direct democracy is that citizen majorities seldom possess the expertise necessary to vote what is best for the community in the long term. The "tyranny of the majority" — the rule of a majority that only seeks its own good at the expense of all others — was an object of great fear for the Founders of the American system of government.

In a representative democracy like America's, government power is divided into legislative, executive and judicial branches — each of which serves as a counterweight to the others —and overall power is limited by a written constitution. The people of the nation vote periodically to elect representatives, who will make laws on the peoples' behalf, and an executive to carry them out. The opinions of the people are supposed to guide representatives (who are elected, theoretically, on the basis of superior wisdom, knowledge, and experience) in their decision making. Laws are made in public sessions, and it is the responsibility of the citizens to make sure their elected representatives know their views on matters requiring a vote. Countries governed by a representative democracy are known as *Republics*, though many repressive governments also call themselves republics.

The danger of republican government lies in the fact that without proper public vigilance, elected representatives can assume dictatorial powers. If the majority of people become apathetic and refuse to accept their responsibilities as citizens, and do not oversee the proceedings of their republic's government, laws can be made that personally benefit corrupt representatives and ultimately harm the people.

One historic example is the political takeover of democratic Italy in the 1920's by Benito Mussolini, who, through his control of the legislature, passed laws that denied citizens the rights of free speech, assembly, and election. Once Mussolini had rendered the people of Italy powerless to remove him from office, he outlawed all opposing political parties and turned Italy's democratic system into a fascist dictatorship.

Benito Mussolini with Nazi Officer

Today, many nations claim to have democratic governments, while in fact they are dictatorships. Most truly democratic governments not only conform to the above description, but also incorporate five principles that relate to the *citizens* of a nation:

1. Popular Sovereignty

The citizens of a democracy exercise self government through the voting process. The actions of government reflect the wishes of the people, and the people hold the power to remove representatives who neglect or abuse their offices.

2. Rule of the Majority

Majorities decide all legislative matters requiring a vote, their power limited by a system of checks and balances aimed at preventing those majorities from running roughshod over minority rights. Thomas Jefferson once noted, "the majority, to be right, must be reasonable."

3. Judicial Recourse

Minorities accept decisions of the majority, but are also free to express their views and to persuade majorities to accept them. Where this process fails, and conflicts ensue, there should be recourse to judicial authority to decide matters according to legal precedent, commonly understood customs and rights, and legal interpretations of whatever written constitution may govern the system.

4. Voting Rights

Though the definition of a "citizen" has varied throughout history, in modern times all citizens of a democracy usually have the right to cast votes that are equal in value, or effect, to those of their fellow citizens. A citizen of a democracy can usually campaign for public office as a member of any political party, or independent of all political parties.

5. Fundamental Rights, Constitutionally Guaranteed

A democratic government, to function properly, is usually based upon a written constitution that guarantees the basic freedoms of citizens and lays out the basic structure of government. America's founders believed a constitution was needed in order to ensure that total power could not fall easily into the hands of any particular faction, and such that majorities would not easily be able to impose their will on minorities. The American constitution uniquely enunciates and limits the power of the central government.

The major advantage of any democratic system is the emphasis on personal freedom. But that freedom must be exercised with wisdom and responsibility for the result to be a society in which all have an equal opportunity to succeed. A major disadvantage of democratic government is that it may be slow to act in times of crisis, as the opinions of the people must be considered in all decisions. Another disadvantage is that unless a democratic society works hard to produce a wise, educated, responsible citizenry, the people will eventually lose the capacity to choose leaders wisely. They can thus place themselves in the hands of unjust rulers, who may promise services and programs to the people that cannot be delivered, or that unfairly take from one group to give to another.

TYPES OF DEMOCRATIC SYSTEMS

Some feel that the central government should have the power to govern on a national basis, and make decisions for the entire nation. Others, such as the majority of the founders of the United States, are distrustful of a strong central government and argue that each individual state of the nation retain the right to govern itself in most areas. Various attempts to balance the competing powers have historically given birth to three basic types of democratic systems; Unitary Government, Confederate Government, and Federal Government.

Unitary Government

In a unitary system of government, the nation's central government is legally supreme. State or local governments possess no powers independent of the national government, and are therefore merely subsidiaries of that government, carrying out local tasks. A unitary system of government may be democratic or dictatorial, depending on its constitution. In Great Britain, for instance, the nation is governed by a monarchy (a king, queen, emperor, etc.), which is a unitary form of government and would normally suggest authoritarian rule. But Great Britain has a *Constitutional* Monarchy in which the monarch's powers are limited by written agreement with the people, and elected officials represent the will of the people in Parliament. The advantage of a unitary form of government is that laws are uniform throughout the nation, which theoretically lessens confusion and conflict between higher and lower jurisdictions. But in practice, when unitary governments rule over very large countries, they are unable to allow for regional differences that dictate different approaches to solving local problems. Unitary governments are therefore typically slow to act in emergencies, and citizens are typically forced to wait until the central government decides what to do. This is why unitary governments are usually successful only in smaller nations.

Confederate Government

Those who distrust the strong central power of a Unitarian system prefer a confederate system of government. In a confederacy, the separate states of a nation govern themselves independently, and cooperate through alliances aimed at mutual political, military, or economic advantage. Any organized central government acts only on matters of common concern, such as defense or foreign relations, and only by the consent of the independent states. These may agree to restrict the central power at any time. While confederacy does prevent the growth of a "big government," it lacks the unity a nation may need in times of emergency. It is much more difficult to maintain national security under a confederacy, since the central government is powerless to act without the consent of all the states. Confederate arrangements currently can be found *between* nations, such as the European Community and the Commonwealth of Independent States (CIS), countries of the former Soviet Union.

Federal Government

The compromise between unitary and confederate systems — and the one chosen by America's founders — is the federal system of government. Under a federal system, political authority is divided between regional governments and the central government. State and local governments have their own spheres of jurisdiction which (theoretically) cannot be infringed by the central government. The power of the central government is typically enumerated in a written constitution (for example, the power to collect federal taxes, print a national currency, or provide for the defense of the nation). The federal system offers the advantages of unity, while allowing individual regions, states, or localities to handle most of their own problems. Jurisdictional conflicts between state and local governments and the national government are typically handled through judicial resolution. Under the Constitution of the United States, for example, any powers not specifically granted to the federal government are presumed to be matters for state jurisdiction.

TYPES OF LEGISLATURES

Parliamentary Systems

The parliamentary system of representation is very popular throughout Europe, and is also used by nations such as Canada, Australia, and Japan. At the center of this system is a "bicameral" body of elected representatives known as the Parliament. The Parliament in Great Britain, for example, consists of an upper house known as the "House of Lords," and a lower house known as the "House of Commons." In Great Britain, members of the upper house are appointed by the nation's monarch (one of the few remaining powers of the king or queen), and the lower house is elected by the public. In Canada, both houses are elected by the public.

In any case, once the parliament is formed, its members then go through a process of selecting the chief executive by a majority vote. The chief executive heads the nation's cabinet and is commonly known in most countries as the "prime minister," but can also be known as the "premier" (France), "chancellor" (Germany), or any other name that the nation's constitution designates. The chief executive is normally the leader of the majority party. In nations such as Italy, which have many different political parties, a coalition of several parties must be formed to make a majority vote possible to name the chief executive. Once named, the chief executive then selects a cabinet from members of the parliament. Therefore the nation's chief executive is not elected by the public but by the parliament; and cabinet members (commonly known as "The Government") also serve as members of the parliament. The nation's Supreme Court members are either selected by the monarch (Great Britain) or the executive cabinet (Canada).

In a democratic parliamentary system, legislation can be submitted by members of parliament, but usually originates from the executive cabinet. Once introduced, legislation becomes law through the majority vote of parliament. An interesting mechanism of the parliamentary process is the "no confidence" system. If the executive cabinet submits major legislation that is opposed by the majority of Parliament, the chief executive and the entire cabinet can be forced to resign. The Parliament need only vote that it has "no confidence" in the cabinet's ability to lead the nation to force its resignation and a nationwide vote for a replacement. In most democratic parliamentary systems, the only way for the executive cabinet to survive a "no confidence" vote is if it calls for a general election to seek public support for the cabinet. In other parliamentary systems, such as Great Britain's, the monarch has the power to supersede a vote of "no confidence," dissolve the parliament on behalf of the Prime Minister, and call for new elections.

There are two main advantages to a parliamentary system. One advantage is that the voting process is simplified, as the public needs only to vote for members of Parliament. Parliament is then responsible for governing and managing the nation, including the selection of the chief executive. The second advantage is in the way the executive cabinet may be held immediately responsible for its actions. This tends to prevent the chief executive from assuming too much power, limits conflict between the two branches of government, and allows the legislature to change policies without waiting for the chief executive's term of office to expire.

The major disadvantage of a parliamentary system is found in the process of appointing the chief executive. If there are substantial disagreements between multiple political parties, it may be difficult to secure a stable executive cabinet. In a time of crisis, the parliament may not be able to take effective action. This problem recurred in France from 1946 to 1958, when the average length of time a French cabinet remained in power was about five months.

Presidential Systems

Presidential systems of government are found throughout the world, but are particularly popular in the Western Hemisphere. Unitary, authoritarian presidential systems are more commonly found in poorer and less advanced nations. Most democratic presidential systems are modeled after the US system, which has the longest and most successful history. The American model consists of a bicameral legislature known as the Congress, an executive cabinet under a chief executive known as the President, and a Supreme Court. The public elects members of both houses of Congress directly, and elects the President indirectly through an electoral college (an institution that normally reflects public opinion, but is not required to).

The president appoints new members to the Supreme Court when vacancies occur, with the "advice and consent" of the Senate, the upper chamber of the US legislature.

In a democratic presidential system, legislation can be submitted by the executive cabinet, but usually originates from members of Congress. Once introduced, legislation becomes law through the majority vote of Congress and approval by the President. The President is free to make certain policies through executive orders and agreements, and can veto legislation at will. Congress can override a presidential veto by a vote of two-thirds of both houses of Congress. Judicial decisions of the Supreme Court may have the effect of overriding the acts of either the legislative or executive branches, except when Congress decides to legislate more specifically on the particular matter in dispute. The advantage of a democratic presidential system is found in its more or less equal distribution of power, and its system of checks and balances, which make it difficult for any one branch of government to assume total power over the others. This mitigates against any one faction or party from taking complete charge over the government. The major disadvantage of a democratic presidential system also relates to the equal distribution of power. The separation of powers between the executive and legislative branches can result in disagreements which cause delays in times of crisis. Sometimes it is hard for the public to determine who is responsible when a given policy fails, or who is preventing action from being taken when disagreements arise between the President and Congress.

While the US political system is not without its critics, it is the system of government that made the US the most prosperous, most free, most creative, and most diverse nation in the world. It has also proven to be the most stable system in the world, having remained intact through a foreign invasion (1812), a civil war, a great depression, two world wars, a cold war, and numerous government scandals. Nearly all of the other government systems in the world have undergone profound changes when faced with only one of these crises. The US system of government has served its country well over the past 200 years, and with the public's support, it will serve the country well for the next 200.

George Washington being sworn-in as the first President of the United States

CHAPTER 3

ECONOMIC SYSTEMS DEFINED

by Dr. Ravi Batra
Professor of Economics – Southern Methodist University

GLOSSARY
for Economic Systems Defined

Aggregate
1. Constituting or amounting to a whole; total: aggregate sales in that market.

Depression
1. A period of drastic decline in a national or international economy, characterized by decreasing business activity, falling prices, and unemployment.

Destitution
1. Extreme want of resources or the means of subsistence; complete poverty.
2. A deprivation or lack; a deficiency.

Egalitarian
1. Affirming, promoting, or characterized by belief in equal political, economic, social, and civil rights for all people.

Equitable
1. Marked by or having equity; just and impartial.

Exploit
1. To selfishly or unethically make use of another person or group.
2. To employ to the greatest possible advantage.

Foreign Exchange Market
1. Foreign exchange methods and instruments used to adjust the payment of debts between two nations that employ different currency systems.
2. In the decades following World War II, international trade was conducted under a gold-exchange standard. Under this system, nations fixed the value of their currencies not to gold but to some foreign currency, which was in turn fixed to and redeemable in gold. Most nations fixed their currencies to the U.S. dollar. During the 1960s, however, a severe drain on U.S. gold reserves led to the introduction (1968) of the so-called two-tier system. In the official tier, the value of gold was set at $35 an ounce; in the free-market tier, the price was free to fluctuate according to supply and demand. At the same time, the International Monetary Fund (IMF) created "Special Drawing Rights" (Also known as "paper gold" and are assigned to the accounts of IMF members in proportion to their contributions to the fund) as a new reserve currency. In the early 1970s new troubles plagued the international monetary system, resulting in the temporary adoption of "floating" exchange rates based largely on supply and demand. Finally, under a 1976 agreement IMF members accepted a system of controlled floating rates and took steps to diminish the importance of gold in international transactions, including elimination of the official price.
A nation's "Balance of Payments" (A systematic record of a nation's total payments to foreign countries, including the price of imports, the outflow of capital and gold, and the total receipts from abroad, including the price of exports and the inflow of capital and gold) has an important effect on the exchange rate of its currency. The rate of exchange is the price in local currency of one unit of foreign currency and is determined by the relative supply and demand of the currencies in the foreign exchange market.

Great Depression
1. The severe U.S. economic crisis of the 1930s, supposedly precipitated by the 1929 stock market crash. Certain causative factors are generally accepted: overproduction of goods; a tariff and war-debt policy that curtailed foreign markets for American goods; and easy money policies that led to overexpansion of credit and fantastic speculation on the stock market. At the depth (1933) of the Depression, one third of the labor force (16 million people) was unemployed.

Inflation
1. A persistent increase in the level of consumer prices or a persistent decline in the purchasing power of money, caused by an increase in available currency and credit beyond the proportion of available goods and services.

Monopoly
1. a. A company or group having exclusive control over a commercial activity. b. A commodity or service so controlled.
2. Exclusive control by one group of the means of producing or selling a commodity or service.

Orthodoxy
1. Adhering to what is commonly accepted, customary, or traditional

Propaganda
1. The systematic propagation of a doctrine or cause or of information reflecting the views and interests of those people advocating such a doctrine or cause.
2. Material disseminated by the advocates of a doctrine or cause

Recession
1. An extended decline in general business activity, typically three consecutive quarters of falling real gross national product.

Revolution
1. The overthrow of one government and its replacement with another.

Smith, Adam
1. Scottish political economist and philosopher (1723-1790). His book, Wealth of Nations (1776), laid the foundations of classical free-market economic theory.

Third World
1. Underdeveloped or developing countries, especially those not allied with Communist countries.
2. Minority groups as a whole within a larger prevailing culture.

ECONOMIC SYSTEMS DEFINED

Dr. Ravi Batra

Professor of Economics – Southern Methodist University

"I place economy among the first and most important virtues, and public debt as the greatest of dangers... We must make our choice between economy and liberty, or profusion and servitude. If we can prevent the government from wasting the labors of the people, under the pretense of caring for them, they will be happy."

— *Thomas Jefferson*

THE BASICS

Corresponding to its political system, each nation also has an economic system. The economy deals with the ways in which people's material needs and wants are met. This covers the production, distribution, and exchange of a nation's goods and services. The economic system determines what goods will be produced and by whom, who will own the means of production, what an individual business owner can decide and what the government decides, and so on.

In most colleges and universities economics is considered a difficult subject. Given the choice, many students would like to graduate without it. In reality, economics was and is a simple discipline, provided logic is mingled with common sense. The subject becomes unintelligible when experts try to justify narrow and self-centered interests. That unfortunately is how the discipline has evolved over time, and not surprisingly the world's economies have been convulsed time and again by recessions, depressions, and inflations. Even today the vast majority of people on our planet live in poverty, not because of a lack of resources, but the lack of proper understanding of how a system may operate smoothly.

Every economy, old or modern, primitive or complex, works through the operation of two forces, demand and supply. Demand and supply are like the two blades of a pair of scissors displayed in Figure 1. The blade moving from A to B represents supply and the one moving from M to N represents demand. The point where the supply and demand blades meet is commonly called the point of equilibrium. Indeed the magnitude of the economic ills can be measured by how far the economy has deviated from its equilibrium point.

Today, there are three major, widely differing, economic systems: Capitalism, Communism, and Socialism. Although each claims to be the best way to a better life and the achievement of social justice, their means of attaining these goals differ. Note, however, that there is no country that is totally communistic, socialistic, or capitalistic. Capitalism and socialism are the main systems prevalent today, while communism, an extreme form of socialism, is undergoing a lingering death. The scissors analogy can be used to see the major difference between the global systems. The blade representing demand is more or less the same under both capitalism and communism, but the one representing supply is drastically different. Under capitalism the supply blade is run by private individuals and markets, whereas under communism it is run by state and central planners.

Like scissors that are loose or rusted, an economy runs into problems if its twin forces are out of balance or restrained. Thus, when the economy is out of equilibrium, poverty, unemployment, and misery follow. Consider, for instance, the national labor market. Here the two blades of the scissors represent supply and demand for employees, with the price scale representing the average wage, and the quantity scale representing the total amount of workers. If the labor market is in equilibrium, there is no unemployment, because the supply *of* labor matches the demand *for* labor. But if the market wage is higher than the equilibrium wage, there is unemployment.

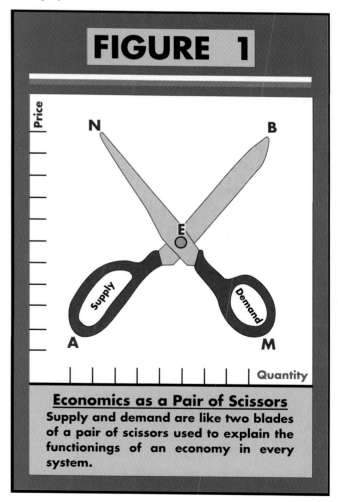

FIGURE 1

Economics as a Pair of Scissors
Supply and demand are like two blades of a pair of scissors used to explain the functionings of an economy in every system.

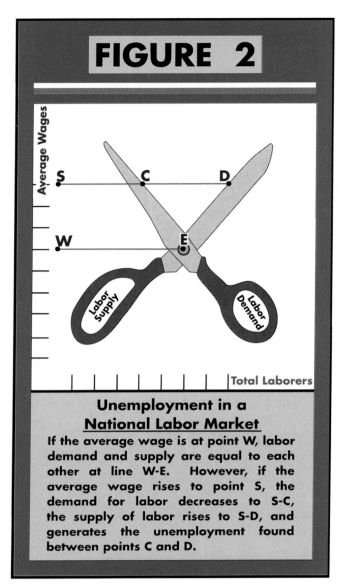

FIGURE 2

Average Wages (vertical axis)

Total Laborers (horizontal axis)

Unemployment in a National Labor Market

If the average wage is at point W, labor demand and supply are equal to each other at line W-E. However, if the average wage rises to point S, the demand for labor decreases to S-C, the supply of labor rises to S-D, and generates the unemployment found between points C and D.

For example, consider that you have $150 to spend on hiring people for the day, and that is all you have, and there are three people seeking work. In this scenario, you could pay all three people $50 each. But, if the three people all demand at least $75 to work for the day, you would only be able to hire two of them, and the third would become unemployed.

A graphic example of this occurence is offered in Figure 2, where the average wage is measured on the verticle axis and the number of laborers seeking employment on the horizontal axis, labor demand (number of jobs offered by employers) and supply (number of workers seeking employment) are equal to the line W-E, if the average wage is W. However, if for some reason the market wage rises to point S, the amount of money available to labor must be distributed to fewer workers. Thus, labor demand is lowered to line S-C, while labor supply rises to the line S-D, with the range between points C and D equaling total unemployment. In addition, the supply of labor rises because a higher wage encourages more people to join the labor force.

What could keep the market wage stuck at point S? In the Third World, wages cannot fall below subsistence level, simply because human survival is then unlikely. Thus, if the subsistence wage is above W, there will be permanent unemployment. Such is the case in many poverty stricken economies of Asia, Africa, and Latin America. There, investment opportunities are so meager that the labor demand blade is too low (i.e. too close to the origin) to absorb labor supply, even at the subsistence wage. The only way to eliminate or reduce unemployment then is to infuse massive investment through foreign aid or local savings. This would shift the labor demand blade upward and generate more jobs. Another area where unemployment is high and has been so since the early 1970's, is Europe. There, the problem is that the market wage is stuck above W because of strong unions. Investment is sufficient but wages are above the equilibrium level. Hence, unemployment persists and is likely to continue for a long time.

In Europe, the unemployment rate is now above 12% of the work force. In the United States, by contrast, the unemployment rate is below 7%. U.S. joblessness has been much lower than the European rate, but U.S. real wages have been falling since 1973 and are now below average salaries in Germany, Sweden, Netherlands, and Switzerland.

Demand for goods and services arises from people's wants and needs, and since human needs are similar across nations, the same laws of demand apply to all systems. In every region, demand for a product rises if its price falls, if income grows, or if population increases. Thus the demand blade is more or less the same under divergent economic systems. But the supply blade differs sharply, as will be demonstrated in the following section.

THE THEORIES

CAPITALISM

Capitalism is an economic system in which the means of production, exchange, and distribution, (industries, banks, and natural resources) are privately owned. Private ownership and control can be by one person, a few persons, or a large group. The production and distribution of goods and services are in the hands of individuals who seek to maximize profits. Driven by self interest, they utilize resources (labor, capital, and technology) in a way to minimize the cost of production. Their product must attract consumers, otherwise goods will be left unsold, resulting in losses.

A pure capitalist system would not impose any government control on various industries, and would allow "the invisible hand of the free market" to control production and distribution, based on the principles of supply and demand. This theory was originally proposed in 1776 by Adam Smith, "the father of economics," in his book, *The Wealth of Nations.* Smith theorized that competition with other privately owned companies would regulate the pricing and quality of products, and competition among workers for higher wages would stimulate worker productivity. The profit motive drives the capitalist system, where charging too little for a product or service can result in maximizing production at little or no profit, and charging too much can produce large profits over a very limited level of production.

These "laws" of capitalism are derived from the fact that consumers (the ultimate user of the products) try to maximize their purchasing power by seeking the highest quality product at the lowest possible price. This is how capitalism relies on everyone's self interest to generate a highly productive economy that meets the needs of its satisfied consumers.

Any imbalance arising in a capitalist economy is normally corrected by the price system, operating through the "supply-demand scissors." This is illustrated in Figure 3, which illustrates the supply-demand workings of the market for automobiles. The graph measures the average car price on the vertical axis and quantity bought by consumers or sold by producers on the horizontal axis. For the scissors to do its job, it is essential that the two blades meet at some point such as E. Similarly, for the auto industry to be profitable and have satisfied consumers, it is essential that price be set at the point where the supply and demand blades meet each other. Thus, if the market price is set at point A, auto demand and supply are equal to each other at the distance of line A-E, which can be projected on to the horizontal, quantity axis.

However, if the market price happens to be set at point B, car demand is decreased to the distance of line B-C, whereas the supply is at line B-D. Here, the price is too high, resulting in a glut of cars equal to the distance between points C and D. In this case, producers will be left with unsold cars and consumers will be dissatisfied because of the high price. Moreover, with a surplus of cars, auto producers will have to cut production and lay off workers, creating unemployment in the process.

This is an example of demand-supply imbalance, which in a capitalist system is corrected by the flexibility of price. With some cars unsold, the suppliers will reduce their price and move toward point A. As the price falls, demand will rise, and supply will fall until the two meet at point E. The demand supply imbalance is then corrected by the willingness of producers to trim the product price, in their own self interest.

The advantage of a capitalist economic system is in the competitive atmosphere that it creates. Capitalist-type economies have the highest production of any system, and this often translates into a higher standard of living for the nation's citizens. The disadvantages are in the lack of central control in the economy. With industries free to do as they choose, they may choose to maximize their profits by underpaying their workers, or exposing them to unnecessary hazards. Several groups or corporations may get together, create a monopoly in a certain industry, and then fix prices at unreasonably high levels. This practice often leads to shoddy products and dissatisfied consumers. The scissors analogy is one of the best ways to explain how industrial monopolies can hurt the nation. The scissors are functional only if the two blades meet at some point such as E in Figures 1, 2, and 3. An agent is needed to nail down the two blades to produce a proper cutting instrument. Similarly, the forces of supply and demand must have a meeting point in order that the economy operates smoothly and efficiently. Price flexibility is normally

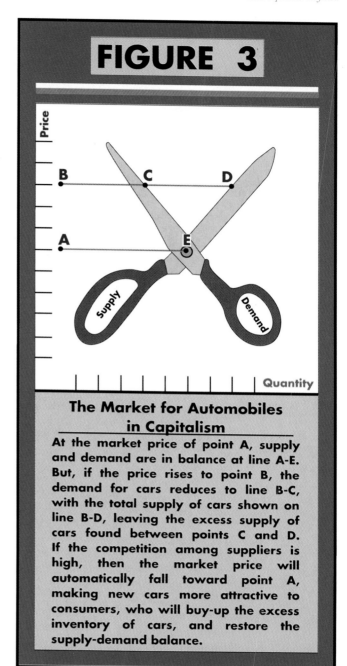

FIGURE 3

The Market for Automobiles in Capitalism

At the market price of point A, supply and demand are in balance at line A-E. But, if the price rises to point B, the demand for cars reduces to line B-C, with the total supply of cars shown on line B-D, leaving the excess supply of cars found between points C and D. If the competition among suppliers is high, then the market price will automatically fall toward point A, making new cars more attractive to consumers, who will buy-up the excess inventory of cars, and restore the supply-demand balance.

the mechanism that equates demand with supply under capitalism. But when monopolies dominate the system, prices are set too high, and there are times when, even in market economies, this equality vanishes. Then the economy, like a broken pair of scissors, does not function properly. Recessions, depressions, inflations, inequality, and low-paying jobs are then the result.

Monopolies may also result in the over-production of certain products beyond the needs of the nation, resulting in the shut-down of many companies, the loss of jobs, and a major economic collapse. Since the capitalist economy is based on supply and demand, workers' income should be adequate to purchase products; because of their low salaries, monopolies have, at times, upset the delicate balance of a free market economy, such as the one that occurred during the 1930's.

COMMUNISM

In theory, communism is an economic system in which all means of production, distribution, and exchange of goods and services are owned by society as a whole. There is no private property, and people work according to their abilities and receive according to their needs. The government plays a central role in directing the economy, and the value of any product is set by the amount of labor needed to produce it. Thus, the person or persons who work to make something should receive that value, not the capitalists who take it from the workers in the form of profits.

The main concepts of communism were outlined by Karl Marx and Friedrich Engels in "The Communist Manifesto" in 1848. Marx and Engels believed that capitalist nations would be unwilling to correct the social injustices that had been brought by industrialization; as a result, the workers would, one day, become discontented and revolt against the wealthy capitalists, causing the fall of capitalism. Ironically, this prophecy came true in several pre-capitalist nations that were under authoritarian rule, such as Russia and China. But in democratic western nations, government addressed the worst grievances of the people, and rectified some wrong-doings on the part of the "predatory capitalists" (wealthy people who enhance their own wealth and power at the expense of their society). So the communist manifesto did not come true on a world-wide scale, and the nations that did turn to communism do not have "true" communism. China has introduced many capitalistic trends through the years, and in the former Soviet Union there were wealthy, privileged people (mostly government officials) who took a larger piece of the communist pie than their fellow comrades, and could be compared to the "predatory capitalists."

The type of flexibility displayed in Figure 3 is absent in a communist economy, where the means of production, exchange and distribution are mostly owned by the government, and production and hiring decisions are made by central planners. A planning body decides how much of each good is produced and then delegates this task to regional planners and local factory managers. Each manager has a production quota to fulfill and he/she hires labor and capital toward that end. Because of the fixed level of the quota, the supply blade, as in Figure 4, is vertical in a communist economy. Under capitalism, private owners vary their production in response to variations in price; that is, they produce more when price goes up and less when the price falls. In a communist system, however, this adaptability is lacking because the production decision is made by the "high command," so that the supply decision, once made at the beginning of the year, is unchanged regardless of prices and consumer preferences. This type of rigid system is inherently inefficient, unproductive, and wasteful.

In Figure 4, the supply blade is vertical at point R, which is where production is set. If the market price happens to be at point A, there is no supply-demand imbalance. But, if the price is at point B, then there is a surplus of cars, which cannot be eliminated until the price drops. However, as the price decision is made by the planning body and not the local manager, the auto price will not come down. Since the balancing market price is difficult to discover, there is a persistent wastage of resources because more cars than are needed, at the prevailing price, will be produced by the economy year after year.

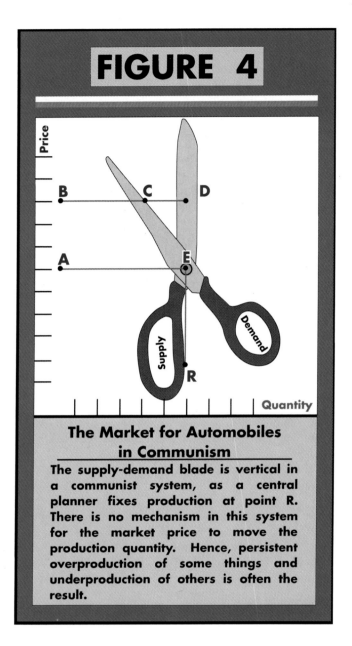

FIGURE 4

The Market for Automobiles in Communism

The supply-demand blade is vertical in a communist system, as a central planner fixes production at point R. There is no mechanism in this system for the market price to move the production quantity. Hence, persistent overproduction of some things and underproduction of others is often the result.

The main advantage of a communist economy is that the government can avoid the evils of private monopolies, such as extreme poverty amidst plenty, thus ensuring an equitable distribution of wealth in the nation. The main disadvantage to a communist system relates to human nature. When a country meets the needs of its citizens, regardless of performance and without the competitive incentive of a capitalist system, people tend to have a lower level of productivity. In addition, local managers have no reason to minimize the production cost because their salaries do not depend on their performance or the quality of production. Hence, the quality, workmanship, and productivity suffer. Thus, communist economies usually turn out shoddy products at high prices that fail to be competitive with products supplied by capitalist systems. All this often results in an egalitarian sharing of low national output, and a lower standard of living for most citizens.

SOCIALISM

A proposed compromise between capitalism and communism is socialism. Under socialism, a nation's important means of production, distribution, and exchange are owned and managed by a democratic government. These usually include the major industries such as coal, steel, transportation, and public utilities. Consumer goods and industries, however, remain under private ownership. Socialism almost always includes some kind of plan drawn by the central government that directs the economy and outlines how resources will be divided. Instead of relying on the law of supply and demand to regulate the economy, or having a "high command" dictate the production decisions, the government will appeal to private businesses to get them to voluntarily agree on the government's plan. Sometimes laws are passed to *make* businesses follow the plan. The main goal of socialism is to distribute wealth more equally, a task often achieved through high taxes on the wealthy, and large welfare programs for the poor.

Socialist-type of economic systems have been popular in the past with European countries such as Sweden, France, Great Britain, Italy, Germany, and others (although many of these nations have recently been privatizing their major industries and moving closer to the US style of "mixed capitalism").

The advantage of a socialist economic system is that the economy may be centrally guided by a democratic government, which eliminates the problems of *laissez faire* (a French term meaning "to allow to do"), and still incorporates the competitive atmosphere of a "free-market" economy. The disadvantages of socialism are related to the high taxes that many socialist countries impose, including stepped taxes that increase as the individual's income increases, thus discouraging citizens who are trying to advance financially. The vast taxes collected by the government are often used up by extensive welfare programs that are commonly abused by both the recipients and the providers. Without proper regulation over this type of abuse, and without a uniform tax structure, socialism will not be able to fully benefit from a competitive free-market economy, and could suffer from the low productivity that occurs when an expansive welfare system eliminates the incentive to work hard and be efficient.

The destruction of the Berlin Wall is a symbol of people's dissatisfaction with communism

The Presidential Cabinet of Franklin Delano Roosevelt

THE U.S. ECONOMIC SYSTEM

The United States has a mixed capitalist economic system, that is, a capitalist system that implements some of the government controls and social services of a socialist system. The difference between our system and a socialist system is that our major industries are privately owned, and (until recently) our tax structure is fairly uniform. During the Great Depression of the 1930s, US workers were discontented, and many communists thought it was time for an anti-capitalist revolt. But President Roosevelt introduced "The New Deal," which addressed many grievances of the workers and rectified some of the wrongdoings of the "predatory capitalists." Much of the resulting growth in government spending was originally inspired by the writings of John Maynard Keynes. The Keynesian theory suggests that demand is at the center of any economy, and recessions or depressions occur when consumer spending is low. In other words, the government must take an active role in ensuring that supply is balanced with demand, by ensuring that the general public has enough money to purchase the goods that are supplied by businesses, and that businesses have enough money for investment. This means that during recessions the government must raise its budget deficit; but, during inflations, the federal budget should be in surplus. This theory is the antithesis of the classical ideology of Adam Smith, as it casts the government in the role of a constant watchdog, indispensable to continued prosperity.

The New Deal introduced many socialist concepts into the US economy, such as a government-imposed minimum wage, unemployment insurance, welfare programs for the poor, and many government controls that would prevent price fixing, unfair business practices, and help distribute the nation's wealth more evenly. The New Deal marked the end of *laissez faire*, the end of "*Communist Manifesto*" predictions, and the beginning of our new, *mixed capitalist*, government-regulated, free-market economy.

In addition to increasing controls over aggregate demand (the sum of spending by consumers, businesses, and the government), the Keynesian theory encourages monetary expansion (producing more money) during recessions to encourage business investment and consumer spending, and tightening of the money supply during economic booms to control inflation. Today, the Keynesian theory has become the orthodoxy to which challenges from other quarters are often posed. The most notable challenge was mounted in the 1960's by Nobel Prize winner Milton Friedman, who pioneered the Monetarist theory. Friedman argued that government intervention does not help, and can actually create economic instability. Monetarists consider money supply to be the single most important determinant of business activity, prices, and employment. Unlike Keynes, they consider the government budget to be unimportant. Monetarists call for a return to deregulated, "laissez-faire" economics, with the government balancing its budget over the business cycle, and permitting an annual monetary expansion that is equivalent to the rate of economic growth (when money and national output grow at the same rate, inflation becomes zero).

Current economic thought reflects what can only be described as a massive state of confusion. To counter the recession of the late 1970's, the government applied classical Keynesian theory in the early 1980's, but called it Supply-Side Economics. Taxes were cut, money was printed, and government spending increased through budget deficits, providing an increase in aggregate demand and, thus, an upswing in the economy. At the same time, Supply-Side Economics applied the Monitarist theory of deregulating industry, but not the Monetarist theory of balancing the federal budget. This resulted in a robust economy by the mid-1980's, with an accompanying national debt of nearly $2 trillion. Both the Keynesian and the Monitarist theories would, at the least, balance the federal budget during the boom. But the government broke from both philosophies and continued to spend beyond its means, while the deregulated banking system invested heavily in risky ventures, and deregulated industry overpaid its executives, underpaid its employees, and merged into giant conglomerates. The swelling bubble of excesses burst in the fall of 1987 with a major stock-market crash, a procession of bank failures, and an overwhelming federal debt of over $3 trillion dollars.

Today, the US economic policy is neither Keynesian nor Monitarist, nor even Supply Side. It is an undefined, hotchpotch policy that applies continued federal deficits against the backdrop of a $5 trillion national debt, low interest rates on a tightly regulated money supply, deregulation of industry during a real-wage decline, and tax increases during a recession. These paradoxical economic policies are a reactionary attempt to deal with the economic mess created by the government's lack of forethought since the 1970's, as well as its failure to accept economic priciples. Yet not all is lost. The United States

is a nation of vast resources and a talented work-force. At its birth, America was stuck with high debt and little industry. Nevertheless, the country emerged to become the world economic leader. We did it once, and we can do it again, by changing our obsolete economic policies.

THE ECONOMIC INDICATORS

To better understand where an economy is headed at any time, one needs to understand the meaning of specific figures that reflect various activities within the economy. These figures are called economic indicators. The major economic indicators are as follows:

INTEREST RATE

The interest rate is the cost of credit that sustains market economies. Almost every expensive item is generally bought on credit. Businesses borrow money to finance their growth or to purchase new equipment. People borrow money to buy a house, car, or appliances. Therefore, when interest rates rise, monthly payments on loans rise, causing the demand for high-ticket goods to fall; this leads to a downturn in the economy. Conversely, when lower interest rates are offered, high ticket goods become more affordable to businesses and people, and this leads to an upturn in the economy.

INFLATION RATE

The rate of inflation is a measure of the increase in prices of goods and services. Every year, some prices decline, while others go up. Hence, an average price is used to see whether goods and services have become more expensive on balance. A well known average price is the consumer price index. People are often confused to see prices rise, even as inflation falls. That is because inflation is the rate at which the average price goes up *annually*. As long as the rate is positive, the price index goes up. A fall in inflation simply means that the average price has risen at a slower rate.

UNEMPLOYMENT RATE

The rate of unemployment is a measure of the number of people unemployed as a percentage of the labor force. The official rate of unemployment, however, grossly understates the true rate. To be considered unemployed, you have to be actively seeking a job, not be a student, and not be working at all. According to the Bureau of Labor statistics, over 18% of the workforce is working only part-time. Furthermore, if someone is a temporary worker or becomes too discouraged to look for a job, he or she is not jobless according to government reporting. However, the US Department of Labor publishes another figure that does take into account the temporary and discouraged workers. At the end of 1993, the true rate was above 10%, whereas the official rate of unemployment provided by the government to the media was only 6.7%. This figure is in stark contrast to the fact that nearly 25% of Americans do not have a full-time job.

RETAIL SALES

This economic figure represents the amount of goods and services that are sold during a given period, and is often compared to a prior period. Retail sales reflect the health of an economy, based upon the theory of "what goes around, comes around." In other words, if sales are up, stores will order more products to fill their shelves; then manufacturers and distributors will get busy providing more products for the market.

The New York Stock Exchange

STOCK MARKET

The health of the New York Stock Exchange is regarded, by some, as another important economic indicator. People buy a stock for its dividends (a portion of the company's profits *divided* among the stockholders) and its potential for capital gains (profits made on the sale of the stock). Dividends, of course, depend on a company's profitability, which improves in a robust economy. Therefore, rising stock prices normally anticipate a healthy economy, because stocks are usually valued by their projected future performance. The most widely followed index of stock prices is the Dow Jones Industrial Average (DJIA), named after Charles Henry Dow, who was the first to compute an average of US stock prices. The DJIA is an average of thirty industrial companies called the "Blue Chip" stocks, such as International Business Machines (IBM) and General Electric (GE), among others. Although the DJIA normally rises in a strong economy, at times it soars during recessions when interest rates fall. This is because falling interest rates make bonds (certificates of debt guaranteeing repayment with interest) unattractive, and investors switch money from bonds into stocks. This is exactly what causes the DJIA to reach all-time highs, and then fall as interest rates rise.

This production activity will, of course, provide jobs and income for the nation's workers, who will, in turn, spend their money on goods and services and refuel the cycle. If retail sales are down, as compared to the month or year before, then one can expect a downturn in the economy. Conversely, if retail sales are up, as compared to the month or year before, then one can expect an upturn in the economy. Another economic indicator that is similar to retail sales, but works the other way, is manufacturing orders. If retail establishments increase their orders from manufacturers, in anticipation of increased purchasing (such as before Christmas), it may indicate a future boost in the economy.

HOUSING STARTS

This economic figure represents the number of new houses under construction during a given period, as well as the number of new building permits. Like retail sales and manufacturing orders, these figures are often compared to a prior period. Since new homes are very high-ticket items, they bring large amounts of capital into the general economy. For this reason, economists watch the growth or decline of new house starts to determine the future health of the economy.

GNP / GDP

The GDP (gross domestic product) is the dollar value of the nation's output of goods and services produced during a year within the national borders, whereas GNP (gross national product) is the total value of production of a country's citizens, who may or may not live at home. Until 1991, the US national accounting system used the concept of GNP, but since then has switched to GDP. In any case, the two concepts are very close to each other. GNP or GDP can be a misleading measure of the nation's living standard, especially if inequality grows in society. When inequality grows, GNP may rise while the average real wage falls. All this means is that the top 15% to 20% of the employees earn so much more than before, that GNP rises despite the falling real earnings of the bottom 80% to 85% of the work force. This is exactly what has been occurring in the US economy since 1973. Rising GNP figures only managed to mask the increasing plight of the vast majority of Americans.

NATIONAL DEBT

When the government spends more than its tax intake, a shortfall results and is called the budget deficit. The government borrows money from households, businesses, banks, and foreign countries to finance this shortfall. The sum total of all that borrowing, over the years, is the national debt. Before 1981, the national debt, accumulated by the federal government, was less than one trillion dollars; but, by the end of 1994, it had reached nearly 5 trillion dollars. Some economists suggest that debt and deficits do not matter; whereas, others detest them for their dire consequences. The truth lies somewhere in the middle.

The national debt imposes a heavy interest cost on current and future generations, which must be paid with increased taxes. Increased taxes, in turn, decrease the amount of spendable income available to the marketplace, which slows the economy. In 1994, the federal government spent over $200 billion to service the interest on its debt. This money could have been used for education, health-care, crime prevention, or a host of pressing problems facing the nation; or, if the debt didn't exist, the average tax rate could be lowered by approximately 20%.

Furthermore, the task of repaying the national debt is not only put off indefinitely by the government, its amount is continuously increased every year. To pay-off the current national debt, it would take an amount equivalent to 25% in federal budget cuts, or a 40% increase in taxes, applied solely to the national debt for 15 years (if the economy could take it for 15 years). Hence, the debt is now a heavy drain on the nation, and its burden is growing every day.

FOREIGN VALUE OF THE DOLLAR

The foreign exchange value of a nation's currency is an indicator of its overall economic strength. For example, from 1950 to 1973, one US dollar bought 360 Japanese yen in the foreign currency exchange market. The dollar was said to be very "strong" (because of its high value) and it reflected the robust health of the American economy. In the late 1960's, US exports failed to keep up with imports, and the trade balance increasingly came under pressure. By 1971, the country had a full-fledged deficit in its foreign transactions. Economists argued that this demand-supply imbalance could be corrected by having the Federal Reserve Bank depreciate the US dollar in the Foreign Exchange Market (see glossary). In theory, the dollar depreciation, or devaluation, raises import prices and lowers export prices. Cheaper exports should increase American sales abroad, and expensive imports should reduce US demand for foreign goods. As exports rise and imports fall, trade becomes balanced.

Ever since 1973, the dollar has been progressively losing its foreign currency value, with a minor interuption occuring between 1981 and 1985. By 1995, US currency devaluation spun out of control, to where one dollar bought less than 85 yen. However, the trade deficit refused to disappear; in fact, by 1995 it reached an all-time high of $165 billion. What happened? Here again, theory failed to reflect reality. Currency depreciation rarely, if ever, eliminates the trade deficit when the country exports services and agricultural products, while importing manufactured items in mass quantities. Until the country becomes a net exporter of manufacturered goods, the trade deficit will not be eliminated by the dollar devaluation.

The proof of this assertion is in the historical record. Presidents Nixon, Ford, Carter, Reagan, and Bush all followed the futile policy of depreciating the dollar to balance America's trade, but with absolutely no success. Now president Clinton is following the same policy to achieve the same objective. Once again, failure is assured.

AVERAGE REAL WAGE

The Average Real Wage is a figure that represents the average weekly wage for a particular group, translated into its equivalent value at a given time in the past. For example, if you make $400 per week in 1994, you will be able to purchase as much as $300 would have purchased in 1984; or, if your salary goes up by 6% and the consumer price index (inflation) rises by 10%, then the purchasing power of your salary, or your living standard, has declined by 4%. This figure offers a baseline against which you can determine a group's standard of living, and is the best measure of a country's well being, because it is not as aggregated as some other measures such as GNP or GDP. For its first two centuries, US real wages rose every decade. This means that salary increases outpaced the rise in prices, or stated another way, wage growth exceeded price growth. Since 1973, however, wage growth for non-management workers has been slower than price growth. According to the US Department of Labor, as much as 75% to 80% of the US work force is in the non-supervisory category. Thus the real wage has plummeted for more than three-fourths of American employees.

People find it hard to believe that the purchasing power of the average American salary, or the real wage, has been falling ever since 1973. But this is exactly what the Economic Report of the President, published in February 1994, reveals. The report shows that the average real wage for production or non-supervisory workers in 1982 dollars was 315 in 1973, but was down to 254 in 1993. This is the most painful affliction of the American economy today. Even if inflation was kept in check during this period, the wage growth fell so much that real wages actually declined.

The shrinking American paycheck is now a great puzzle to economists, who are suddenly awakened to a phenomenon that has been brewing for more than two decades. Those aware of this phenomenon blame it on a number of factors. They cite falling savings, investment, educational standards, and rising female participation in the job market as the reasons for the plummeting living standard. These factors do impact the wage rate, but only through the medium of productivity. However, productivity continues to rise. The index of labor productivity, according to the Economic Report of the President, was 95 in 1973 and 118 in 1993. With productivity continuing to grow, the factors commonly cited for the real wage debacle are not at fault.

Others blame the oil shock of 1973 that quadrupled the petrol price for initiating the wage debacle. On closer inspection, all these turn out to be specious theories divorced from reality. As a simple example, consider the price of oil which did soar periodically during the 1970s, but has been declining since 1981. If the rising price of petrol was responsible for initiating the decline in the real wage in 1973, then the decline should have been reversed after 1981 when the oil price began to fall. Adjusted for inflation, US gasoline is now cheaper than in 1973. Yet the real wage decline not only continued after 1981, but actually accelerated after 1989. Today, the pre-tax real earnings have fallen by 20% when compared to their 1973 peak, and the after-tax earnings have fallen by more than 30%. What is really tragic is that real wages have been sinking while the productivity of the American worker has continued its historic rise, albeit at a slower pace. If you become less productive, through injury or old age, you readily accept a fall in your income. But if you work harder and become more efficient, then the wage decline really hurts. Common sense suggests that one of the major causes for the plight of the American worker is associated with rising imports and rising taxes, as the following will detail.

TAX POLICY

A nation's tax policy can also be an important economic indicator. As I discussed before, increased taxes decrease the amount of spendable income available to the marketplace, which slows the economy. An historic example of this theory can be found in the monumental shifts in the government's tax policy prior to the Great Depression. Until 1913 high taxes on foreign goods (tariffs) were the chief source of revenue for the government. Under the umbrella of these tariffs, the United States had become the world economic leader. Woodrow Wilson was the first American President who ushered a major shift in the tax policy. In the name of free trade he began to reduce taxes on foreign goods, and then, to make up for the lost revenue, introduced the income tax. From 1913 to 1919, tariffs came down steadily from an average of 44% to 16%, whereas the top-bracket income tax rate went up from a low of 6% to 66%.

In 1920, Warren Harding was elected president. He realized that it was bizarre to lower taxes on foreign goods and then raise them on the American people. Americans, after all, could avoid tariffs by avoiding imports, but could not elude the income tax. He reversed Wilson's policy, raised tariffs, and lowered income tax rates. By 1929, the average tariff had increased to 40%, but the top income tax rate had declined to 23%. And this policy produced the "Roaring 20s", as the rate of unemployment came down from 11% in 1920 to 3% in 1929.

At the end of 1929, the New York stock market crashed and a recession ensued. President Herbert Hoover raised tariffs in 1930 in the infamous Smoot-Hawley Tariff Act, just as Warren Harding had done earlier in 1921, when the economy was also in recession. But, unlike Harding, who had periodically reduced income tax rates, Hoover raised the top-bracket tax from 23% to 57% in 1932. By 1933, the recession had turned into the Great Depression. Economists immediately blamed the tariff, which rose from 40% in 1929 to 60% in 1932, for the economic disaster. Their argument was that the new tariff act caused a trade war around the world, as other countries followed suit with their own tariffs. This caused such a sharp drop in US exports that many export industries collapsed, thereby transforming a recession into a depression.

Ever since 1933, this argument has become the folklore of mainstream economics. As recently as November of 1993, during a debate with H. Ross Perot, Vice President Al Gore stated that "In 1930...the Congress passed the Smoot-Hawley protection bill...they raised tariffs and it was one of the principal causes, and many economists say *the* principal cause, of the Great Depression in this country and around the world."

A study of history shows that this reasoning is not only baseless, but smacks of a cover-up. Take a look at Table 1, which presents the official GNP data from 1929 to 1933, the worst years of the Great Depression. By definition, GNP equals domestic demand plus net exports. GNP fell from $104 billion in 1929 to $56 billion in 1933. But net exports (exports minus imports) fell by only $700 million, in spite of the so-called trade war. The fall in net exports was only 1.5% of the fall in GNP, which is so small that statistically it is considered zero (in Gallup poll results, for instance, a difference of plus or minus 3% is considered negligible). Thus, the effect of reduced trade on GNP was more or less nil. Hence, there is absolutely no way the Smoot-Hawley tariff could have caused the depression.

What really happened was that under the hammer blow of the income tax rise from 23% to 57%, domestic demand plummeted, and that generated the Great Depression. Later, President Roosevelt compounded Hoover's blunder. He resumed the bizarre tax policy that Woodrow Wilson had initiated. In the name of free trade, Roosevelt began to switch taxes from foreign goods to the American people. First, he reduced the average tariff, then he raised the top-bracket income tax rate to 68%, and finally, he introduced the Social Security tax. All this crushed domestic spending and created a catastrophic imbalance between supply and demand. Thus, it is free trade, not protectionism, that prolonged the Great Depression.

By now the US tax policy has become ridiculous. Taxes on foreign goods have been reduced again and again, while those on American goods, companies and people have been repeatedly raised. Today, in 1995, the average tariff is only 5%, whereas the top income tax rate is 39%, the corporation income tax is 35%, the Social Security tax is over 15%, sales tax averages 8% in most states, and on and on it goes. In the name of free trade, the tax burden has been switched from foreign goods to the American people.

The negative effect of the government's policy of switching taxes from foreigners to Americans is also now felt on GNP growth and budget deficit. Until 1972 when trade was low, GNP growth averaged 4% annually. Between 1973 and 1995, the growth rate averaged only 2.5%. With the fall in growth came a decline in tax revenue growth, which is one reason why the country is now saddled with a $5 trillion debt and a persistent budget deficit.

TABLE 1

GNP = Domestic Demand + Net Exports

1. **Fall in GNP = $48 billion between 1929 and 1933**

2. **Fall in Net Exports = $700 Million between 1929 and 1933 (= 1.5% of the fall in GNP)**

3. **Fall in Domestic Demand = $47.3 billion between 1929 and 1933**

Hence, the Hoover-Roosevelt income tax rise from 23% to 57% that crushed domestic spending caused the Great Depression.

Source: Economic Report of the President, 1991.

TRADE BALANCE

The balance of trade is also an important economic indicator. Here, the balance means that exports *to* foreign nations offset imports *from* foreign nations. Most countries seek a trade surplus where the country exports more goods and services than it imports. But some countries fall prey to one-sided trade negotiations, which result in trade deficits, where the country ends up importing more goods and services than it exports. In a trade deficit situation, the country literally loses a portion of its net worth to the nations that enjoy a trade surplus. In addition, if the supply of goods and services is partly satisfied by foreign companies, then the demand for domestic labor is reduced. The analysis of Figure 2 shows that if the labor demand blade shifts up, wages, as well as employment, rise in the new equilibrium. Conversely, the trade deficit trims the demand for labor and brings down both the real wage and employment.

As I have argued earlier, when an economy deviates from its equilibrium of demand and supply, it gets into trouble. The trade deficit is another instance of such disequilibrium. Ever since 1973, US trade (imports plus exports), as a percentage of GNP, has been soaring. Historically, the trade/GNP ratio averaged 12% until 1973 when it began to rise. By 1994, it had jumped to 25%, more than twice the historical average. The deficit reached a peak in 1995 at $165 billion, with no solution in sight.

A deficit of such magnitude implies that the US demand for labor is lower by at least 3.3 million workers (it takes about $50,000 today for a company to create a high-paying job - divide the deficit amount by $50,000 and you get at least 3.3 million new, high-wage jobs in the United States). If trade were balanced, US production would be larger by the amount of the deficit. For example, in 1994 alone, GNP would have been higher by $165 billion. If the US had the type of trade surpluses that are enjoyed by China or Japan, it could create at least 5 million new, high-paying jobs. In this way, the US trade deficit also plays a major role in the shrinking real wage.

Figure 5 displays the official data on trade and real earnings after the Second World War. It is divided into two parts, with the lower part exhibiting the contribution of trade to GNP and the upper part presenting the real weekly earnings of non-supervisory workers in all industries, as well as in manufacturing and retail services. All the earnings lines reveal an upward trend until 1973 and a downward trend thereafter. From 1950 to 1972, the contribution of trade to GNP, as measured by the trade/GNP ratio, was rather low (around 10%), insignificant to the American economy, and flat. During these years, real earnings climbed steadily in all industries, including manufacturing and services. But, as soon as trade shot up after 1973, the purchasing power of wages fell everywhere in America. Thus, when trade was low and insignificant, the living standard rose for all Americans; but with rising trade has come a collapse of the real wage for non-supervisory workers, who are as much as 80% of all employees.

Economists frequently offer two arguments in favor of free trade, which means opening your national markets to foreign competition by lowering tariffs and other barriers to imports. With rising imports, exports, and hence, trade (so goes the thesis), every country specializes in its export industries;

this specialization raises national productivity and the living standard. Secondly, the prices of importable goods fall, so that the consumer benefits. The consumer enjoys quality goods at lower prices. These arguments are almost universally accepted today, except that they are illogical and have no emperical backing.

The consumerism argument for free trade is a phony. Every potential purchaser is first a worker and then a consumer. Therefore, a satisfied consumer is one with a satisfying high-wage job. What really matters to a consumer is not just low-priced imports, but the overall purchasing power of his or her salary, commonly called the real wage. If rising imports bring real wages down, the consumer suffers, even if the rate of inflation tumbles. As for the specialization argument, there is absolutely no evidence that rising trade has raised productivity growth in the United States. In fact, productivity growth began to fall as trade started to rise in the early 1970's. This should not come as a surprise, because the national productivity argument of free trade is based on an outrageous assumption: namely, that manufacturing and services pay the same wages. In general, manufacturing wages pay 50% more than the average wage in service industries. Therefore, countries such as Japan, Germany, South Korea, and Taiwan, that have specialized in manufacturing, have benefitted from rising trade; whereas others such as Canada, Australia, and the United States, that have specialized in low-wage services, have been the losers.

If a student, for example, specializes in law, medicine, or engineering, he or she gets a high-paying job upon graduation; whereas if he or she specializes in art, English or journalism, a low salary is often the result. Therefore, it matters what you are specializing in. Similarly, when specialization in exports creates high-wage manufacturing jobs, the nation benefits; but when exports generate low-wage jobs in services, agriculture, or mining, the nation loses from trade. Remember that exports create jobs, but imports destroy them. Therefore, when exports create low-wage jobs and imports destroy high-wage jobs, as in the United States, the country loses from rising trade.

Ever since the early 1970's, the United States has been a net importer of manufactured goods and a net exporter of services and farm products. That is to say, the counry's manufacturing imports have far exceeded its manufacturing exports.

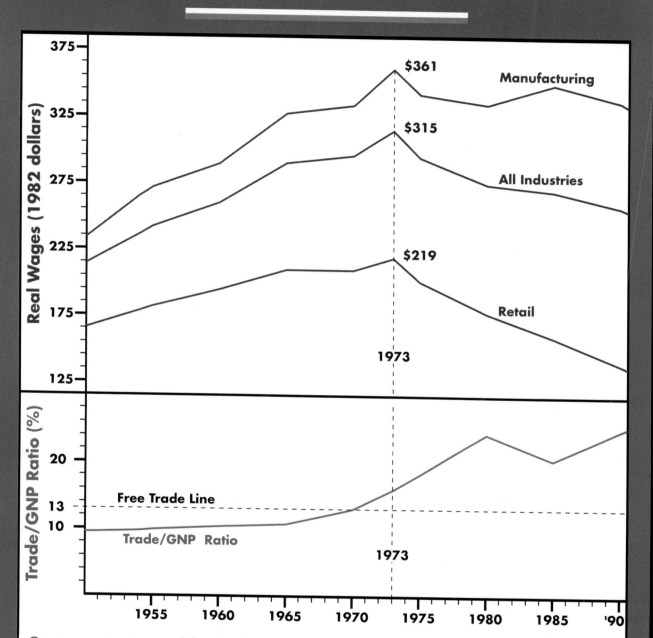

FIGURE 5

Government statistics reveal that for all practical purposes, the US became a free trade country in 1973 for the first time in its history. Until then, either tariffs were exorbitant or foreign trade was too small to impact the US economy. The figure, drawn only for the post-war period, shows that until 1973, trade as a percentage of Gross National Product (GNP) was below 13%, which historically marks the free-trade line. At nearly the exact same time as trade shot-up, real earnings began to tumble.

Data source: Ravi Batra, The Myth of Free Trade, Scribners, N.Y., 1993. Real earnings are adjusted for inflation, representing constant 1982 dollars.

Thus, the United States has been a loser from its free trade policy. Common sense suggests that manufacturing industries are the main source of prosperity. In every city, the mayor likes to bring industry to his area; every governor seeks to attract big business to his state. This is because manufacturing pays wages much higher than service industries such as Wal-Mart, McDonald's, and Sears. Since the early 1970's, the United States has imported manufactured goods in vast quantities. Cars, motorcycles, bicycles, air conditioners, refrigerators, televisions, VCRs, fax machines, and cameras from abroad have flooded the American market. Today, 17 million workers are employed in manufacturing, while ironically 18 million people work for the government. Millions of industrial jobs have disappeared, and workers, laid off from these jobs, had to move to service industries. As a result, real wages first fell in manufacturing, and then in services, because of the influx of the unemployed manufacturing workers.

One might ask: "Why, then, is free trade so popular?" Because it makes wealthy corporations, their corporate officers, and those that can still afford to invest in them, wealthier. When tariffs were high in the United States, American companies had a great incentive to keep factories at home, because they had to pay high taxes on imported goods. But now, businesses are free to shift plants overseas and earn the high profit that results from paying dollar-an-hour wages. These profits are enjoyed by the CEOs, corporate officers, and stockholders of these corporations; they give generously to the political campaigns of candidates who are supportive of free-trade policies, and provide numerous reports supportive of free trade to the media. While American wages shrivel from this practice, 20% of the US population enjoys short-term benefits, and as much as 80% of Americans needlessly forfeit the American dream.

CONCENTRATION OF WEALTH

When a large percentage of a nation's net worth is held by a small percentage of population, there is concentration of wealth. In an economic system where "what goes around, comes around," it is worrisome when concentrated wealth prevents the money from going around in the first place.

Suppose, for the sake of argument, that the $6 trillion US GDP were equally distributed among 120 million employees. It would provide an annual pre-tax income of $50,000 per worker. But with over 40% of the nation's wealth concentrated with 1% of the population, the richest Americans had an average income of $500,000 in 1994, while nearly 40 million people subsisted below the poverty income of $9,000. Of course completely equal distribution of income and wealth is neither possible nor desirable from the viewpoint of work incentive and even social justice. Yet the figure serves to show that with just the current level of GDP, no American needs to subsist in poverty, provided inequality is just below the prevailing level.

For instance, in 1973, US GDP per person was $15,000, while 11% of individuals lived in poverty. By 1994, the per capita GDP, after an adjustment for inflation, had jumped to $20,000. Clearly, this should have lowered the rate of poverty; instead, the poverty rate climbed to 15%.

Such are the depredations of extreme wealth disparity. This is a perversion of economic growth, where poverty paradoxically rises with rising productivity and output per person.

As both the Keynesian and Monitarist philosophies suggest, a healthy economy is the result of an abundant supply of consumer spending. When consumers spend more, more products need to be produced, creating more jobs, which means that more people have more money to spend. This ongoing cycle is hindered when a large portion of the nation's wealth starts to concentrate within a minority of the population. This is mainly because each person, basically, has the same needs. One closet of clothes per person, one home per family, one refrigerator per home, 20 square feet of food products per refrigerator, and so on. When an individual aquires a great deal of wealth, he or she still only needs this average amount of goods and services. The wealthy may splurge and buy two or three homes and many clothes and consumer goods for their family; but if their wealth is 100 times greater than the average wealth, there is little chance that their demand will be 100 times the amount of consumer goods bought by the average person. The concentration of wealth, therefore, results in a loss of consumer spending from the nation's marketplace; and the negative effect is compounded when individuals acquire wealth that is one thousand, ten thousand, or a million times that of the average person.

The problem with concentration of wealth, as mentioned above, is somewhat manageable when the wealthy are fair-minded citizens; but when the rich get greedy and use their wealth to exploit the working class, destitution is often the result. Such is the case in many third-world countries such as Brazil, India, and Mexico, where much of the nation's wealth is held by a handful of families, and the majority of the populace lives in abject poverty. In such countries, the wealthy are referred to as the ruling class, because of their absolute control of the government, police, and military. Any attempt by the working class to strike for higher wages, better working and living conditions, or a more democratic government, is quickly crushed by the government, on behalf of the rulers.

The abuse of wealth, and the power it buys, is not exclusive to third-world nations. Even in a democratic society, the wealthy can buy themselves into the position of the ruling class, provided that the electorate is not paying close attention. Their money can buy government support and tax breaks through campaign finance and media manipulation, orchestrated by biased think-tanks and commercial advertising. In groups, they can form monopolies that fix prices at high levels, force wages to low levels, and prevent hard working entrepreneurs from creating competitive products. Any remaining obstacles are often easily overcome by trickling a small portion of the spoils to 10% or 15% of the population. Eventually, the above mentioned ruling class will begin to feed on each other by manipulating the stock market, acquiring competing corporations through aggressive stock purchasing, and forcing competing corporations to merge with dominant ones. This "feeding frenzy" activity may continue until the victors have acquired and hoarded so much wealth, that there is not enough consumer spending left to sustain a healthy economy.

As the number of persons with little or no assets rises, demand for loans rises, the number of banks that need to write questionable loans to cover the interest on their deposits rises, speculative investments by the rich and desperate people rise, the presence of illegal schemes and scams increases; all while the consumer base shrinks. Recessions, depressions and widespread poverty are often the result, with urban blight, high crime, and social unrest being the by-products of the failing economy. This cycle is completed when the general public is pushed to its breaking point and the ruling class is overthrown, either through the peaceful application of law, or through a violent revolution. Then it's back to the drawing board for the wealthy elite, and the cycle begins all over again.

This basic pattern has occured in cycles, in almost every culture in the world, for much of the world's history. It is simply people's primitive instinct to "hunt and gather" as much as they can; hunting animals into extinction - overfarming fields into deserts - acquiring wealth until there is no viable economy. Retired Digital Equpment Corp. Chairman Ken Olsen, summed it up in a recent venture forum where he commented: "Going public means putting a company's fate in the hands of, often, short-sighted investors...owners today have no loyalty to the company. They don't care about the company or the country. They would do anything to have $1 more at the end of the quarter." This simple statement sums up the economic policies of multinational corporations that lay off American furniture makers, to exploit Third-world workers who earn less than $1 per hour, to provide cheap furniture to the remaining consumer base in America, until very few people in either nation can afford to *buy* furniture.

Taking all this into consideration, it is easy to see why the concentration of wealth can be an important economic indicator; because what goes around, comes around... if it goes around.

By fully understanding all of these economic indicators, and analyzing them with the help of the scissors analogy, basics, and theories presented earlier in this chapter, you can assess the current situation and make economic predictions with reasonable accuracy. In this way, you can scrutinize the forecasts and propaganda offered by government representatives and the media; and you may form your own educated opinions and prophecies, based upon the economic indicators and some plain old common sense.

CHAPTER 4

THE U.S. CONSTITUTION DEFINED

by Mr. Vin Weber
Vice Chairman – Empower America

GLOSSARY
for The US Constitution Defined

Acquiesce
1. Passive assent or agreement without protest.

Ambassador
1. A diplomatic official of the highest rank appointed and accredited as representative in residence by one government or sovereign to another, usually for a specific length of time.
2. A diplomatic official heading his or her country's permanent mission to certain international organizations, such as the United Nations.

Amendment/Amending
1. The act of changing for the better
2. A correction or an alteration, as in a manuscript.
3. a. Formal revision of, addition to, or change, as in a bill or a constitution. b. A statement of such a change: The 19th Amendment to the Constitution gave women the right to vote.

Assent
1. Hasty, typically servile agreement with another's opinions.

Consanguinity
1. Relationship by blood or by a common ancestor.
2. A close affinity or connection.

Despotism
1. A government or political system in which the ruler exercises absolute power.

Electoral College
1. A body of electors chosen to elect the President and Vice President of the United States.

Executive
1. A person or group having administrative or managerial authority in an organization.
2. The chief officer of a government, state, or political division.
3. The branch of government charged with putting into effect a country's laws and the administering of its functions.

Founding Fathers
1. The members of the convention that drafted the U.S. Constitution in 1787.

Impeachment
1. To make an accusation against or to charge (a public official) with improper conduct in office before a proper tribunal.

Judicial
1. Of, relating to, or proper to courts of law or to the administration of justice: the judicial system.
2. Decreed by or proceeding from a court of justice: a judicial decision.
3. Belonging or appropriate to the office of a judge

Jurisdiction
1. The territorial range of authority or control.
2. Law. The right and power to interpret and apply the law: courts having jurisdiction in this district.
3. a. Authority or control: islands under U.S. jurisdiction; a bureau with jurisdiction over Native American affairs. b. The extent of authority or control: a family matter beyond the school's jurisdiction.

Middle Ages
1. The period in European history between antiquity and the Renaissance, often dated from A.D. 476 to 1453.

Militia
1. An army composed of ordinary citizens rather than professional soldiers.
2. A military force that is not part of a regular army and is subject to call for service in an emergency.
3. The whole body of physically fit civilians eligible by law for military service.

Quartered
1. To furnish with housing: quartered the troops in an old factory.

Redress
1. To set right; remedy or rectify.
2. To make amends to.

Roman Empire
1. An empire that succeeded the Roman Republic during the time of Augustus, who ruled from 27 B.C. to A.D. 14. At its greatest extent it encompassed territories stretching from Britain and Germany to North Africa and the Persian Gulf. After 395 it was split into the Byzantine Empire and the Western Roman Empire, which rapidly sank into anarchy under the onslaught of barbarian invaders from the north and east. The last emperor of the West, Romulus Augustulus (born c. 461), was deposed by Goths in 476, the traditional date for the end of the empire.

Treasury
1. A place in which private or public funds are received, kept, managed, and disbursed.
2. The department of a government in charge of the collection, management, and expenditure of the public revenue.

Tyranny
1. Absolute power, especially when exercised unjustly or cruelly
2. Use of absolute power: A tyrannical act.

Unalienable
1. Not to be separated, given away, or taken away.

Usurpation
1. A wrongful seizure or exercise of authority or privilege belonging to another; an encroachment

THE U.S. CONSTITUTION DEFINED

Mr. Vin Weber
Vice Chairman - Empower America

"The men who founded your republic had an uncommonly clear grasp of the general ideas that they wanted to put in here, then left the working out of the details to later interpreters, which has been, on the whole, remarkably successful. I know of only three times, in the western world, when statesmen consciously took control of historic destinies: Periclean Athens, Rome under Augustus, and the founding of your American republic."

— *Alfred North Whitehead*

THE HISTORY OF OUR CONSTITUTION

Although our American government is unique in many ways, it was not established from a set of new ideas. Instead, its creation was the result of the founding fathers' reliance upon democratic ideals that had been evolving for over 2000 years.

As early as 500 BC, the citizens of the ancient Greek city of Athens enjoyed sovereignty, the ability to elect public officials and the benefit of constitutional government. Similarly, in the latter years of the Roman Empire, representative democracies were formed, where elected representatives would carry out the functions of government for the people who elected them. These experiments with democratic government in the ancient world (although far different from the type of government we enjoy today) laid the foundations for the democratic ideals that eventually led to our nation's founding.

The signing of the Magna Carta in 1215 was an important step in the protection of the basic rights of English citizens.

During the Middle Ages, philosophers developed the idea of "natural law," which was viewed as the law of nature or the law of God. This was the beginning of the idea that a government that violated the "natural rights of man" should be replaced with one that respected natural law and natural rights. Therefore, reasoned the philosophers, monarchs, governments, and all laws should conform to the natural law; if they did not conform, they should not have to be obeyed. This shift in thought changed the way people viewed the nature of power.

The roots of American democracy can be found in 13th Century England. In the year 1215, King John was faced with a revolt of powerful nobles, causing him to sign a document that began the evolving creation of the British constitution.

This document, the Magna Carta, forced King John and his successors to recognize "Natural Law," and thus the rights of the individual noblemen. Fifty years later, Parliament emerged as the main institution of representative government in Great Britain, and slowly began assuming powers that had formerly been held by the crown. In 1628, King Charles I was forced by Parliament to sign the Petition of Right, which prevented the king from levying taxes without permission of the Parliament; prevented him from declaring martial law, and prohibited him from imprisoning people without a trial.

Ultimately, in 1689, the British Bill of Rights was signed by William and Mary giving Parliament supreme authority over the monarchy, and guaranteeing citizens the rights of free parliamentary elections, freedom to petition, freedom of speech, etc.

AMERICA'S BEGINNINGS

When Great Britain colonized North America, most of the thirteen states were royal colonies under direct control of the British crown. In each royal colony, a governor and council, known as the Upper House, was appointed by the monarch, and an assembly of representatives elected by the colonists made up the Lower House. Many disputes arose between the two houses in each colony concerning voting rights, unfair trade laws that restricted importing and exporting of goods, unfair taxation without representation, and colonists' rights under "natural law." It became ap-

American colonists, dressed as Indians, throw British tea overboard into the Boston Harbor to protest unfair taxation

parent that the lower houses had little power over the upper houses, and the monarchy held the ultimate power over the people of the American colonies. When the colonists realized that they were not being treated as British citizens, and did not enjoy the same rights that were granted to the citizens in England, the movement for American separation from British rule began. In 1765, delegates from nine colonies met in New York City and quickly approved a document known as the "Declaration of Rights and Grievances." This declaration, and others like it, demanded that American colonists be given the same rights as English citizens, and that Parliament repeal British imposed taxes. Boycotts of British goods were instituted and acts of protest, such as the "Boston Tea Party" were executed to support the declarations. As a result, the British Parliament passed laws designed to punish the colonists (which the colonists entitled "intolerable acts"). A final formal request for rights was presented to the King from the 1st Continental Congress, which, again, had no positive effect. The delegates from the thirteen colonies, then, assembled again as the 2nd Continental Congress, and adopted the "Declaration of Independence" on July 4, 1776, which separated the colonies from Great Britain. This document also acted as a temporary constitution for the new nation, presenting the philosophies of "natural law" such as equality, safety, life, liberty and the pursuit of happiness as the basis of the new government. Great Britain responded to this act of defiance with military action, thus beginning the American Revolution.

An artist's rendering of a battle fought during the American Revolution

During these turbulent times, the 2nd Continental Congress served as the new nation's central government; organizing an army to fight the British, establishing a new currency, and negotiating with foreign countries. Each of the thirteen colonies drafted individual constitutions that outlined how their state would be governed, and on November 15, 1777, the Continental Congress approved a formal plan for a confederate form of central government known as "The Articles of Confederation" (not approved by all the states until March, 1781). This loose association soon proved troublesome for the young nation. Economic problems arose from the fact that each state had its own currency, while the national currency had little to no value. In addition, the national government lacked the power to regulate commerce or settle conflicts between states. Some states negotiated treaties with foreign countries, although this was forbidden by the Articles, and the Continental Congress found it had no way to force the states to obey laws that had been passed. By 1784, the nation was in such disorder that George Washington described the confederate plan as "...a half starved, limping government, that appears to be always moving upon crutches, and tottering at every step." By the summer of 1786, the nation's condition had become so displeasing that many feared an additional armed revolt against the new government. It was decided, at the 1787 Constitutional Convention, that a federal system of government must be implemented to govern the nation as a whole. Thus, the US Constitution was written and submitted for approval by the individual states on September 28, 1787. Many Americans were suspicious of a strong central government and resisted the change to a federal system. As a result, it took three years for the US Constitution to be ratified by all the states, with Rhode Island being the last hold-out state (ratifying by a close 34 to 32 vote) to give in to the new federal system. The federal government, outlined in that Constitution, became the "law of the land" as of May 29, 1790, and still is to this day.

THE ADVANTAGES OF OUR CONSTITUTION

The Constitution of the United States is the oldest written national constitution, still in operation, in the world today. Undoubtedly, a large part of the success of our Constitution lies in the fact that it is flexible, and can be altered to meet new conditions as they arise; at the same time, it still provides a durable framework for the federal government. On one hand, a constitution that is too flexible may not provide the stable government that a country needs, and will constantly be modified to reflect even temporary whims of various political groups. On the other hand, a constitution that is too rigid prevents the government from effectively meeting new needs, and will ultimately be replaced by one that is more flexible. A balance between the two is accomplished, in our Constitution, by providing a brief and concise set of guidelines, while excluding any overly specific details (our national Constitution is a brief 7,000 words, while the average state constitution is approximately 30,000 words, and the Alabama state constitution is 172,000 words).

While the basic meaning of ne\arly every article of our Constitution is clear, the language is general and allows for a generous amount of interpretation so as to meet new conditions, without the need for formal amendments. To further allow for future change, amendments can be made to the Constitution through the legislative process.

The Constitution outlines a government based on federalism, in which power is shared between the federal government and the individual states, in a way that the central government will have sufficient power to maintain order, yet be restricted in its actions, so that it cannot threaten individual freedom, or the freedom of the states to govern themselves. This power is shared through the "rule of law," in which the states may govern themselves, as long as their individual laws do not conflict with the Constitution. All laws, both state and federal, must pass the test of our courts, and if found to be in conflict with the principles of the Constitution (i.e. found to be unconstitutional), a judicial review may cause the law to be repealed. Other basic principles were also written into our Constitution to avoid the growth of an authoritarian central government. These principles institute a separation of powers, which prevents the danger of an excessive concentration of power in any single branch of the federal government. To achieve this goal, the various powers of the federal government are divided into three separate branches: executive, legislative, and judicial. A system of "checks and balances" is then implemented in which each branch of government "checks" on the other, to insure a true "balance" of power, insuring that no single branch of our government can attain an excessive amount of power.

Finally, an important principle of the Constitution is the guarantee of individual freedom. So fearful were the founding fathers that the federal government might abuse its power, that seven states demanded that a bill of rights be added to protect the people from the potential tyranny of the federal government. In recent years, however, the Bill of Rights has been used to protect the rights of individuals against abuses by the states. These and other features of our Constitution have given it durability and vitality. The unique governmental system created by this Constitution has allowed every person to develop his or her God-given talents and abilities, without being burdened by the heavy hand of arbitrary government or ancient traditions of class or station. Our Constitution is indeed a watershed in the history of man's struggle to govern himself.

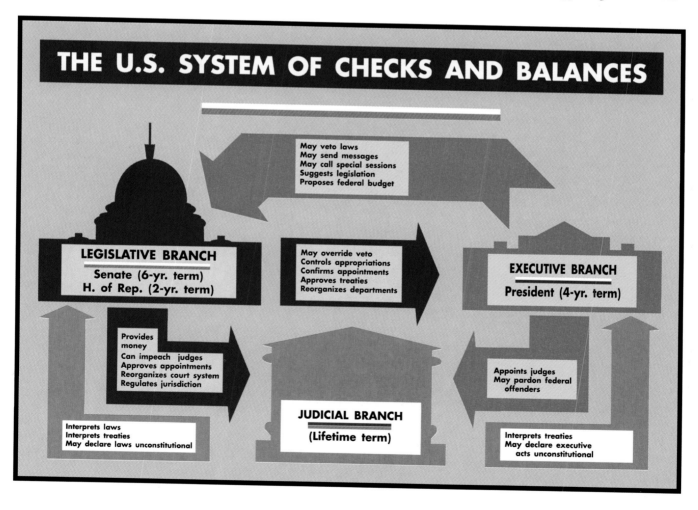

THE U.S. SYSTEM OF CHECKS AND BALANCES

May veto laws
May send messages
May call special sessions
Suggests legislation
Proposes federal budget

LEGISLATIVE BRANCH
Senate (6-yr. term)
H. of Rep. (2-yr. term)

May override veto
Controls appropriations
Confirms appointments
Approves treaties
Reorganizes departments

EXECUTIVE BRANCH
President (4-yr. term)

Provides money
Can impeach judges
Approves appointments
Reorganizes court system
Regulates jurisdiction

Appoints judges
May pardon federal offenders

Interprets laws
Interprets treaties
May declare laws unconstitutional

JUDICIAL BRANCH
(Lifetime term)

Interprets treaties
May declare executive acts unconstitutional

THE US DECLARATION OF INDEPENDENCE

Text of the Declaration of Independence

When in the Course of human events, it becomes necessary for one people to dissolve the political bands which have connected them with another, and to assume among the Powers of the earth, the separate and equal station to which the Laws of Nature and of Nature's God entitle them, a decent respect to the opinions of mankind requires that they should declare the causes which impel them to the separation.

We hold these truths to be self-evident, that all men are created equal, that they are endowed by their Creator with certain unalienable Rights, that among these are Life, Liberty and the pursuit of Happiness. That to secure these rights, Governments are instituted among Men, deriving their just powers from the consent of the governed, That whenever any Form of Government becomes destructive of these ends, it is the Right of the People to alter or to abolish it, and to institute new Government, laying its foundation on such principles and organizing its powers in such form, as to them shall seem most likely to effect their Safety and Happiness. Prudence, indeed, will dictate that Governments long established should not be changed for light and transient causes; and accordingly all experience hath shown, that mankind are more disposed to suffer, while evils are sufferable, than to right themselves by abolishing the forms to which they are accustomed. But when a long train of abuses and usurpations, pursuing invariably the same Object evinces a design to reduce them under absolute Despotism, it is their right, it is their duty, to throw off such Government, and to provide new Guards for their future security.—Such has been the patient sufferance of these Colonies; and such is now the necessity which constrains them to alter their former Systems of Government. The history of the present King of Great Britain is a history of repeated injuries and usurpations, all having in direct object the establishment of an absolute Tyranny over these States. To prove this, let Facts be submitted to a candid world.

He has refused his Assent to Laws, the most wholesome and necessity for the public good.

He has forbidden his Governors to pass Laws of immediate and pressing importance, unless suspended in their operation till his Assent should be obtained; and when so suspended, he has utterly neglected to attend to them.

He has refused to pass other Laws for the accommodation of large districts of people, unless those people would relinquish the right of Representation in the Legislature, a right inestimable to them and formidable to tyrants only.

He has called together legislative bodies at places unusual, uncomfortable, and distant from the depository of their Public Records, for the sole purpose of fatiguing them into compliance with his measures.

He has dissolved Representative Houses repeatedly, for opposing with manly firmness his invasions on the rights of the people.

He has refused for a long time, after such dissolutions, to cause others to be elected; whereby the Legislative Powers, incapable of Annihilation, have returned to the People at large for their exercise; the State remaining in the mean time exposed to all the dangers of invasion from without, and convulsions within.

He has endeavoured to prevent the population of these States; for that purpose obstructing the Laws of Naturalization of Foreigners; refusing to pass others to encourage their migration hither, and raising the conditions of new Appropriations of Lands.

He has obstructed the Administration of Justice, by refusing his Assent to Laws for establishing Judiciary Powers.

He has made Judges dependent on his Will alone, for the tenure of their offices, and the amount and payment of their salaries.

He has erected a multitude of New Offices, and sent hither swarms of Officers to harass our People, and eat out their substance.

He has kept among us, in times of peace, Standing Armies without the Consent of our legislature.

He has affected to render the Military independent of and superior to the Civil Power.

He has combined with others to subject us to a jurisdiction foreign to our constitution, and unacknowledged by our laws; giving his Assent to their acts of pretended legislation:

For quartering large bodies of armed troops among us:

For protecting them, by a mock Trial, from punishment for any Murders which they should commit on the Inhabitants of these States:

For cutting off our Trade with all parts of the world:

For imposing taxes on us without our Consent:

For depriving us in many cases, of the benefits of Trial by Jury:

For transporting us beyond Seas to be tried for pretend offences:

For abolishing the free System of English Laws in a neighboring Province, establishing therein an Arbitrary government, and enlarging its Boundaries so as to render it at once an example and fit instrument for introducing the same absolute rule into these Colonies.

For taking away our Charters, abolishing our most valuable Laws, and altering fundamentally the Forms of our Governments:

For suspending our own Legislature, and declaring themselves invested with Power to legislate for us in all cases whatsoever.

He has abdicated Government here, by declaring us out of his Protection and waging War against us.

He has plundered our seas, ravaged our Coasts, burnt our towns, and destroyed the lives of our people.

He is at this time transporting large armies of foreign mercenaries to complete the works of death, desolation and tyranny, already begun with circumstances of Cruelty & perfidy scarcely paralleled in the most barbarous ages, and totally unworthy the Head of a civilized nation.

He has constrained our fellow Citizens taken Captive on the high Seas to bear Arms against their Country, to become the executioners of their friends and Brethren, or to fall themselves by their Hands.

He has excited domestic insurrections amongst us, and has endeavoured to bring on the inhabitants of our frontiers, the merciless Indian Savages, whose known rule of warfare, is an undistinguished destruction of all ages, sexes and conditions.

In every stage of these Oppressions We have Petitioned for Redress in the most humble terms: Our repeated Petitions have been answered only by repeated injury. A Prince, whose character is thus marked by every act which may define a Tyrant, is unfit to be the ruler of a free People.

Nor have We been wanting in attention to our British brethren. We have warned them from time to time of attempts by their legislature to extend an unwarrantable jurisdiction over us. We have reminded them of the circumstances of our emigration and settlement here. We have appealed to their native justice and magnanimity, and we have conjured them by the ties of our common kindred to disavow the usurpations, which, would inevitably interrupt our connections and correspondence. They too have been deaf to the voice of justice and of consanguinity. We must, therefore, acquiesce in the necessity, which denounces our Separation, and hold them, as we hold the rest of mankind, Enemies in War, in Peace Friends.

We, therefore, the Representatives of the United States of America, in General Congress, Assembled, appealing to the Supreme Judge of the world for the rectitude of our intentions, do, in the Name, and by Authority of the good People of these Colonies, solemnly publish and declare, That these United Colonies are, and of Right ought be Free and Independent States; that they are Absolved from all Allegiance to the British Crown, and that all political connection between them and the State of Great Britain, is and ought to be totally dissolved; and that as Free and Independent States, they have full Power to levy War, conclude Peace, contract Alliances, establish Commerce, and do all other Acts and Things which Independent States may of right do. And for the support of this Declaration, with a firm reliance on the Protection of Divine Providence, we mutually pledge to each other our Lives, our Fortunes and our sacred Honor.

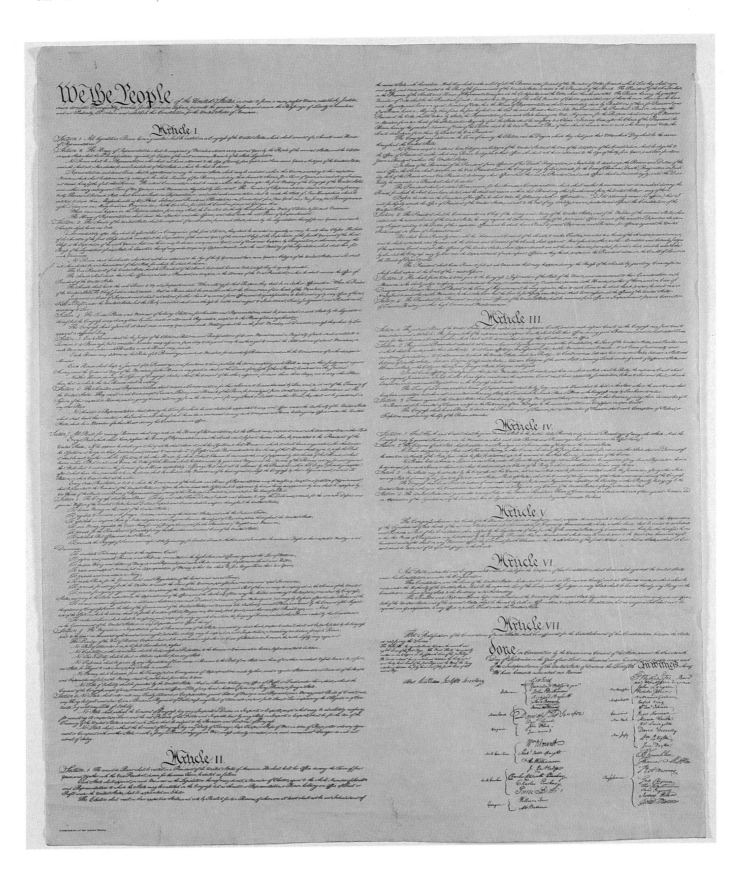

THE US CONSTITUTION

The U.S. Constitution Defined

ARTICLE I
{The Federal Legislative Branch}

Section 1.   The Legislative Body

As a compromise between the southern and northern states, a bicameral legislature consisting of a Senate and a House of Representatives was created to serve as the nation's legislative body. Representation in the House of Representatives depends upon population, whereas each state has an equal representation in the Senate.

Section 2.   The House of Representatives

a.   The members of the House of Representatives are elected for a two year term of office.

b.   House of Representatives members must be at least 25 years of age, be a US citizen for at least 7 years, and be a resident of the state that he/she will be representing (a long-standing practice in the House is that representatives also be residents of the *district* they are representing).

c.   Congress will determine the number of representatives to be assembled in the House of Representatives, each representing a district of a given state (in 1929, Congress passed a law establishing a permanent apportionment of 435 seats, to be redistributed after every census). Each district will be equivalent in population size so as to ensure equal representation for all voters, and there must be at least one representative per state, regardless of population. Districts must be re-established by population count (census) every ten years.

d.   When vacancies occur, the Executive Authority of the state that is deficient will order an election to fill the vacancy.

e.   The House of Representatives will choose their speaker and other officers; and shall have the sole power of impeachment of those officers.

Section 3.   The Senate

a.   The Senate of the United States is composed of two senators from each state, elected by the people of that state.

b.   Each senator will serve for a term of six years, and each senator shall have one vote.

c.   The Senate is separated into thirds, with each third elected every second year, creating a rotation of newly elected senators in two year increments (thus preventing the entire Senate from completely changing every 6 years).

d.   When vacancies occur, the Executive Authority of the state deficient will order an election to fill the vacancy, and may appoint a temporary Senator to represent the state, until such election can produce a newly elected Senator.

e.   US Senators must be at least 30 years of age, be a US citizen for at least nine years, and be a resident of the state that he/she will be representing.

f.   The Vice President of the United States will be the President of the Senate, and will only vote when the Senate is equally divided (to break the tie).

g.   The Senate will choose their officers, including a "President pro tempore" to act as President of the Senate in the absence of the Vice-President of the United States.

h.   The Senate has the sole power to try all impeachments (under oath or affirmation) including Supreme Court Justices and the President of the United States. When the President of the United States is tried, the Chief Justice will preside over the trial. No person can be convicted without the concurrence of two-thirds of the members present. Judgments of impeachment do not extend beyond removal from office, and disqualification from any other government office, but, the party may still be subject to indictment, trial, judgment, and punishment, according to the law.

Section 4.   Congressional Elections

a.   The time, place, and manner of holding elections for Senators and Representatives shall be prescribed by each individual state legislature, but Congress may at any time, by law, make or alter such regulations, except as to the places and choosing of Senators.

b.   The Congress will assemble at least once every year, and such meeting will be on the third day of January (as prescribed by the Twentieth Amendment), unless they shall, by law, appoint a different day.

Section 5.   Congressional Rules

a.   Each House of Congress shall be the judge of the elections, returns and qualifications of its own members.

b.   A majority of the members, in either house, must be present (constituting a Quorum) in order for that House to do business. Some members may adjourn from day to day, and others may be authorized to compel the attendance of absent members.

THE POWERS OF CONGRESS

LEGISLATIVE POWERS

Monetary:	**Taxing Power, Spending Power** **Coining Money, Borrowing Money**
Commerce & Regulatory:	**Regulate Interstate Commerce & International Trade** **Set Rules for Naturalization** **Establish and Maintain a Postal Service** **Provide for Patents and Copyrights** **Set Standards of Weights and Measures** **Set Uniform Laws of Bankruptcy**
Judicial:	**Set up Federal Courts** **Decide Punishment for Federal Crimes**
War:	**Declare War** **Maintain Armed Forces**
Implied:	**Make All Laws Necessary and Proper To** **Carry Out its Duties**

NON-LEGISLATIVE POWERS

Investigative:	**Determine Effectiveness & Proper Administration of Laws** **Gather Information Useful in Making New Laws**
Amend Constitution:	**Propose Amendments** **Call Convention to Propose Amendments at the** **Request of the States**
Electoral:	**Elect President (House) and Vice President (Senate)** **if No Candidate Wins Majority in National Election**
Judicial:	**Bring Impeachment Charges Against Federal Offices** **in the Executive and Judicial Branches (House)** **Try Impeachment Cases (Senate)**
Executive:	**Give Advice & Consent on Presidetial Appointments** **and Treaties**
Governing:	**Admit New States and Territories** **Administer Federal Lands**

Section 5.   **Congressional Rules**
                   (continued)

c.   Each House may determine the rules of its proceedings, punish its members for disorderly behavior, and, with the concurrence of a two-thirds majority, expel a member.

d.   Each house will keep a journal of its proceedings and publish it, from time to time, (omitting any parts which the House deems that secrecy is required), and the Yeas and Nays of either House on any question will be entered on the journal, at the desire of one-fifth of those present.

e.   Neither House, during the session of Congress, shall, without the consent of the other, adjourn for more than three days, nor to any other place other than the Capitol building.

Section 6.   **Congressional Pay & Privilege**

a.   The Senators and Representatives shall receive a compensation for their services, to be ascertained by law and paid out of the Treasury of the United States.

b.   Congressmen shall in all cases, except treason, felony, and breach of the peace, be privileged from arrest during their attendance at the session of, or going to and from their respective Houses; and for any speech or debate in either House, they shall not be questioned in any other place.

c.   No Senator or Representative shall hold any other government position during his/her continuance in office.

Section 7.   **Legislation**

a.   All bills (Bill: a draft of a law presented for approval to a legislative body) for raising revenues shall originate in the House of Representatives; but the Senate may propose or concur with such Bills or amendments.

b.   Every bill must pass both Houses before being presented to the President of the United States.

c.   The President of the United States has ten days, from the time the bill was presented to him or her, to approve the bill, which then becomes law. If the bill is not returned by the President within the ten days, it will become law, as if he or she had signed it (unless Congress, by their adjournment, prevents its return)

d.   If the President should reject the bill, he/she must return it to the House in which it originated, along with his/her objections to the bill, which will be entered into that House's journal. That House will then reconsider the bill, and if passed by two-thirds (or more) of that House, the bill will then pass to the other House. If the second House, after reconsidering, should also pass the bill by two-thirds (or more), the bill will become law, despite the President's disapproval.

Section 8.   **Expressed Powers**

This section provides the powers that are expressly given to Congress, through the Constitution. They are the powers to:

a.   Raise money through taxes, duties, and excises to pay debts and provide for the common welfare.

b.   Borrow money on the credit of the United States.

c.   Regulate commerce among the states and with foreign nations.

d.   Establish uniform laws, throughout the nation, regarding bankruptcy and naturalization.

e.   Coin money, regulate the value thereof, and establish a standard of weights and measures.

f.   Establish the punishment for counterfeiting the securities and coinage of the United States.

g.   Establish post offices.

h.   Establish patents and copyrights.

i.   Create courts inferior to the Supreme Court (i.e. our federal court system).

j.   Establish maritime law.

k.   Declare war.

l.   Raise and support armed forces; also create the rules governing such forces.

m.   Govern the District of Columbia and other federal properties.

n.   Make any laws which are necessary and proper for the carrying out of the powers issued to all branches of the government through the Constitution (known as the "necessary and proper" clause, this portion of the Constitution is often invoked by legislators searching for a justification for their legislation).

Section 9.   **Powers Denied to Congress**

This section outlines the powers forbidden to Congress. Through this section Congress may not:

a.   Suspend the privilege of the writ of habeas corpus (right of a jailed individual to be released if charges cannot be brought against him), except in time of rebellion, invasion, or such that the public safety may require.

b.   Pass a bill of attainder (a law directed at a single individual) or ex post facto law (a law criminalizing an act done prior to the creation of the law).

CONSTITUTIONAL DIVISION OF POWER

POWERS OF THE NATIONAL GOVERNMENT

To reguate foreign trade and commerce between states

To borrow and coin money

To conduct foreign relations with other nations

To establish post offices and roads

To raise and support armed forces

To declare war and make peace

To govern territories and admit new states

To pass naturalization laws and regulate immigration

To make laws that are "necessary and proper" for the government

CONCURRENT POWERS

To collect taxes

To borrow money

To establish and maintain courts

To make and enforce laws

To provide for the health and welfare of the people

POWERS RESERVED TO STATE GOVERNMENTS

To regulate trade within the states

To establish local governments

To conduct elections

To determine voter qualifications

To establish and support public schools

To incorporate business firms

To license professional workers

To ratify amendments

To keep all the "reserved powers" not granted to the national government nor prohibited to the states

POWERS DENIED TO THE NATIONAL GOVERNMENT

To tax exports

To suspend writ of habeas corpus

To change state boundaries without consent of states involved

To abridge the Bill of Rights

POWERS DENIED TO BOTH NATIONAL AND STATE GOVERNMENTS

To pass ex post facto laws

To pass bills of attainder

To deny due process of law

To grant titles of nobility

POWERS DENIED TO STATE GOVERNMENTS

To coin money

To enter into treaties

To tax agencies of the federal government

To tax imports or exports

Section 9.   Powers Denied to Congress
                   (continued)

c. Give preference by regulation to the commerce of any state.

d. Draw money from the Treasury without the benefit of an appropriation law and a regular statement and account of expenditures.

e. Grant titles of nobility.

Section 10.   Powers Denied to the States

In order to eliminate many of the problems inherent in the loose association of the states under the Articles of Confederation, the authors of the Constitution made sure to delineate certain powers that the states were not allowed to possess. Under this section, states are proscribed from:

a. Making separate treaties or alliances.

b. Printing money.

c. Passing any bill of attainder or ex post facto law.

d. Granting titles of nobility.

e. Taxing imports or exports without the consent of Congress (an exception exists for amounts to cover the cost of inspection).

f. Keeping troops or warships in time of peace.

g. Entering into any agreement with another state or foreign power.

h. Engage in war, unless actually invaded.

ARTICLE II
{The Federal Executive Branch}

Section 1.   The President & V.P.

a. The power of the Executive Office is vested in the President of the United States.

b. The President and Vice President are elected to serve a four year term of office.

c. Each state appoints a number of electors equal to the total number of Senators and Representatives of that state. These electors (see "The Electoral College" – pg. 147) will meet in their respective states, and vote by ballot for the President and Vice President of the United States. The Congress may determine the time of choosing the electors, and the day on which they shall give their votes, which day shall be the same throughout the United States.

d. Only natural-born citizens of the United States are eligible for the office of President. He/she must also be at least 35 years old, and have resided in the US for at least 14 years.

e. In case of the removal of the President from office by legislative action, or as a result of his/her death or resignation, the Vice President shall become President. Also, whenever there is a vacancy in the office of Vice President, the President shall nominate a new Vice President, who shall take office upon confirmation by a majority vote of both Houses of Congress.

f. The President will be compensated for his/her services by an amount that neither increases or decreases during his/her term, and will not, during his/her term, receive any other compensation or profit from the United States, or any individual state.

g. Before a newly elected President can enter on the execution of office, he/she shall take the following Oath or Affirmation: – "I do solemnly swear (or affirm) that I will faithfully execute the office of President of the United States, and will, to the best of my ability, preserve, protect, and defend the Constitution of the United States."

Section 2.   Presidential Powers

a. The President shall be the Commander in Chief of the Armed Forces of the United States, including state militias when called into the actual service of the United States.

b. The President may require the opinion, in writing, of the principal officer in each of the executive departments, upon any subject relating to the duties of their respective offices.

c. The President has the power to grant reprieves and pardons for offenses against the United States, except in cases of impeachment.

Section 2. **Presidential Powers**
(continued)

d. The President has the power, with the advice and consent of the Senate, to make treaties (provided two-thirds of the Senate present concur), and can, also with the advice and consent of the Senate, appoint ambassadors and other public ministers and consuls, judges of the Supreme Court, and all other officers of the United States.

e. The President has the power to temporarily fill any vacancies that may happen during the recess of the Senate, which shall expire at the end of the Senate's next session.

Section 3. **Presidential Responsibilities**

a. The President will, from time to time, give to the Congress information about the state of the union, and recommend to their consideration such measures as he/she judges necessary and expedient.

b. The President may, on extraordinary occasions, convene both Houses of Congress, or either of them, and in case of disagreement between them concerning the time of adjournment, he/she may specify such time as he/she shall think proper.

c. The President will receive ambassadors and other public ministers.

d. The President will take care that the laws be faithfully executed, and commission all the officers of the United States.

Section 4. **Executive Jeopardy**

a. The President, Vice President and all civil officers of the United States will be removed from office on impeachment for, and conviction of, treason, bribery, or other high crimes and misdemeanors.

THE POWERS OF THE PRESIDENT

Executive:	Enforces Laws, Treaties and Court Decisions Issues Executive Orders in Carrying out Policies Presides Over the Executive Cabinet Appoints and Removes Officials Assumes Emergency Powers
Legislative:	Give Annual State of the Union Address to Congress Issue Annual Budget and Economics Reports Signs Legislation into Law and Vetoes Bills Proposes Legislation Uses Influence to Get Bills Passed Calls Special Sessions of Congress
Diplomatic:	Appoints Embassadors and Other Diplomats Makes Treaties and Executive Agreements Meets Other Leaders at International Conferences Grants Diplomatic Recognition to other Governments
Judicial:	Appoints Members of the Federal Judiciary Grants Reprieves, Pardons and Amnesty
Military:	Commander in Chief of the Armed Forces Has Final Decision Making Power in Matters of National Defense and Security Provides for Domestic Order

ARTICLE III
{The Federal Judicial Branch}

Section 1.   Judicial Establishment

a. The judicial power of the United States is vested in one Supreme Court, and also in the inferior courts established by the Congress.

b. The Judges, both of the Supreme and inferior courts, will hold their offices during good behavior, until retirement or death.

c. The Judges, both of the Supreme and inferior courts, will be compensated for their services, and such compensation will not diminish during their continuance in office.

Section 2.   Judicial Jurisdiction

a. The Judicial power extends to all cases, in law and equity, arising under this constitution. All laws and treaties of the United States will be made under this Judicial authority.

b. The Judicial power extends, also, to all cases involving ambassadors and other public ministers and consuls, cases of admiralty and maritime jurisdiction, controversies to which the United States shall be a party, controversies between two or more states, between a state and citizens of another state, between citizens of different states, and between a state, or the citizens thereof, and foreign states, citizens, or subjects.

c. The Supreme Court will have original jurisdiction over all cases affecting ambassadors and other public ministers and consuls. In all the other cases before mentioned, the Supreme Court will have appellate jurisdiction, both as to law and fact, with such exceptions, and under such regulations as the Congress shall make.

d. The trial of all crimes, except in cases of impeachment, shall be by jury, and such trial shall be held in the state where the said crimes may have been committed, but when not committed within any state, the trial shall be at such place or places as the Congress may by law have directed.

Section 3.   Cases of Treason

a. Treason shall consist only in levying war against the United States, or in adhering to their enemies, giving them aid and comfort. No person will be convicted of treason unless on the testimony of two witnesses to the same overt act, or on confession in open court.

b. The Congress will have power to declare the punishment of treason, but no forfeiture of civil rights shall be applied to the blood relatives of the accused.

THE FEDERAL JUDICIARY

The Supreme Court and the lower federal courts are independent for constitutional and historical reasons. There are limits, however, on the independence of the federal judiciary.

Independence
Supreme Court justices and other federal judges are appointed by the President for lifetime terms (with the Senate's consent) during which their salaries cannot be lowered. This allows justices to apply the law without political concern.

Reasons for Independence
An independent judiciary can check the executive and legislative branches and temporary popular majorities, and provide a remedy when those branches of government fail to act; in addition to protecting individual rights, controlling crime, resolving conflict, promoting general welfare, limiting government, and setting social goals.

Limits of Independence
Members of the judiciary can be impeached by Congress; a Supreme Court decision can be reversed by an amendment to the constitution; lower courts must base their decisions on the precedents set in other courts (stare decisis); federal courts must have the support of most of the people most of the time.

ARTICLE IV
{State Governments}

Section 1. State Proceedings and Records

a. All of the United States shall have confident belief and trust in the decisions of any individual state, pertaining to public acts, records, and judicial proceedings.

b. Congress may, by general laws, prescribe the manner in which such acts, records, and proceedings shall be proved to other states, such as by certified copies of state documents, authenticated copies, etc.

Section 2. State Constitution

a. The citizens of each state shall be entitled to all privileges and immunities of citizens in the several states.

b. A person who has been charged with a crime in any state, who has fled from justice to another state, shall on demand of the Executive authority of the state from which he/she fled, be delivered up and removed (extradited) to that state having jurisdiction of the crime.

Section 3. State Boundaries

a. New states may be admitted by the Congress into this union. But, no new state will be formed within the jurisdiction of another state, or formed by the junction of two or more states, without the consent of the legislature of the states concerned, as well as of the Congress.

b. The Congress has the power to dispose of and make all needful rules and regulations respecting the territory or other property belonging to the United States.

Section 4. State Protection

a. The United States will guarantee to every state in the union a republican form of government, and will protect each of them against invasion, and, on application of the legislature, or of the executive (when the legislature cannot be convened), protect that state against domestic violence.

ARTICLE V
{Amending the Constitution}

An amendment to the Constitution must be proposed and ratified. An amendment may be proposed as follows:

a. by two-thirds vote of both houses of Congress, or

b. a constitutional convention called by Congress at the request of two-thirds of the state legislatures (this method has never been used).

The ratification of a proposed amendment is accomplished by a positive vote by:

a. three-fourths of the state legislatures, or

b. special conventions in three-fourths of the states.

ARTICLE VI
{Constitutional Supremacy}

This section of the Constitution establishes the Constitution as the "supreme law of the land." This supremacy also applies to the federal laws made in pursuance of the Constitution.

The sixth Amendment also requires that all government officials either swear or affirm to uphold the principles and procedures of the Constitution, stating; "The Senators and Representatives before mentioned, and the Members of the several State Legislatures, and all executive and judicial officers, both of the United States and of the several States, shall be bound by Oath or Affirmation, to support this Constitution; but no religious Test shall ever be required as a Qualification to any Office or public Trust under the United States."

ARTICLE VII
{Ratification}

The framers of the Constitution provided that 9 of the 13 states must ratify the Constitution by conventions held in each respective state in order for it to become the governing instrument. This requisite number was reached on June 21, 1788.

AMENDMENTS

When the Constitution was sent to the states for ratification, there arose numerous objections that the document failed to enumerate personal liberties. Many states ratified the Constitution, with the understanding that a bill of rights would be added. Twelve amendments were drawn up as the original bill of rights, but only ten of these were ratified by the states. These original ten amendments make up what we now refer to as The Bill of Rights. Amazingly, since the passage of the Bill of Rights in 1791, there have only been an additional sixteen amendments added to the Constitution.

Congreſs OF THE United States

begun and held at the City of New-York, on

Wednesday the Fourth of March, one thousand seven hundred and eighty nine

THE Conventions of a number of the States, having at the time of their adopting the Constitution, expressed a desire, in order to prevent misconstruction or abuse of its powers, that further declaratory and restrictive clauses should be added: And as extending the ground of public confidence in the Government, will best ensure the beneficent ends of its institution.

RESOLVED by the Senate and House of Representatives of the United States of America, in Congress assembled, two thirds of both Houses concurring, that the following Articles be proposed to the Legislatures of the several States, as amendments to the Constitution of the United States, all, or any of which Articles, when ratified by three fourths of the said Legislatures, to be valid to all intents and purposes, as part of the said Constitution; viz.

ARTICLES in addition to, and amendment of the Constitution of the United States of America, proposed by Congress, and ratified by the Legislatures of the several States, pursuant to the fifth Article of the original Constitution.

Article the first.... After the first enumeration required by the first Article of the Constitution, there shall be one Representative for every thirty thousand, until the number shall amount to one hundred, after which, the proportion shall be so regulated by Congress, that there shall be not less than one hundred Representatives, nor less than one Representative for every forty thousand persons, until the number of Representatives shall amount to two hundred, after which the proportion shall be so regulated by Congress, that there shall not be less than two hundred Representatives, nor more than one Representative for every fifty thousand persons.

Article the second. No law, varying the compensation for the services of the Senators and Representatives, shall take effect, until an election of Representatives shall have intervened.

Article the third. Congress shall make no law respecting an establishment of religion, or prohibiting the free exercise thereof; or abridging the freedom of speech, or of the press; or the right of the people peaceably to assemble, and to petition the Government for a redress of grievances.

Article the fourth. A well regulated militia, being necessary to the security of a free State, the right of the people to keep and bear arms, shall not be infringed.

Article the fifth. No Soldier shall, in time of peace be quartered in any house, without the consent of the owner, nor in time of war, but in a manner to be prescribed by law.

Article the sixth. The right of the people to be secure in their persons, houses, papers, and effects, against unreasonable searches and seizures, shall not be violated, and no Warrants shall issue, but upon probable cause, supported by oath or affirmation, and particularly describing the place to be searched, and the persons or things to be seized.

Article the seventh. No person shall be held to answer for a capital, or otherwise infamous crime, unless on a presentment or indictment of a Grand Jury, except in cases arising in the land or naval forces, or in the militia, when in actual service in time of War or public danger; nor shall any person be subject for the same offence to be twice put in jeopardy of life or limb, nor shall be compelled in any criminal case to be a witness against himself, nor be deprived of life, liberty, or property, without due process of law; nor shall private property be taken for public use without just compensation.

Article the eighth. In all criminal prosecutions, the accused shall enjoy the right to a speedy and public trial, by an impartial jury of the State and district wherein the crime shall have been committed, which district shall have been previously ascertained by law, and to be informed of the nature and cause of the accusation; to be confronted with the witnesses against him; to have compulsory process for obtaining witnesses in his favor, and to have the assistance of counsel for his defence.

Article the ninth. In suits at common law, where the value in controversy shall exceed twenty dollars, the right of trial by jury shall be preserved, and no fact tried by a jury, shall be otherwise re-examined in any Court of the United States, than according to the rules of the common law.

Article the tenth. Excessive bail shall not be required, nor excessive fines imposed, nor cruel and unusual punishments inflicted.

Article the eleventh. The enumeration in the Constitution, of certain rights, shall not be construed to deny or disparage others retained by the people.

Article the twelfth. The powers not delegated to the United States by the Constitution, nor prohibited by it to the States, are reserved to the States respectively, or to the people.

ATTEST,

Frederick Augustus Muhlenberg, Speaker of the House of Representatives.

John Adams, Vice President of the United States, and President of the Senate.

John Beckley, Clerk of the House of Representatives.

Sam. A. Otis Secretary of the Senate.

THE US BILL OF RIGHTS

The Bill of Rights Defined

First Amendment

Perhaps the most cited Amendment, it provides that Congress shall make no law establishing a national religion or interfering with the free practice of religion. In addition, the Amendment protects the freedom of speech, the freedom of the press, the right to assemble peaceably, and the right to petition the government for a redress of grievances.

Second Amendment

This amendment states that "A well regulated militia, being necessary to the security of a free state, the right of the people to keep and bear Arms, shall not be infringed." The exact meaning of this amendment, particularly in regard to personal gun ownership, has recently been a source of much debate, and has yet to be satisfactorily determined.

Third Amendment

Provides that no soldier shall be quartered in any house, without the consent of the owner, in times of peace. In times of war, troops may only be quartered as prescribed by law. This amendment came as a result of the British practice of quartering troops during the colonial period.

Fourth Amendment

Establishes the right of individuals to be free from unreasonable searches and seizures of themselves, their houses, their papers, and other personal property. This amendment also requires the government to show probable cause before issuing a warrant.

Fifth Amendment

The fifth amendment provides that no person shall be held to answer for a capital or other serious crime, unless he or she has been indicted by a grand jury (an exception is provided for the armed forces). It also provides that no one may be subject for the same offense twice (double jeopardy); no one may be compelled to be a witness against himself/herself; no one may be deprived of life, liberty, or property, without due process of law; and, no one may have his or her private property taken for public use without just compensation.

Sixth Amendment

An individual being tried for a criminal offense has the right to a speedy trial, before a jury of his/her peers. Along with this, the individual has the right to know the charges brought against him; the right to confront witnesses against him; the right to subpoena witnesses favorable toward him; and the right to have counsel assist him at trial.

Seventh Amendment

In civil actions, where the amount in controversy exceeds twenty dollars, an individual has the right to request a trial by jury. A decision, issued by the jury, is binding, although it may be appealed through the federal process (this only applies to federal actions).

Eighth Amendment

The government cannot set excessive bail, nor impose excessive fines upon an individual. In addition, cruel and unusual punishment may not be inflicted upon any individual.

Ninth Amendment

This amendment provides that the rights listed in the Constitution are not the only ones enjoyed by the citizenry. As the amendment states, "the enumeration in the constitution of certain rights shall not be construed to deny or disparage others retained by the people."

Tenth Amendment

The powers not delegated to the federal government are to be reserved to the states or the people. Among these are the power to set up state courts, establish civil and criminal laws, tax, etc.

The Remaining Amendments

Amendment 11 (January 8, 1798)

No suit brought against an individual state may be tried in the federal courts (this alters Article III, Section 2); instead, the suit must be brought in the courts of that state.

Amendment 12 (September 25, 1804)

This amendment altered the way in which we elect the President and Vice President. It established an electoral process by which the electors meet in their respective states and vote by ballot for President and Vice President. Distinct lists are made of the persons voted for, and this is sent to the president of the Senate. Should no presidential candidate receive a majority of the electoral votes, the House of Representatives elects a President from the leading three candidates. This amendment is a mere formality in the modern world, where we know the outcome of an election upon the closing of the ballot boxes.

Amendment 13 (December 18, 1865)

This amendment formally ended slavery. Section 1 of the amendment states that neither slavery nor involuntary servitude may exist in this country, except as punishment for a convicted criminal. Section 2 is known as the "enabling clause," and allows Congress to enforce this amendment through appropriate legislation.

Amendment 14 (July 28, 1868)

The power of this amendment comes from the language stating, "no state may deny any person, under its government, equal protection of the law." Known as the "equal protection clause," this amendment was used extensively in the civil rights struggles, which occurred about 100 years after the passage of this amendment. The amendment also provides language designed to punish states that interfered with the right of African-Americans to vote (this part of the amendment was never enforced); additionally, punitive measures toward the Confederacy were included.

Amendment 15 (March 30, 1870)

This amendment protected the right of African-Americans (males only, prior to ratification of the 19th amendment) to vote. The language provides that, "the right of the citizens of the United States to vote cannot be taken away because of a person's race, color, or previous condition of servitude."

Amendment 16 (February 25, 1913)

Established the right of the federal government to collect income taxes (this altered Article I, Section 2).

Amendment 17 (May 31, 1913)

This amendment changed the way in which US. Senators are elected. Prior to the amendment, Senators were elected by the state legislatures, but this amendment allowed for their election by a popular vote of the people.

Amendment 18 (January 29, 1919)

Prohibited the manufacture, sale, and transportation of intoxicating liquors in the United States. This amendment was voided by the twenty-first amendment.

Amendment 19 (August 26, 1920)

Prohibited the denial of the right to vote based on a person's sex. In essence, this extended the right to vote to all women. Prior to this amendment, only nine states allowed women the opportunity to vote.

Amendment 20 (February 6, 1933)

Changed the dates upon which the President, Vice President and members of Congress begin their terms in office. This amendment did away with the long delay between election and assumption of office.

Amendment 21 (December 5, 1933)

Repealed the 18th amendment, thereby repealing prohibition.

Amendment 22 (February 26, 1951)

Restricted the number of terms an individual can serve as President. No one may be elected to the office more than twice; additionally, if a person has acted as President for more than two years of a term to which some other person was elected then that person may only be elected once.

Amendment 23 (April 3, 1961)

Extends the right to vote in Presidential and Vice-Presidential elections to those living in the District of Columbia. The District is now represented by as many electors in the electoral college as its population calls for. But, it may never have more electors than the least populated state.

Amendment 24 (February 4, 1964)

Provides that no citizen can be denied the right to vote in federal elections due to the failure to pay any poll or other tax.

Amendment 25 (February 10, 1967)

This amendment makes provisions should the President die, resign, or become incapacitated. Should the President become incapacitated by injury or illness, the Vice President and a majority of the President's Cabinet may inform the president pro tempore of the Senate and the Speaker of the House, in writing, and the Vice President immediately becomes Acting President. The President may resume his/her position when he/she informs the president pro tempore and the speaker that he/she is again capable of carrying out the duties and powers of the office. If this is contradicted by the Vice President and a majority of the cabinet, then it becomes a question for Congress. The amendment also provides for replacement of the Vice President should that office become vacant during his/her term in office.

Amendment 26 (June 30, 1971)

Brought about by the Vietnam War, this amendment lowered the voting age to eighteen by providing that "citizens of the United States eighteen years or older may not be denied the right to vote by the United States or any state, on account of age."

Amendment 27 (1992)

Originally proposed in 1789 as the second of the original twelve articles proposed as the Bill of Rights, this amendment states: "No law, varying the compensation for the services of the Senators and Representatives, shall take effect, until an election of Representatives shall have intervened."

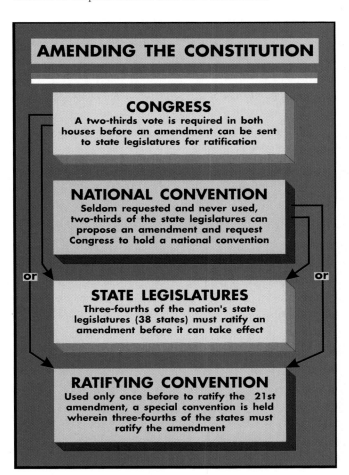

AMENDING THE CONSTITUTION

CONGRESS
A two-thirds vote is required in both houses before an amendment can be sent to state legislatures for ratification

NATIONAL CONVENTION
Seldom requested and never used, two-thirds of the state legislatures can propose an amendment and request Congress to hold a national convention

or   or

STATE LEGISLATURES
Three-fourths of the nation's state legislatures (38 states) must ratify an amendment before it can take effect

RATIFYING CONVENTION
Used only once before to ratify the 21st amendment, a special convention is held wherein three-fourths of the states must ratify the amendment

CHAPTER 5

HOW CONGRESS WORKS

by Ms. Roberta Weiner
Vice President – Americans for Democratic Action

GLOSSARY
for How Congress Works

Activism
1. To take action or effectuate change
2. The theory, doctrine, or practice of assertive, often militant action, such as mass demonstrations or strikes, used as a means of opposing or supporting a controversial issue, entity, or person.

Amendment/Amending
1. The act of changing for the better
2. A correction or an alteration, as in a manuscript.
3. a. Formal revision of, addition to, or change, as in a bill or a constitution. b. A statement of such a change: The 19th Amendment to the Constitution gave women the right to vote.

Appropriations
1. Something appropriated, especially public funds set aside for a specific purpose.
2. A legislative act authorizing the expenditure of a designated amount of public funds for a specific purpose.

Autocratic
1. Rulership of unlimited power or authority; despotism.

Baby Boomers
1. Member of a baby-boom generation; commonly referring to those born in the US between 1946 to 1963.

Caucus
1. A meeting of the local members of a political party especially to select delegates to a convention or register preferences for candidates running for office.
2. A closed meeting of party members within a legislative body to decide on questions of policy or leadership.
3. A group within a legislative or decision-making body seeking to represent a specific interest or influence a particular area of policy: a minority caucus.

Chair
1. A piece of furniture consisting of a seat, legs, back, and often arms, designed to accommodate one person.
2. A seat of office, authority, or dignity.
3. An office or position of authority, such as a professorship.
4. A person who holds an office or a position of authority, such as one who presides over a meeting or administers a department of instruction at a college; a chairperson.

Colloquy
1. Characteristic of or appropriate to the spoken language or to writing that seeks the effect of speech; informal.
2. Relating to conversation; conversational.

Committee
1. A group of people officially delegated to perform a function, such as investigating, considering, reporting, or acting on a matter.

Constituents
1. Resident of a district or member of a group represented by an elected official.

Delegation
1. A person or group of persons officially elected or appointed to represent another or others.

District
1. A division of an area, as for administrative purposes.

Enterprise Zone
1. An impoverished area in which businesses are exempt from certain taxes and are given other economic advantages as an inducement to locate there and employ residents.

Filibuster
1. The use of obstructionist tactics, especially prolonged speechmaking, for the purpose of delaying legislative action.
2. An instance of the use of this delaying tactic.

Fortune 500
1. The five hundred most successful corporations in a given year, as determined by Fortune magazine (founded in 1936 by Henry Luce as a business monthly).

Germane
1. Being both pertinent and fitting.

Grassroots
1. People or society at a local level rather than at the center of major political activity.
2. The groundwork or source of something.

Jurisdiction
1. The territorial range of authority or control.
2. Law. The right and power to interpret and apply the law: courts having jurisdiction in this district.
3. a. Authority or control: islands under U.S. jurisdiction; a bureau with jurisdiction over Native American affairs. b. The extent of authority or control: a family matter beyond the school's jurisdiction.

Legislative/Legislation
1. The act or process of legislating; lawmaking.
2. A proposed or enacted law or group of laws.

Lobbying/Lobbyist
1. To try to, or one who tries to, influence the thinking of legislators or other public officials

Lot
1. The use of objects in making a determination or choice at random: chosen by lot.
2. The determination or choice so made.

Mark-up
1. A session of a U.S. congressional committee at which a legislative bill is put into final form.

this glossary is continued on page 74

HOW CONGRESS WORKS

Ms. Roberta Weiner
Vice President – Americans for Democratic Action

"Democracy is based upon the conviction that there are extraordinary possibilities in ordinary people."
— *Harry Emerson Fosdick*

MS. CARTWRIGHT GOES TO WASHINGTON

It's December, more than a month before she will be sworn in, and newly elected first-termer Rep. Monica Cartwright has arrived in Washington, ready to conquer her new world.

Rep. Cartwright, 45, a liberal Democrat from a mid-size northeastern city, is part of a new breed of women Members of Congress who have come to politics through community activism. Soon after helping to spearhead a successful local effort to save her city's deteriorating historic district, she became the first woman to serve on its City Council, and eventually, moved on to the state legislature, where, after three terms, she was elected Deputy Majority Leader of the State Senate. Married to an architect and the mother of two college-age children, she combines a deep commitment to improving the quality of urban life, with the kind of political savvy that's needed to get things done.

She ran for an open seat, in the most diverse district in the state, an old city on a river with a declining industrial base. Her constituents range from public-housing tenants, to "baby boomers" who have settled in the restored historic district; from retired ethnic factory workers, to a growing African-American and Asian-immigrant minority community. Her opponent, a traditional Republican who ran on a platform focused on crime, taxes, and "family values," received 46% of the vote.

Rep. Cartwright understands that her dry, constitutional mandate is to make laws in the areas of monetary power, commerce and regulatory affairs, judicial functions, and war. But, her personal mandate is to help renew her city's economy, to create new kinds of jobs for those displaced by old industries, to help develop programs that will prevent crime, and to improve the quality of life for <u>all</u> her constituents. Yet, despite her idealism, she is a pragmatist, and her years in the legislature and its leadership have taught her about the real politics and artful compromises she will have to make, to achieve her goals.

It was not an easy race, and while Rep. Cartwright won with a definitive majority, she will have to devote time, over the next months, to building bridges in parts of the district. I know. I have come back to Washington, after running her campaign, to serve as her Chief of Staff. Like many of my colleagues, I have spent my professional life moving between campaigns and the Hill, finding both arenas fulfilling and the variety exciting. It's important for the Congresswoman-elect to have someone with her who is knowledgeable about the political nature of her new job, knows the whys-and-wherefores of setting up an office, and can put together an effective and congenial staff.

While her swearing in is a month away, Rep. Cartwright is here, now, to learn how to be a Member of Congress. She will spend the next ten days attending seminars, both on the Hill and at Harvard, making preparations—intellectual, administrative and political—for this highly complex new phase of her life. She will be taught the intricacies of the legislative process, focus on the legislative priorities of the new session, explore the newly-tightened do's-and-don'ts of ethics and office management, and learn about computer systems and constituent services.

She will caucus with her fellow Democrats, incoming freshmen, and women. She will be shown around her new "home town," and wined and dined by corporations and colleagues. And, if that weren't enough, she will try to find an affordable apartment close to the office. (While Members of Congress now earn $129,500 per year, it is difficult for many to maintain two homes and two cars, and although Rep. Cartwright is fortunate in having a working spouse, they have two children in college.)

Meanwhile, working out of a cubby-hole, with a computer set up in one of the House cafeterias, I will focus on the details. Office locations are determined by chance, so I will draw a "lot" for office space, decide with Rep. Cartwright what kind of office systems we want, keep track of her schedule, and even decide what color the office should be painted. Most importantly, I must begin sifting through the hundreds of resumes that have come across my desk, first separating out those people that are clearly wrong for our office. Like everyone else, we're looking for bright, knowledgeable, and energetic people who share Rep. Cartwright's political views and are committed to her goals.

Of course, I'm also looking for people who are willing to work for a pittance—each member receives the same limited amount of money for staff, and can hire a maximum of 18 people, not a lot, considering that we are planning to have two offices in our district. We must make some careful decisions about allocating our resources. While I will begin recommending people to Rep. Cartwright now for jobs, such as press secretary, office/systems manager, and caseworkers, I want to wait until after she receives her committee assignments before we hire legislative staff.

COMMITTEE ASSIGNMENTS

Soon after the election, Rep. Cartwright sat down with her political mentor, Rep. Steve Moore, a Member of Congress from the District adjoining hers. An 18-year veteran of the House, he is currently the Chair of her state delegation caucus. Members of the delegation get together twice a month for lunch, in the capitol, to discuss the impact of current legislation on the state; to hear from representatives of the governor's office and city and county governments about their current legislative concerns; and to develop, where possible, a coordinated strategy on priority issues. Like other non-official caucuses, this is an arena where local or other priorities can outweigh partisan politics. The delegation also votes on recommendations to the Steering and Policy Committee on committee assignments.

Rep. Cartwright was anxious to make a decision about her committee assignments, and the application and lobbying process begins early and moves forward intensively. Fortunately, Rep. Moore, as a member of the House leadership (he is one of six regional Assistant Chief Whips), is in a position to both offer wise advice and play a significant role in assuring that she receives the assignments she wants. They focused on those committees that will make use of her expertise and are related to the committees on which she served in the state legislature; Committees that impact on the issues that are important for her District—issues she emphasized during the campaign—and that mesh with her urban affairs priorities.

Banking, Finance, and Urban Affairs is her first choice, for several reasons: its housing and community development jurisdiction; her interest in the creation of urban enterprise zones and community development banks; and the possible opportunity to expand her horizons to international relations, through the committee's oversight of international lending institutions such as the World Bank. Her back-up choices are Public Works and Transportation, or Education and Labor, both because they have jurisdictions in which she can influence legislation to benefit her district.

Rep. Moore knows who from their state is on each committee, where there will be vacancies due to retirements and electoral losses, and where new members with her expertise are needed. Believing she has a good chance of getting onto Banking, he offered to call Rep. Henry B. Gonzalez, the Committee's chairman, to set up an appointment for both of them to visit with him. He also gave her a list of key members of the Steering and Policy Committee to contact. The Steering and Policy Committee makes all Democratic committee assignments, which must later be ratified by the whole House, and it is important that she meet with those Members who have a hand in deciding her fate. The Senate makes its committee assignments in a similar manner.

STANDING COMMITTEES OF CONGRESS

SENATE

Aging
Agriculture, Nutrition, and Forestry
Appropriations
Armed Services
Banking, Housing, and Urban Affairs
Budget
Commerce, Science, and Transportation
Energy and Natural Resources
Environment and Public Works
Ethics
Finance
Foreign Relations
Governmental Affairs
Indian Affairs
Intelligence
Judiciary
Labor and Human Resources
Rules and Administration
Small Business
Veterans Affairs

JOINT COMMITTEES

Economic   Library
    Printing   Taxation

HOUSE OF REPRESENTATIVES

Agriculture
Appropriations
Banking and Financial Services
Budget
Commerce
Economic and Education Opportunities
Government Reform and Oversight
House Oversight
Intelligence
International Relations
Judiciary
National Security
Merchant Marine and Fisheries
Resources
Rules
Science
Small Business
Standards of Official Conduct
Transportation and Infrastructure
Veterans Affairs
Ways and Means

Before her December trip to Washington, she spoke with most of the members of the state's delegation, and is optimistic about their support for her assignment to Banking. She also wrote to members of the House leadership and Steering and Policy Committee, indicating her preferences and requesting meetings during the December session, which she feels also went very well.

Rep. Cartwright leaves Washington for the holidays, with two new staff members on board—a press secretary and an office manager, and an armload of reading and resumes. She is confident about her committee assignments and excited about the new adventure on which she is to embark.

THE CONGRESSPERSON'S JOB

We returned to Washington on the first workday of the New Year, and although Rep. Cartwright was sworn in, surrounded by her family and hundreds of supporters who came by bus for the occasion, the legislative business of the House did not begin until three weeks later. The intervening weeks were used by the Steering and Policy Committee and the Democratic Caucus for meetings to determine committee assignments, establish the rules for the organization of the House for the 103rd Congress, and determine the legislative priorities for the session's first weeks.

Rep. Cartwright was grateful for the time, during which she began to set up her offices (there will be two constituent services offices in the district—a main office downtown and a satellite office across the river, in the poorest part of the District), hire staff, and bone up on the important legislative issues that are beginning to emerge. We were fortunate in finding an office manager wise in the ways of office systems, and we will have a single computer network connecting all our offices in order to keep track of correspondence and maintain contact with our constituents.

We were thrilled when Rep. Moore stopped by with a bottle of champagne to let Rep. Cartwright know that her homework had paid off and she was scheduled to be assigned to the Banking Committee (she will also serve on the Small Business Committee and the Space, Science and Technology Committee—both also of potential benefit to economic development in her district), and she began immediately to meet, informally, with her new colleagues, to determine where her priorities and the Committee's intersect.

The Democratic Caucus controls the balance between Democrats and Republicans on each committee—it is now about two-to-one. In the past few years, the Democratic makeup of the Banking Committee has shifted from moderates, with close ties to the banking industry, to liberal, urban members—many of them women and minorities—with an interest in community development and consumer issues. The Republicans' ranking minority member is Rep. Jim Leach (IA), who, while he has been outspoken on the need for hearings on the Whitewater scandal, often has more in common with the Democrats than with his many more conservative colleagues. Its chairman, Henry B. Gonzalez, is a quirky Texas populist who, after 31 years on the Committee, is a staunch supporter of housing, and could be a natural ally of Rep. Cartwright. He is much less autocratic (and wields less power in the House)

The US House of Representatives

than his predecessor, Rep. Ferdinand St. Germain, who was voted out of office as a result of his central role in the savings and loan scandal.

As soon as the word was out that Rep. Cartwright would be on the Banking Committee, the phone began ringing with requests for appointments. Representatives of organizations, ranging from the Department of Housing and Urban Development and the World Bank to the National Coalition for Public Housing and the US League of Savings Institutions made requests to make courtesy calls on the Congresswoman, but we waited until we had a knowledgeable staff person on board before she began seeing them.

The role of good staff cannot be underestimated, and, as with Members, it is the relatively few who have abused the system who have given the job a bad name. About 13,000 bills are introduced in each house every Congressional session. Unless there is someone who can help bring a specific bill to the top of the pile, the legislation will languish. Nor can a Member be an expert on the extraordinary range of issues those bills incorporate. Legislative Assistants (LAs) are specialists who focus on one, or only a limited number, of issues, and an LA with both expertise and political savvy is a most valuable asset.

We were very fortunate in finding, through the grapevine (senior staff is rarely hired from resumes sent cold), a ten-year Hill veteran who had handled Banking Committee work for a just-retired Democratic member. Rosalie Burr is philosophically *simpatico* with the Congresswoman and has an intimate knowledge of the issues and the players. She knows the Committee members and both friendly and opposition lobbyists, and is universally respected and well-liked.

Rep. Cartwright finds time in a tremendously busy and pressured schedule of hearings, meetings, and floor debates, to meet regularly with each of her four LAs, to discuss her priorities and legislative strategy, to get reports on meetings and hearings she has not been able to attend in person, and to check on constituent response on an issue. She also signs off on all written materials—*Congressional Record* inserts, letters, etc.—that go out of the office over her signature. She has assigned her staff to meet with and represent her views (with some exceptions), with other members' staff, lobbyists, and constituents.

GETTING A BILL TO
THE FLOOR OF THE HOUSE

On each of her committees, the Congresswoman has been assigned to either two or three subcommittees: on Banking, she will serve on Consumer Credit and Insurance, Housing and Community Development, and International Development, Finance, Trade and Monetary Policy. Her appointment to Consumer Credit and Insurance is a boon to her deep interest in Community Enterprise Zones, which can make low-interest loans to small businesspersons and provide tax incentives and breaks for those opening businesses within such a Zone, usually in an inner city area. The legislation has already been introduced, and while she and Rosalie Burr generally favor the bill's provisions, they have introduced a bill that would mandate a child care center within each Enterprise Zone, where at least 35% of employees are single parents. The center would be financed by the employers within the Zone.

After deciding on the specific provisions that the bill should include, Rosalie went to see the Legislative Counsel assigned to the committee. He understands every nuance of federal housing and community development law, and was able to help the Congresswoman prepare a bill that was legally correct and very specific. At the same time, Rosalie began meeting with other members' staff—starting with members of the Banking Committee and the Congressional Caucus on Women's Issues—to seek co-sponsors for the bill, the Enterprise Zone Child-Care Act of 1993, and by the time it is introduced we already have 12 co-sponsors. The bill is given a number, HR (House Resolution) 271, and is referred to the Banking Committee.

The Congresswoman immediately made an appointment with the subcommittee's chairman to discuss how best to proceed with the bill. They decide that it can be offered as an amendment to the Enterprise Zone legislation, and he tells her that after minor modifications he will support her provision, and include witnesses in support of HR 271 when he holds hearings within the next few weeks.

In the meantime, Rosalie has reached out for support to the Enterprise Zone Task Force, a coalition of several grass-roots, public-interest organizations that have come together to support the legislation. The Task Force, like many similar groups, is made up of labor unions and organizations concerned with housing, welfare reform, children's and women's issues, and equal opportunity, and can be extremely helpful to us in engendering grass-roots support for the bill. They immediately responded to Rep. Cartwright's bill and agreed to include the provisions of HR 271 in the mailings each organization will send to its members, urging them to write their Members of Congress to support the bill. She also spoke with the Congressional Liaisons from HUD and the White House, both of whom were enthusiastic in their response and agreed to lobby for the bill.

Among the groups opposing HR 271 were the National Association of Independent Businesses, concerned about the cost to small business, and the Christian Coalition, which opposes any legislation they consider anti-family. But we were surprised to find that the National Association of Women Business Owners is among our opponents, claiming that the legislation will place undue financial burden on the women business owners that the Enterprise Zone legislation is designed to help. In a conversation with the Congresswoman, their representative asserted that they would be willing to support the bill if the percentage of single parents is raised to 51%. Representative Cartwright could not agree.

Hearings are scheduled, and along with representatives from the Department of Housing and Urban Development, the Department of Commerce, and the Small Business Administration, all of which support the bill, we will hear testimony from, among others, the AFL-CIO, the Minority Business Council, several opponents of the bill, and, at my request, the Children's Defense Fund and a large corporation that has provided on-site child care for its employees for many years. At the end of the day before the hearing, Rosalie received a briefing book from the subcommittee, containing the testimony of the witnesses who were to appear. Based on the testimony, she worked late into the night preparing questions for the Congresswoman to ask at the hearing.

The hearing, one of two on her schedule that morning, presented a compelling case for the legislation. Opposition witnesses did not have strong arguments, but it was clear from the tenor of the questions that support for the bill, and for HR 271, like so much legislation, would break down along party lines, with opponents claiming the bill will add to the deficit and do little to help the deteriorating communities it is designed to serve.

Prior to mark-up (placement on the house calendar) two weeks later, the transcript of the hearing was printed and distributed to subcommittee members, along with copies of the amendments that would be offered to the bill. For three hours the members of the subcommittee, seated in a small hearing room filled with staff and lobbyists, debated and voted on every provision of the bill. After a contentious discussion, Congresswoman Cartwright's child-care provision was included, with, as expected, only a single Republican vote in its favor. The bill was voted out of subcommittee, and referred to the full committee. The bill, while somewhat modified, was still strong enough to have the support of its sponsors.

After the mark-up, the subcommittee issued a Report on the bill, containing a provision-by-provision analysis of the legislation, a history indicating how particular provisions should be interpreted, and comments by the Majority and Minority on their views of the legislation. Individual members can also include comments, and Rep. Cartwright has included her views on the importance of the child-care provision.

Although full committee hearings are optional, the full Banking Committee has decided that, because the legislation is innovative, it will hold another set before it marks up the bill. During the intervening weeks, while the Congresswoman met with sympathetic colleagues to strategize for a positive outcome, both the Coalition and groups opposing the bill sent their grass-roots representatives to visit with each member of the Committee when they were in their home districts, and Washington lobbyists worked with sympathetic staff, on both sides, to get their pet provisions included.

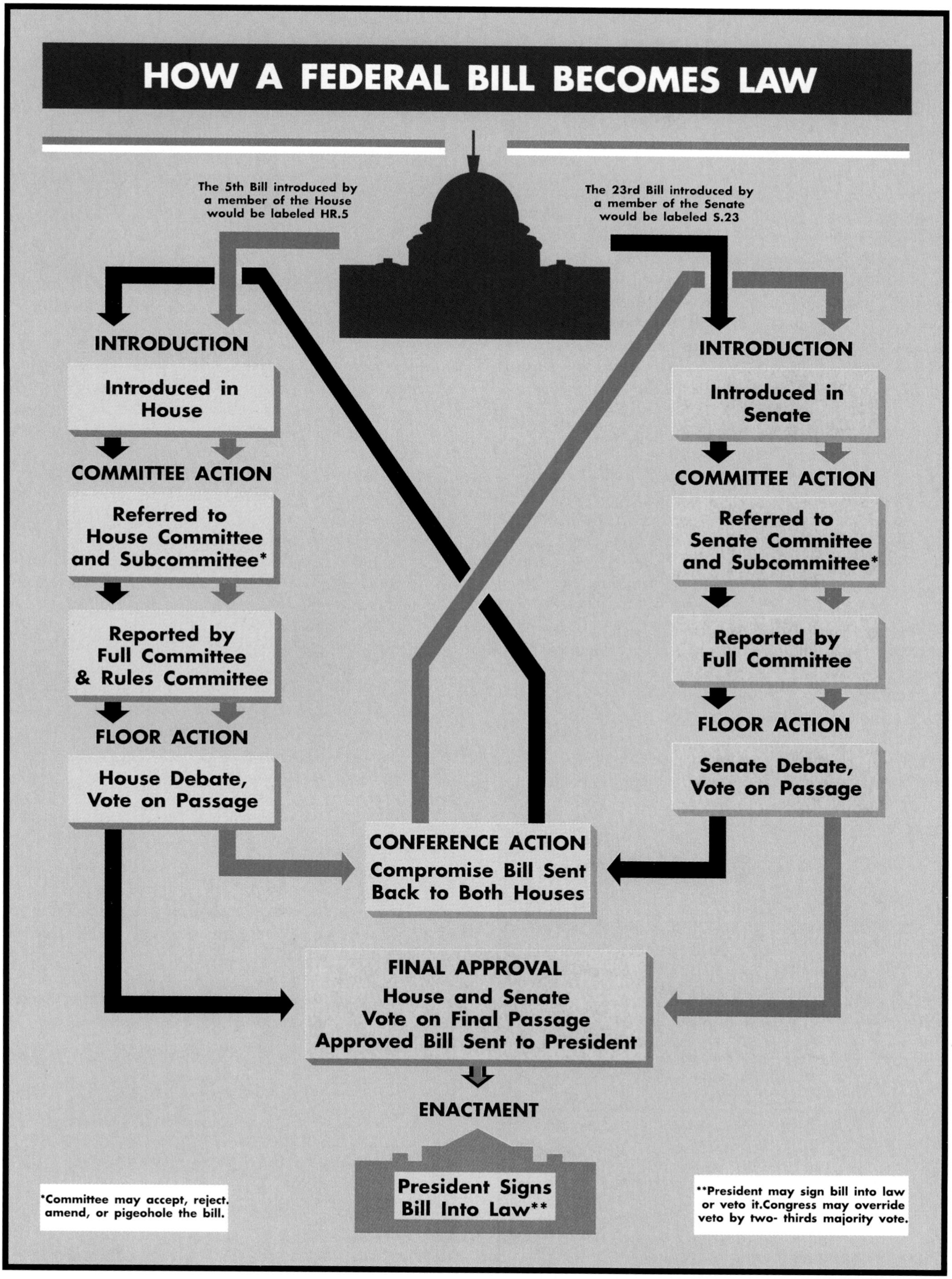

HOW A FEDERAL BILL BECOMES LAW

The 5th Bill introduced by
a member of the House
would be labeled HR.5

The 23rd Bill introduced by
a member of the Senate
would be labeled S.23

INTRODUCTION

**Introduced in
House**

COMMITTEE ACTION

**Referred to
House Committee
and Subcommittee***

**Reported by
Full Committee
& Rules Committee**

FLOOR ACTION

**House Debate,
Vote on Passage**

INTRODUCTION

**Introduced in
Senate**

COMMITTEE ACTION

**Referred to
Senate Committee
and Subcommittee***

**Reported by
Full Committee**

FLOOR ACTION

**Senate Debate,
Vote on Passage**

CONFERENCE ACTION
**Compromise Bill Sent
Back to Both Houses**

FINAL APPROVAL
**House and Senate
Vote on Final Passage
Approved Bill Sent to President**

ENACTMENT

**President Signs
Bill Into Law****

*Committee may accept, reject.
amend, or pigeohole the bill.

**President may sign bill into law
or veto it.Congress may override
veto by two- thirds majority vote.

As a new member of the Small Business Committee, the Congresswoman was feeling intense pressure from small businesspersons and their organizations in her district, opposing the bill through a letter-writing campaign. She decided that she could show her support for the small business community through her work on the Small Business Committee, but there was no way she could compromise on this bill, and she informed their representatives when they came to see her. But if our mail was any indication, the Coalition's strategy was a good one, as our legislative correspondent answered 575 letters from our constituents in support of the bill—in one week!

The hearing mark-up and lobbying process were repeated in the full Committee, and the bill was reported out favorably, somewhat weakened by its opponents. An attempt was made to delete the child care provision, but it was defeated. Once again, the vote was mostly along party lines; this time two Republicans were in favor of it, but three conservative Democrats were against it.

THE RULES COMMITTEE

Four months after the subcommittee mark-up, the leadership and Chairman Gonzalez decided that the bill should move to the floor, and a Rules Committee hearing was scheduled to determine the terms under which the bill will be debated. Because it authorizes money, The Community Enterprise Zones Act will be put on the Union Calendar, and must be debated by the Committee of the Whole House.

The rule specifies the amount of time that will be allowed for the debate, and how a bill can be amended. There are three kinds of rules for amending a bill: **open**, which allows amendments from the floor; **closed**, which prohibits any amendments; and a **modified closed** rule, which lists specific amendments that will be allowed, or specific sections of a bill that can be amended. The resolution may also include prohibition of points of order against parts of the bill that violate established House rules (such as offering policy provisions in an appropriations bill.)

A US House of Representatives Committee Hearing

The Rules Committee, by deciding which bills and amendments are in order, plays a particularly important role as arbiter and power broker, and the rule given to a bill can make or break its chances of passage. In agreement with the House leadership and the subcommittee chairman, Rep. Gonzalez has requested and been granted an open rule, with four hours of debate divided equally between the majority and minority. The subcommittee's chairman and ranking minority member will be the floor managers of the bill, allotting their allowed time to Members to amend and debate the bill.

The final push was on. Congresswoman Cartwright sent every member of the House a Dear Colleague letter, one of eight they received on various aspects of the bill, stressing its importance to the nation's economy and urging their support for the child-care provision. She also spent extra time on the House floor, lobbying her colleagues for support of her amendment. To her regret, each member of Congress also received, among other letters in opposition, one from the National Association of Women Business Owners, supporting the legislation—except for the Congresswoman's amendment.

The day before the bill was scheduled, Members received, from the Democratic Study Group and the Republican Policy Committee, analyses of the legislation, proposed amendments, and recommendations on certain provisions. The President also sent a letter stating strongly that this was a major priority of his administration. Rosalie and the Congresswoman spent a half hour discussing the comments she would make on the floor, and Rosalie once again burned the midnight oil, drafting a speech and preparing another briefing book, including detailed projections on what the child-care centers would cost, extrapolated from existing programs by the Congressional Research Service, an arm of the Library of Congress.

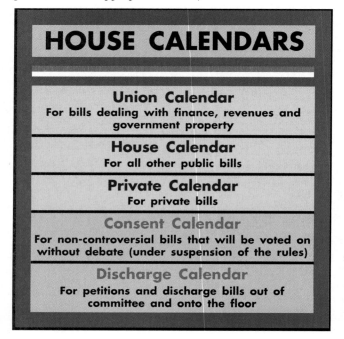

HOUSE CALENDARS

Union Calendar
For bills dealing with finance, revenues and government property

House Calendar
For all other public bills

Private Calendar
For private bills

Consent Calendar
For non-controversial bills that will be voted on without debate (under suspension of the rules)

Discharge Calendar
For petitions and discharge bills out of committee and onto the floor

SENATE CALENDARS

Calendar of Business
For all legislative business

Executive Calendar
For action on nominations and treaties

THE FLOOR DEBATE

The House went into session at noon, with a daily prayer by a visiting Chaplain, followed by a series of one- and two-minute speeches by Members. The Member in the Chair, transacted House business while several Clerks carried out their responsibilities at the desk below the podium.

Lining the doors outside the House chamber, as members arrived, was a bantering line of lobbyists who were there to remind their Congressional allies how to vote on each amendment, as the time came.

At about 2 p.m., the bill was called up by the Clerk of the House. The formality of reading it from beginning to end was dispensed with, the rule for its debate was approved, and the House resolved itself into the Committee of the Whole House on the State of the Union (a special parliamentary procedure). This enables debate on legislation with a quorum of less than 218, and most debate on legislation occurs in the Committee of the Whole.

In a scene familiar to all C-SPAN viewers, the floor managers took their positions near the front of the well, and relying heavily on House rules and precedents, they recognized their colleagues, alternating from one side to the other, to debate the legislation. Amendments are introduced and debated, and each is voted on, as it is debated, either by voice, or, if a recorded vote is requested by at least one-half of those present, an electronically-recorded vote is ordered.

Members have 15 minutes to come to the House floor to cast their vote. (Many members, busy with meetings and appointments, often watch the debate from their offices.) These periods, when there are many members on the floor, are actually periods when a great deal of Congressional business is accomplished as members seek support from their colleagues for pending legislation and discuss other matters of Congressional business.

The discussion is lively and contentious, and goes on longer than expected as the amendments are being debated under the five-minute rule, a parliamentary device through which debate on an amendment can be extended five minutes longer than scheduled. Late in the afternoon, an amendment is offered to delete the child-care amendment, and the Congresswoman offers a spirited defense. The amendment is defeated by voice vote.

However, another is immediately offered raising the trigger number for the child care centers to 40%. The Congresswoman outlines the cost projections under both plans, showing that losses from absenteeism and turnover will offset any possible gain from a higher number of eligible single parents. Despite her presentation, and impassioned speeches from several of her colleagues, the amendment passes in a recorded vote by only four votes. Frustrated and disappointed, but it is some consolation when the bill, surprisingly not substantially changed from the time it was introduced, passes the House by a large margin.

The Committee of the Whole rises, the person in the Chair is replaced by the Speaker, and the House then votes on final passage of the amended legislation.

KEY LEGISLATIVE AGENCIES

Congressional Budget Office
Provides expert technical and computer service to congress; analyzes the budget proposal of the office of management and budget; determines the economic consequences of legislation.

General Accounting Office (GAO)
Checks to see that government spending is proper and reasonable; headed by the Comptroller General who is appointed by the President, with the senate's approval, for a 15- year term.

Government Printing Office
Prints the Congressional Record, does all the national government's printing; distributes government publications and reprints documents for public purchase

Library of Congress
Serves national, state & local government, as well as the public; contains over 20 million books; The Congressional Research services and the Copyright Office are important divisions of the Library of Congress

Offices of Legislative Counsel
Provide legal assistance to Congressional Committees in drafting bills

Office of Technology Assessment
Studies new scientific developments and the likely effects of technological change on society

SENATE ACTION

During the same period, a similar, but not identical bill has worked its way through the Senate, receiving the same detailed consideration as the House legislation—with Senators receiving the same intense lobbying pressures from the same groups. However, floor procedures differ considerably from that in the House.

There is no Senate equivalent of the House Rules Committee, and legislation is brought to the floor by the unanimous consent of its members. The unanimous consent order will include the rules of debate established by the Senate and Committee leadership, including time limits and the amendments that can be offered. Debate occurs at the end of morning business for each "legislative day," which is not 24 hours, but the length of time allowed to debate a bill.

Unlike in the House, when Senators are recognized they may speak for as long as they wish, giving up the floor only when he or she wishes to yield to another. It is that device that permits a filibuster by a Senator blocking legislation, and it requires a three-fifths vote (60) to cut off debate.

Amendments may be offered, also without limits on debate, and after the first three hours of debate they need not be germane to the pending legislation, a parliamentary ploy that has produced some of the most controversial legislation of our day.

CONFERENCE

The Community Enterprise Zones legislation that is voted out of the Senate differs substantially from the House version, and a Conference will be necessary to resolve the differences. There is little that is controversial, but each bill contains provisions absent from the other, including Congresswoman Cartwright's amendment.

The members of a Conference Committee, and the number of conferees, are determined by the Speaker in the House and the Majority Leader in the Senate, in consultation with the Committee Chairmen. A Committee usually includes the legislation's floor managers and those who have been intimately involved with the legislation. While conferees represent both sides of the issue, a majority must represent the prevailing side. The Congresswoman, because of her amendment, was asked to serve as a conferee, a compliment from the Chairman for her hard work and good political judgment on her first major piece of legislation.

Conference Committee meetings must be open, and the conferees are limited in their discussions to those points of disagreement between the two bills - e.g. if there is difference between two numbers, those are the only two numbers that can be legitimately discussed. There are four recommendations that can be made on a point of disagreement:

1. The Senate can recede from its amendment(s);
2. The House can recede from its amendment(s);
3. The Senate can agree to the House amendment(s), with amendment;
4. The House can recede from its amendments to the Senate amendment(s).

Often, the third option can produce a compromise acceptable to both Houses.

Once again the lobbyists visit the conferees, promoting their positions one last time. The National Association of Women Business Owners has agreed with the new "trigger" figure and lobbies in favor of the child care amendment, much to the Congresswoman's pleasure.

The Conference Committee meets in an elegant room in the Capitol, which lends dignity to the debate. The Conference on the Enterprise Zones legislation is marked by good-natured colloquy and a serious effort to reach compromise on what many of the conferees believe is landmark legislation. After a well-reasoned defense by Congresswoman Cartwright, the child-care amendment is accepted by the Senate. With only two, two-hour meetings, agreement is reached on a bill that, while far from perfect, is stronger than either was when voted out.

The US Senate

A conference report is then prepared delineating the changes made in conference to each bill, and the report, approved by all members of the Conference Committee, is then returned to each body for another debate. Any non-germane Senate amendment that has been included is subject to a point of order and rejection by the House. And either body may reject any amendment accepted by the conferees, and insist on their own. If that happens, the conference report can either be accepted without the disputed amendment(s), or can be returned to conference for further discussion. The new conference report on the Community Enterprise Zone Act of 1994, however, was, after some debate, accepted and approved, and an enrolled copy was prepared on parchment for presentation to the President for his signature.

Several weeks later, Congresswoman Cartwright was invited to the White House Rose Garden for the bill-signing ceremony. It was a beautiful spring day, and the President had invited a large and diverse group of people, who will potentially benefit from the legislation, to be present. He had thoughtfully included four small-business people from the Congresswoman's district, and she was delighted to be able to escort them to the ceremony, a fitting end to her first foray into the byways of Congress.

WHY CONGRESS FAILS

by Mr. Bill Bartman

Associate Editor - VOTE USA

"I was from Connecticut, whose Constitution declares that 'all political power is inherent in the people, and all free governments are founded on their authority and instituted for their benefit...' Under that gospel, the citizen who thinks he sees that the commonwealth's political clothes are worn out, and yet holds his peace and does not agitate for a new suit, is disloyal; he is a traitor."

— Mark Twain, from A Connecticut Yankee in King Arthur's Court

We the people, of this Republic, elect politicians to public office to manage our nation's affairs. They are elected because they have convinced us that they posses superior knowledge in the area of public policy, that they are of high moral character, and mainly, because they have promised that, under their leadership, we will all enjoy greater prosperity and happiness. Yet, the nation's overall standard of living has steadily declined for over 20 years, crime has nearly doubled over the same period, our education system is failing, our taxes are rising, our federal debt is staggering (and continuously growing), and many of the nation's people have lost faith in the "American Dream." Along with all of this, one of the greatest failures of Congress, as a whole, has been its inability to retain the public's respect and trust.

Contempt for government, and the reasons for it, seem to have a recurring theme. The famous Roman orator and statesman, Marcus Tullius Cicero (106-43 BC), stated over 2,000 years ago that "the budget should be balanced, the treasury should be refilled, public debt should be reduced, and the arrogance of public officials should be controlled." Through the "Roaring '20s" that preceded the Great Depression, a *Baltimore Sun* columnist named H.L. Mencken perfected the art of constituent revulsion, calling the US Congress "the Asses Carnival," a swarm of "unconscionable knaves" with a "talent for pishposh," claiming that "The American people have got so used to quacks in high office that they have come to feel uneasy in the presence of honest men."

More recently, in a November 1993 Parade Magazine interview, Barry Goldwater (R-AZ - US Senator from 1953 to 1986 and 1964 Presidential candidate) commented: "The men in politics, whom I knew when I was a boy, a young man, were very highly respected. They were looked up to...When Jack Kennedy and I went to the Senate in 1953, we had what we called 'giants': Senators like Walter George and Richard Russell of Georgia, Bob Taft, Lehman of New York - very intelligent, honest men. When they went on the floor to make a speech, damn near every member of the Senate went to listen to them. Today, you make a speech, and you're the only one on the damn floor. Nobody's there to listen, because they know you're not going to say anything. And what you say has been written by somebody else. Today, we have a bunch of bums running for office. We have a Congress that should not be allowed anyplace."

Goldwater added, in a separate interview, that "today's 'Hill staffers' write most of the legislation and speeches, they do all kinds of work that the members of Congress should be doing. In fact, it is safe to say that the US Congress is now run by paid staffers, not by people elected to do the job."

Such a circumstance is hardly unusual on Capitol Hill; close observers of Representatives and Senators, watching them while they are on their way into a chamber to vote, will notice many of them quickly glancing to the side where their aides stand. The aide's simple yes or no gesture becomes all the information the elected representative needs.

Goldwater's statements reflect the sweeping public resentment toward Congress which never seems to run out of fuel. In its "government reform" legislation, Congress has consistently exempted itself from the regulations it imposes on the executive branch and American businesses, including the disability act, OSHA act, equal opportunity act and fair labor standards act. Exceptions also include sexual harassment and gift reporting laws. The recent check-bouncing scandals at the House bank, middle-of-the-night pay raises, and the numerous abuses of Congressional perks have also served to further enrage the public.

A *Wall Street Journal/NBC News* survey was in line with other polls, when it found 67 percent of Americans disapprove of Congress. Yet, even in the 1992 and 1994 elections, those banner years of "change," over 90 percent of incumbents who ran were re-elected. These figures reflect an old joke about how the average constituent states that "Congress is filled with a bunch of bums - except for my Congressman, of course."

In the text that follows, we will review the sources of the nation's discontent, in the hope that you will investigate the activities of your district's representatives, to see if any of these scenarios apply.

LEGISLATIVE RIDERS

When Congress voted to give Altoona, PA, a moveable sidewalk, at a cost of $10 million, folks in Jacksonville, FL, were probably pretty darn miffed. But then Congress gave Jacksonville $10 million to build something even "cooler" — an automated skyway express system. This just goes to show: one community's wastefulness is another's economic stimulus.

As critics are increasingly pointing out, this mentality of raiding the federal treasury, is only aggravating the alarmingly huge $5 trillion federal deficit.

One of the most blatant examples of government waste are "pork-barrel" programs — named for their way of not addressing public grievances, but simply serving to "bring home the bacon" for a senator or representative. Once such programs are funded, warns the group Citizens Against Government Waste, they "grow like a cancer, consuming more and more tax dollars every year."

The "pork" game begins when legislation is released by a congressional committee for a vote. This provides the politicians an opportunity to pass their favorite pork-barrel programs as legislative "riders," which are, in effect, minor attachments to a major bill, prior to the final vote. If the major legislation passes, the attached "riders" pass with it. Most of these "riders" would never pass as separate legislation, as they are often trivial wastes of taxpayer money. But wily politicians will hold their vote for ransom, voting for the major bill only if their beloved "rider" is attached.

The result is hundreds of nonessential programs, ranging from the construction of multi-billion dollar dams and tunnels, multi-million dollar subsidies for local industries, and the construction of museums that feature antique trains, planes, and entertainers such as Lawrence Welk. There is even a $19 million program to study cow flatulence.

While these programs are effective in bringing some federal tax money back home (which usually results in a higher favorability rating for the incumbent politician) multiplying this kind of government spending by hundreds of federal representatives results in billions of tax dollars being squandered that may have been better applied to far-reaching social programs, debt reduction, or tax decreases.

Brian Kelly, author of "Adventures in Porkland" — a reference to wasteful, "pork-barrel" spending, claims that wasteful congressional spending amounts to $100 billion a year and is "killing this country," and that "the same mentality that led Congress to fund a museum honoring late band leader Lawrence Welk also gives the country its staggering deficit."

Occasionally, a few porkbusters emerge among the freshmen, but they're never able to overcome the system. For example, when junior senator Robert Smith (R-NH) tried, several years ago, to trim some pork from the transportation appropriations bill, the savvy old-timers twisted arms on the Senate floor, and his effort failed miserably, 84-14.

Rep. Harris W. Fawell (R-IL) says the fight is extremely difficult. "Let another member go after a colleague's hometown park or bike trail, and the ranks close behind the victim." Taking away another member's vote-attracting appropriations is "not something you should be doing" as far as most other representatives are concerned.

Most new members of Congress look forward to becoming appropriators of pork themselves. This avalanche of spending, to look good back in the home district and thus be re-elected again and again, often creates ludicrous and undemocratic scenes.

Viewed in total, citizens understand that wasteful congressional spending is "driving up their taxes and digging America into a hole," said Marol Lewis of Citizens Against Government Waste. "Yet, time after time, they re-elect the big-spending princes of pork, reasoning that at least this way they can get back some of the tax dollars they've sent to Washington. Many also understand that their representative or senator cannot bring home the bacon without pilfering tax dollars from other districts or states. Yet they tolerate, or even applaud, this practice, reasoning that as long as "everybody" in Congress engages in pork piracy, they should, at least, elect someone who's proficient in the craft. Some constituencies become so hooked on 'pork steroids' that they would never dream of turning the rascals out."

As a result, Lewis reasons, responsible citizenship is undermined, as voters sell out to the highest bidder, so to speak. When citizens vote for a candidate, not because he or she is the best person for the job but because that person is the best at bringing home the bacon, large numbers of voters have been implicated "in a kind of anonymous bribe-taking."

Newsweek magazine put it this way: "After years of living high on the hog, Americans have come to think like politicians: they want their share, which means entitlements."

Lewis says this situation corrupts democratic government, at its grassroots, by encouraging citizens "to take a cynical, self-serving view of their role in the political process," and by legitimizing "a politics of plunder, enticing citizens to demand special favors, at the expense of other districts and states."

The end result of it all, comments the group Citizens Against Government Waste, is that each and every day that Washington "dawdles and dickers over the nuances of deficit reduction, the nation slips nearly a billion dollars closer to bankruptcy." CAGW believes that taxpayers have accepted higher taxes recently due to a promise that has been broken before — deficit reduction. "Each time taxes have risen, spending has grown even more. And what kind of return do taxpayers get on their investment? Waste, inefficiency and mismanagement remain pervasive in the federal government, claiming an estimated 34 cents of every individual income tax dollar."

POLITICAL FAVORS

Another phenomenon in Congress is the intricate web of political favor trading that occurs. When it all started is unknown, but the phenomenon is basically made-up of politicians who vote for bills that they don't particularly agree with, because they owe a favor to someone. They are reminded of the favor they owe, in return for support they received on a bill they were pushing in the past. If no favor is owed, the politician receives a credit for a "political favor" in the future.

The existence of both the legislative riders and the political favors creates a problem where major legislation may not be voted upon based on its merit, or based upon its effect on the nation, but upon the level of political positioning it can provide for the politician.

The most notorious example of political favors in recent times involved passage of the highly controversial North American Free Trade Agreement (NAFTA), which opened up a free-trading block between the US, Canada, and Mexico. According to NAFTA opponent, Ralph Nader, the noted consumer and political activist, "The Clinton administration had to make billions of dollars worth of pork barrel deals just to get a faulty NAFTA agreement passed. Trade agreements should be judged on the merits, not on the basis of personal favors, unfundable promises, and narrow special interest deals." Nader's group, Public Citizen, uncovered 21 deals made to garner NAFTA votes, and ten of them were totally unrelated to trade, such as:

★ In an interview with the Journal of Commerce, Rep. E.B. Johnson (D-TX) stated that her commitment to NAFTA was firmly tied to a commitment, by an unnamed Clinton administration official, to purchase six C-17 cargo planes from the McDonnell Douglas plant, in her district, at a cost of approx. $500 million each. To add insult to injury, the C-17's design is known to be flawed, with cargo doors that open in mid-flight and wings that continue to buckle in flight testing despite costly redesigns. The C-17 is a perennial target of Congressional investigators and critics of Pentagon spending. Rep. Johnson stated that "I am not going to say who it was. It was a confidential conversation. But, there will be six, I can say that!"

★ An announcement by Energy Secretary Hazel O'Leary to place a $10 million government-funded laboratory, dedicated to exploring the "positive side of plutonium," in Rep. Bill Sarpalius'a (D-TX) district.

★ A private commitment by Transportation Secretary Frederico Pena to Rep. Howard P. McKeon (R-CA), to link the Golden State and Antelope Valley freeways.

★ A pledge from President Clinton that Rep. Lewis F. Payne's (D-VA) district would receive "top level consideration" for a manufacturing technology center.

★ By comparison to these requests, Reps. Marty Meehan (D-MA) and Mel Reynolds (D-IL) were relatively easy to please. All that they wanted was Vice President Al Gore's attendance at Rep. Meehan's $250 per person Boston fund-raiser, and Chief of Staff Mac McLarty's attendance at Rep. Reynold's Chicago fund-raiser.

All told, no one knows how many favors are owed within the halls of Congress, or how many pork-barrel programs are influencing the direction of the nation's policies. What is known is that as long as these practices exist, there will be less representation and more political shenanigans than the public deserves.

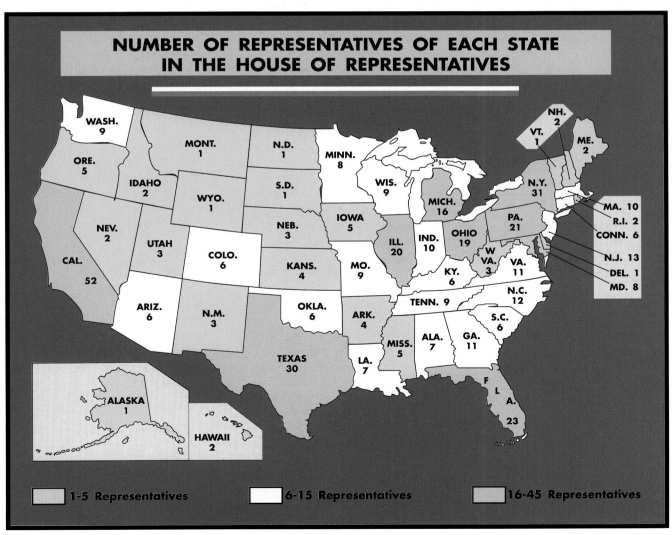

NUMBER OF REPRESENTATIVES OF EACH STATE IN THE HOUSE OF REPRESENTATIVES

WASH. 9
ORE. 5
MONT. 1
N.D. 1
MINN. 8
NH. 2
VT. 1
ME. 2
IDAHO 2
WYO. 1
S.D. 1
WIS. 9
MICH. 16
N.Y. 31
MA. 10
R.I. 2
CONN. 6
NEV. 2
UTAH 3
NEB. 3
IOWA 5
ILL. 20
IND. 10
OHIO 19
PA. 21
N.J. 13
DEL. 1
MD. 8
CAL. 52
COLO. 6
KANS. 4
MO. 9
KY. 6
W VA. 3
VA. 11
ARIZ. 6
N.M. 3
OKLA. 6
ARK. 4
TENN. 9
N.C. 12
S.C. 6
MISS. 5
ALA. 7
GA. 11
TEXAS 30
LA. 7
FLA. 23
ALASKA 1
HAWAII 2

1-5 Representatives   6-15 Representatives   16-45 Representatives

EMPTY LEGISLATION

We can watch our representatives scurry around Congress endlessly, passing more than 600 new pieces of legislation per year, but the issues that threaten our nation's security (poverty, crime, high taxes, federal debt) never seem to change. Many accuse the Congress of passing "empty legislation" that serves only as window dressing for politicians to campaign on in their next election, and not as real solutions to the nation's problems.

In a March 1, 1994 speech to the Congress, Senate Majority Leader George Mitchell, the retiring Maine Democrat, made some telling comments about his peers regarding the Balanced Budget Amendment, which he opposed. "Not one of them, not one single Senator who will vote for this amendment, has publicly specified what he or she would do to balance the budget - not one! That would be the honest thing to do. But, it would also be very difficult and very unpopular. And this amendment is intended to create the illusion of concern about the deficit, while avoiding any meaningful action *on* the deficit. It is a further irony that the authors of this amendment, which originally required a balanced budget in 1999, insisted on changing that date... But, they didn't alter the date to bring it closer to the present. Instead, they moved the date of a balanced budget further into the future, into the next century, to the year 2001... Senators serve for six years. This is an election year. Senators, successful in winning election this year, will serve until the year 2000. If they required a balanced budget to be produced in 1999, every Senator supporting this amendment and running for reelection this year would have to face the prospect of actually voting for a balanced budget. And that is the one thing the supporters of this amendment won't do: vote for an actual balanced budget... That is what this amendment is all about: creating the illusion of action about the deficit, to conceal the unwillingness of its sponsors to actually do anything about the deficit. It is no coincidence that the big talkers about the deficit are also the big spenders, the ones who will rarely, if ever, vote to cut spending. This amendment is their cover. They vote for more and more spending. They rarely, if ever, vote to cut spending. And when they're asked about that, they say: 'But I am for the Balanced Budget Amendment.' It is not an answer; it is political cover..."

Another way politicians pass "empty legislation" is to pass laws that appear to appease a public outcry, creating an image for themselves as an effective public servant. But, they will often leave the interpretation of how the law will be enforced to an executive agency. This "Regulatory Process," where the law is interpreted into actual regulations and enforcement procedures, is often done behind closed doors, out of public sight, where lobbyists are often happy to "help" the agencies in structuring the regulations. For instance, the American Bankers Association (ABA) drafted the S&L bailout legislation before the 1988 elections (while most politicians were denying that it was a major problem), and the S&L bailout legislation that was passed, after the election, was almost verbatim to the ABA proposal, where the bailout expenses were paid by the American taxpayers and not by the banking industry.

Former Rep. Vin Webber (R-MN) commented on the subject of hollow laws in a "Frontline" interview, stating "...that regulatory process is really, sort of even more an extreme example of the insider game, the special interest game, that people don't like about Washington...In theory, I suppose, the elected officials are supposed to represent the people. But, really, it's a special interest game by and large...it's a fairly regular two-step that elected officials go through, I'm sorry to say, in which they'll tell the public that they're for something to protect the environment, or whatever, and then, on the other hand, make sure that they tell a narrowly organized interest group, 'don't worry about it, we'll take care of you in the regulatory process'"

This scenario is exemplified by cases in which the rate of serious injuries in the workplace is actually higher than when the worker safety laws were passed in 1970 (an average of 10 Americans die on the job every day); in which the automobile manufacturers were able to stall the inclusion of airbags, into new cars for over 20 years; and where, in over 20 years, the EPA (Environmental Protection Agency) has managed to regulate only seven of the 275 toxic chemicals omitted by factories into populated areas, and has cleaned only 73 of the 1,200 "Superfund" sites.

Lois Gibbs, Director of the Clearinghouse for Hazardous Waste, stated in a "Frontline" interview, "The way it (Superfund Legislation) was written is that a pool of money would be put aside by industry, and if there was another "Love Canal" (an environmental disaster in NY where toxic waste dumping caused the deaths of many people), EPA would rush right in, clean up that dump and then go look for the responsible parties, those who should pay back the EPA for the damages. What a terrific idea. I supported that. And now, ten years later, you look at Superfund, what happened? They go in and negotiate with the responsible parties about 'how much are you willing to pay for the cleanup?' In some cases, communities were told by the Environmental Protection Agency — 'you have the worst site in this country, you are a Superfund site' — ten years ago, and have had nothing done. In writing it sounds terrific, I mean anybody could support it, but in reality it doesn't work that way."

ON THE TAKE?

The comments of Senate Majority Leader George Mitchell would lead one to believe that the Congress is mostly made-up of cowards, but the comments of Rep. Vin Webber are much more disturbing, as they suggest collusion with special interests. Those who suspect such collusion point to the numerous gifts, vacations, and luxuries that are provided to elected representatives who are "sympathetic" to the needs of wealthy special interest groups. Not only is life more pleasurable for those who "play ball," but campaign finances are often more plentiful to those who "cuddle-up" to the well-backed lobbyists.

Even Congress's greatest detractors won't deny that its members are hard working. The problem is that most of the work involves getting the financing to stage an impressive re-election campaign. And the need for campaign cash is what is drawing the influence peddlers in unprecedented numbers.

This sentiment is echoed by US Representative Jim Leach (R-IA) in a "Frontline" interview: "Increasingly, the private sector, at the influence level, has come to dominate Washington so that it's a fairly wealthy community, and the lifestyle of members is not that of the average citizenry...you have a series of commitments, that is to large powerful groups who, by definition, have money, instead of the average citizen who, by definition, doesn't. And that is very different than anyone ever intended the system to be...Judgment has been lost, we elect people that are good at getting elected and not as good at representing, and then when they come to Washington, their friends become those who have special agendas, those who live fairly impressive lifestyles...and so the island aspect of Washington DC has become more and more accentuated...they don't question the value structure so much for one simple reason, and that is because everyone else does it. And if everyone else does it, how can it be wrong?"

In his book *The Best Congress Money Can Buy,* Philip M. Stern offered startling examples of Leach's allegation. Late one June night in 1984, Stern noted, Sen. Bob Dole, now the Republican majority leader in the Senate, did a 180-degree flip-flop and helped pass a special tax provision potentially worth at least $300 million to 333 wealthy commodities traders. That averaged $866,000 per trader. In the three months prior to Dole's action, Stern reported, the commodities industry and various individual traders gave $10,500 to a political action committee set up and run by Dole. Just three weeks prior to his flip-flop, individual traders gave $3,600 to a fund-raiser hosted by Dole's PAC.

The most notable example of the "Congress for sale" phenomenon is the famous "S&L scandal." In the 1980s, the savings and loan institutions got greedy and successfully lobbied for as much deregulation as they could get, enabling them to invest in projects outside their traditional mandate of consumer home-building loans and savings accounts. The chairman of the powerful House Banking Committee, Ferdinand St. Germain, one, in fact, who proclaimed himself a consumer advocate, took full advantage of the very material benefits of doing the bidding for a specific industry, including expensive meals, travel, and, of course, campaign contributions. The more thrifts (a type of bank) that were allowed to move beyond their traditional mandate, the more shaky investments they made, and the more excessive the lifestyles of many of their executives became. Finally, when the banks began to collapse and their congressionally-approved insurance couldn't cover the losses, their officials came running to Congress for a bail out.

Adding further injury to insult, Congress complied, first by providing multi-billion dollar loan guarantees, and then by establishing the Resolution Trust Corporation and providing billions of dollars to buy out the thrifts' troubled assets — money the government will never recover because of the fire-sale prices at which those assets are being sold. In designing bad legislation that the thrift institutions wanted (promulgated at the behest of their lobbyists) St. Germain and several of his colleagues in the House and Senate (Rep. Frank Annunzio (D-IL), former Sen. Alan Cranston (D-CA), Sen. Jake Garn (R-UT) and Sen. Don Reigle (D-Mich), as well as members of their staffs, have cost American taxpayers billions of unrecoverable dollars.

In his 1994 State of the Union address, President Clinton raised *his* concerns about the integrity of the Congress, stating that health care reform "will raise critical questions about the way we finance our campaigns and how lobbyists wield their influence. The work of change, frankly, will never get any easier until we limit the influence of well financed interests who profit from this current system. So I must now call on you to finish the job both houses began last year, by passing tough and meaningful campaign finance reform and lobby reform legislation this year." Meanwhile, two of the leading Democratic players on health care reform, the chairman of the House Energy and Commerce Committee, John Dingell (D-MI), and the chairman of its health subcommittee, Henry Waxman (D-CA), were top recipients of campaign finance from the health and insurance industries.

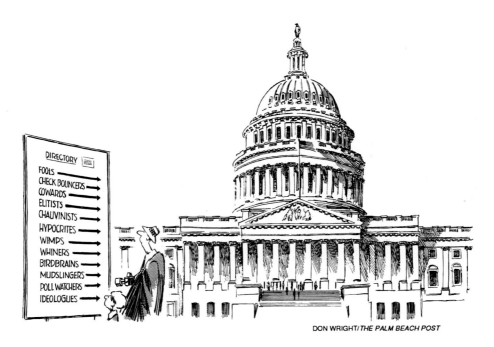

DON WRIGHT/*THE PALM BEACH POST*

PAC'S BEGINNINGS

By the early 1970s, the very fabric of America had been changed in the areas of civil rights, consumer's rights, worker safety, and environmental protection. While these changes were eventually embraced by both major parties, they originally came as a result of "grass-roots" movements for change.

Most of the issues that were won by these grass-roots movements came at a great cost to corporate America. Many of the Fortune 500 companies reacted to the growing grass-roots movement by creating their own privately funded think tanks whose purpose is to produce biased policy studies and other propaganda, for dissemination to the various news agencies. They also formed lobbying alliances that could more effectively influence federal representatives, and increased the total number of their registered federal lobbyists from less than 200 in 1971, to over 2,000 in 1981 (there are over 3,000 lobbyists in Washington today). The underfunded grass-roots organizations became overwhelmed by this influx of corporate capital, and looked to Congress for help in leveling the playing field.

In an effort to strengthen the grass-roots movements and provide them with means to counter the influences of industry, Congress passed the Campaign Reform Act of 1974, allowing groups, including business groups, to form Political Action Committees, or PACs, that can raise unlimited amounts of money for the purpose of influencing political campaigns. This law allows PACs to contribute up to $15,000 per candidate ($5,000 in the primary election, $5,000 in the general election, and an additional $5,000 if there is a run-off election).

This legislation may have leveled the playing field if there was only one PAC per group. But corporate America quickly went to work to form as many PACs as legally possible. Powerful DC attorneys refused to take on clients unless they formed a PAC that the attorney controlled. With a large number of these "pseudo PACs" under the control of a single attorney, it became easy for a special interest to funnel massive amounts of campaign finances to selected candidates, far exceeding the $15,000 limit. For instance, if your favorite attorney controls 67 PACs, you could funnel up to $1 million to each candidate who represents your interests. But, with that kind of financial assistance on the table, at a time when high-priced TV advertising was winning elections, the candidates were tempted to adopt the positions that attract the most campaign finances.

Soon thereafter, the tail started to wag the dog, and a growing number of representatives, on both the federal and state levels, became quite defensive of the special interests that supported their campaigns, citing reams of biased information, provided by the PAC-controlled think tanks. Today, the influence of PACs, along with "soft money" and "big-dollar dinners," has created a system that gives even more influence to the moneyed interests than they had before 1974.

Today, there are nearly 5,000 PACs, and each one can give each congressman or challenger $10,000 or $15,000 — $5,000 for the primary race and $5,000 for the general election (and another $5,000 if there is a run-off election). During the congressional election of 1992, the average House member took in $260,000 from PACs. So fluid was the money flow that the congressmen could not spend it all, and at the end of the election they had a $76 million surplus. The resulting appreciation for this cash windfall means that the special interests who contributed it take precedence over the Representative's or Senator's own constituents. For example; Sen. Rudy Boschwitz of Minnesota, who was defeated in 1992, blatantly gave a book of "access" stamps to every person who gave him a $1,000 gift. By placing one of these stamps on a letter to the Senator, it would receive special attention, superior to that of the average constituent.

The Campaign Reform Act of 1974 has accomplished the exact opposite effect than was originally intended, causing many representatives to pay more attention to the needs of their financiers than to their constituents. And the social decay of the nation that has ensued since 1974 is considered, by many, to be a direct result of this phenomenon.

REVOLVING DOOR

Political Action Committees can be effective ways to bribe committee chairs and members who are interested in maintaining a lifelong political career. But, there are politicians who either don't want to stay in public office forever, or know that their constituency won't let them. Since retiring politicians can no longer take their campaign finance "war-chests" home with them (as the spoils of politics), as they had been able to do until just recently, the wily lobbyists had to find another way to make these "short-term" politicians sympathetic to their special interests' needs. The technique for influencing such politicians is called, simply enough, the "revolving door." It permits wealthy special interests to "buy" a politician by offering him or her a cushy, high-paying position within a company, or maybe a "no-show" job within a lobbying firm.

Public Citizen's "Congresswatch" group spent ten months tracking 319 former members of Congress, congressional staffers, and executive branch officials who left office in 1992. They found that at least 101 of these former government officials had taken jobs with lobbying firms, another 79 took jobs with law firms (the vast majority of which have lobbying practices), and 23 went to work for corporate interests.

Another suspected way for special interests to use the "revolving door" is to get all of the individual companies that are members of an association to agree to hire the legislator to speak at functions, for perhaps as much as $25,000 per appearance, once they are out of office.

These techniques are suspected to be highly effective ways for special interests to influence our nation's leaders. And since most politicians return to the world of private industry anyway, it is extremely difficult for anyone to actually prove wrongdoing. Why wouldn't a politician join a firm that they have been supportive of for so many years? Where is the crime in that? Why wouldn't a retired politician accept a $1 million offer to speak in Japan? Maybe the politician's support of an unbelievably lop-sided trade agreement with Japan, while in office, is just a coincidence. Maybe the Japanese industry leaders are, simply, very interested in what the retired politician has to say. And maybe politicians don't lie.

PACS IN ACTION

In order for special interests to get results from their special-interest money, they need not pay off everyone in Congress - just those who chair or are members of the committees that impact their interests. The situation was succinctly presented by Rep. Mike Synar during an interview on PBS's "Frontline." The Oklahoma Democrat recalled numerous instances where he attempted to gain support for legislation or an amendment, but found heavy resistance from colleagues who would explain "that vote would go against the goals of my PAC, and would cost me $30,000 - the $15,000 I don't get, and the $15,000 my opponent gets." Theoretically, at least, even politicians who don't accept PAC money can be influenced by a special interest group that promises not to give PAC funding to their opposition.

The reason that PACs work so well for well-heeled interests is due to the high cost of modern political campaigns. The most recent congressional campaigns cost a record $678 million, a 52-percent increase over 1990's all-time record. The incredible cost of modern campaigns is due to the cost of high-technology mass media — mostly television — which permits an effective mind-molding tool for influencing the majority of voters, who know precious little about how government works, or the details of the various political issues.

Therefore, sound bites on TV and radio, and highly emotional print and brochure advertising are used to communicate a simple but expensive message to the electorate. No new taxes - yet, somehow, no cut in government services. Family values. More prisons. A balanced budget. Whatever the electorate seems to want to hear.

Whether these promises are true or not, and they usually are not, seems to matter little since, as a rule, the public pays little attention to Congressional activities between elections. And even in the rare instance that they do, their lack of political knowledge makes them tremendously easy to mislead. Therefore, all a candidate needs to do to get into office, and stay there, is to focus primarily on the special interests that keep the campaign finance flowing, which keeps the politician's snappy TV ads running during those expensive prime-time hours.

THE GREAT REFORMERS

The costly policies of the 1980's slid the nation into massive debt, and as the quality of life eroded, voters reacted by turning out incumbent President George Bush, and sending 110 new members, or "freshmen," to the House of Representatives. These "freshmen" had vowed massive reforms when elected in 1992. And with over one-hundred "storming the Capitol," the possibilities seemed promising. Then the system worked its self-protective magic: a mix of threats and seduction. As the *New York Times* reported, "Wooed by the old-guard leadership from the moment they arrived, some already have tempered their enthusiasm for change in the interests of getting along."

It took only one year, a few minor concessions, 20 committee appointments, 90 sets of political threats, and 3,000 lobbyists to bring the freshmen "reformers" in line and get Congress back to "business as usual." No major government reforms, no balanced budget, no committee staff cuts, no term limits on committee chairs, no elimination of PACs, no decrease in congressional gift limits, and basically no challenge to the congressional seniority. Within a year of the most informative election in US history, little had changed in American society and the public began to realize that they had been fooled again.

Their response in 1994, once again, was to turn to new leadership. This time by electing a majority of Republican Party candidates who promised, among other things, a balanced budget amendment, tax cuts, and government reform.

Once again, it wasn't long before the newly elected leadership showed their true colors by proclaiming to their constituents that they merely promised to *introduce* such legislation, with no guarantee of passage. Thus the immensely flawed balanced budget amendment went down in flames, the tax cuts turned out to be predominantly for the wealthy, and "sunshine rules" were introduced in place of any meaningful government reforms. The most recent *ABC/Washington Post* polls show the approval rating of the new Congress has dropped to 32%, down from the 58% they boasted when elected.

Once again, the American public's passive actions have resulted in another insult and further injury, reinforcing their feelings of political disgust and national hopelessness.

In the circular trinity of American democracy, where elected representatives regulate the government agencies, the government agencies regulate the populace, and the populace, in turn, regulates the elected representatives, it is clear that it is time for the populace to "step up to bat."

Grass-roots groups such as Common Cause, National Taxpayer's Union, Public Citizen, and United We Stand America have presented numerous proposals for ending campaign finance abuse, restricting gifts to members of Congress, eliminating wasteful government spending, and stopping unfair taxation.

But none of these ideas will come to fruition without spirited public support. Freshman outsiders cannot be expected do the job alone, against an entrenched political machine, without the support of constituents in and out of their districts. If citizens want to stop wasteful spending with such legal tools as a balanced budget amendment; if they want to end a tax burden that has, in many cases, tripled since 1950; if they want to end the overpowering influences of lobbyists and PACs; if they want to save the Social Security fund, not to mention Medicare, the answer is through grass-roots political involvement that *begins* at the ballot box, and ends in victory over the forces that threaten the "American Dream."

The "Founding Fathers" sign the Declaration of Independence in 1776, to pursue the dream of a more perfect Union.

GLOSSARY
for How Congress Works
(continued)

Moral
1. Of or concerned with the judgment of the goodness or badness of human action and character: moral scrutiny; a moral quandary.
2. Conforming to standards of what is right or just in behavior; virtuous: a moral life.
3. Arising from conscience or the sense of right and wrong: a moral obligation.

Parliamentary
1. A body of rules governing procedure in legislative and deliberative assemblies.

Pragmatist
1. A person who implements a practical, matter-of-fact way of approaching or assessing situations or solving problems.

Promulgated
1. To make known (a decree, for example) by public declaration; announce officially.
2. To put (a law) into effect by formal public announcement.

Quorum
1. The minimal number of officers and members of a committee or an organization, usually a majority, who must be present for valid transaction of business.

Recede
1. To move back or away from a limit, point, or mark: The flood waters finally receded.
2. To withdraw or retreat.

Rules Committee
1. A committee of the US House of representatives that prescribes an authoritative direction for conduct, regulation, and governing procedure of the legislative body.

Simpatico
1. Of like mind or temperament; compatible.
2. Having attractive qualities; pleasing.

Special Interests
1. A person, a group, or an organization attempting to influence legislators in favor of one particular interest or issue.

Subcommittee
1. A subordinate committee composed of members appointed from a main committee.

Sunshine Rules
1. increased public access to legislative proceedings.

Think Tank
1. A group or an institution organized for intensive research and solving of problems, especially in the areas of technology, social or political strategy, or armament.

Whip
1. A member of a legislative body, such as the U.S. Congress, charged by his or her party with enforcing party discipline and ensuring attendance.

CHAPTER 6

HOW THE WHITE HOUSE WORKS

by Mr. Russell J. Verney
Executive Director – United We Stand, America

UNITED WE STAND AMERICA sm
7616 LBJ Freeway, Suite 727
Dallas, Texas 75251

GLOSSARY

for How The White House Works

Administration

1. Those who constitute the executive branch of a government.

Appointment

1. The act of appointing or designating for an office or position.
2. The office or position to which one has been appointed.

Aristocracy

1. A hereditary ruling class; nobility.
2. Government by a ruling class.
3. Government by the citizens deemed to be best qualified to lead.
4. A group or class considered superior to others.

Bureaucracy

1. Administration of a government chiefly through bureaus or departments staffed with nonelected officials.
2. The departments and their officials as a group.
3. Management or administration marked by diffusion of authority among numerous offices and adherence to inflexible rules of operation.
4. An administrative system in which the need or inclination to follow complex procedures impedes effective action: innovative ideas that get bogged down in red tape and bureaucracy.

Cabinet

1. A body of persons appointed by a head of state or a prime minister to head the executive departments of the government and to act as official advisers.

Cold War

1. A state of political tension and military rivalry between nations that stops short of full-scale war (often used to define the tensions that existed between the Western Capitalist nations and the Eastern Communist nations from 1948 to 1991).

Consulates

1. The residence or official premises of a consul (an official appointed by a government to reside in a foreign country and represent his or her government's commercial interests and assist its citizens there).

Embassies

1. A buildings containing the offices of ambassadors and staff.

Executive

1. A person or group having administrative or managerial authority in an organization.
2. The chief officer of a government, state, or political division.
3. The branch of government charged with putting into effect a country's laws and the administering of its functions.

Fiscal

1. Of or relating to government expenditures, revenues, and debt

Inaugural

1. Of, relating to, or characteristic of an inauguration (A formal beginning or introduction into office).

Judiciary

1. The judicial branch of government.

Legislative/Legislation

1. The act or process of legislating; lawmaking.
2. A proposed or enacted law or group of laws.

Mandates

1. To make mandatory, as by law; decree or require: mandated desegregation of public schools.

Pork

1. Government funds, appointments, or benefits dispensed or enacted by politicians to gain favor with their constituents.

Regulation

1. The act of regulating or the state of being regulated.
2. A principle, rule, or law designed to control or govern conduct.
3. A governmental order having the force of law (also called executive order).

Rhetoric

1. A style of speaking or writing, especially the language of a particular subject: fiery political rhetoric.
2. Language that is elaborate, pretentious, insincere, or intellectually vacuous: His offers of compromise were mere rhetoric.
3. Verbal communication; discourse.

Special Interests

1. A person, a group, or an organization attempting to influence legislators in favor of one particular interest or issue.

Spin

1. To tell, especially imaginatively: to spin a tale
2. Interpretation, especially of a politician's words, promulgated to sway public opinion.

Spin-Doctor

1. A representative for a person, especially a politician, who publicizes favorable interpretations of that person's words or actions: "Some inconspicuous remark . . . could come back to haunt either candidate; the pundits and 'spin-doctors' remarks could change public perceptions of the debate" (Newsweek).

Subsidies

1. Monetary assistance granted by a government to a person or group in support of an enterprise regarded as being in the public interest.

Unconstitutional

1. Not in accord with the principles set forth in the constitution of a nation or state.

Unilateral

1. Of, on, relating to, involving, or affecting only one side.
2. Performed or undertaken by only one side.
3. Obligating only one of two or more parties, nations, or persons, as a contract or an agreement.

HOW THE WHITE HOUSE WORKS

Mr. Russell J. Verney
Executive Director – United We Stand, America

"The task is above my talents ... and ... I approach it with ... anxious and awful presentiments."
— *Inaugural Address, President Thomas Jefferson, March 4, 1801*

Thomas Jefferson was fully aware of the task he was about to undertake as he spoke of an unfortunate reality for every president who has ever led this nation. As one president succeeded another, the complexities and duties of running the United States, became increasingly more difficult. For many people this duty would be unthinkable, but for one person this is the challenge that must be faced day in and day out, for a minimum of four years. Just think what this would be like. **You** have just taken the oath as the next President of the United States of America.

Inaugural day was a tremendous success and the media has described the inaugural address as an inspiration for every citizen. Your first full day on the job awaits you. Instead of Jefferson's rhetoric, your mind is full of names for possible nominations and a variety of numbers — from polls to budgets — that your advisors are constantly mentioning. As the head of the executive branch of this massive, corporate-like bureaucracy, the first order of business is to appoint the people who will assist you in pursuing your goals. You will most likely pick and choose your personal staff from respected and loyal friends, and members of the Washington establishment.

When Franklin Roosevelt took office, the White House was believed to be understaffed with a few hundred employees. In 1939, the Executive Office of the President (EOP) was formed as a result of the recommendations made by the Committee on Administrative Management. As FDR explained, the EOP was needed for the president "to carry out his constitutional duty as chief executive, because he is overwhelmed with minor details and needless contacts arising directly from the bad organization and equipment of the Government."

Now, over 50 years later, your White House support staff will exceed 1,000 people. As the Executive Office of the President grew, so did its importance and power. The names of the sections within the Executive Office reveal the power, influence, and importance of their functions: the Office of Administration, Office of Management and Budget, Council of Economic Advisers, Office of the United States Trade Representative, Council on Environmental Quality, Office of Science and Technology Policy, and the White House Office. History has proven the power that these offices wield. Everything from Watergate to the criticism surrounding the lack of direction during the Carter administration, can be attributed to an Executive Office of the President that was either out of control or inexperienced.

As Chief Executive, you are also responsible for appointing and, to varying degrees, overseeing administrators and executives of countless agencies. The 61 agencies that you have control over range from the Peace Corps to the Central Intelligence Agency, from the National Aeronautics and Space Administration to the Postal Service, and from the Resolution Trust Corporation to the Office of Government Ethics. Because your influence over these agencies is shared with Congress, many of your initiatives will meet political opposition, and a power struggle between the executive and legislative branch will ensue.

SELECTING A CABINET

In the process of delegating authority, no decisions will be more important than the people you choose to sit on your cabinet, which will be composed of the 14 people you choose to head each of the 14 cabinet-level agencies in the executive department. These men and women, who are the secretaries of the departments they head, will be your closest and most important advisors. Picking and choosing these people is not a simple task. For each secretary on the cabinet there is a dominion of thousands of appointments that must be made, and under each appointed position there are thousands of career employees who make up the giant bureaucracy of the federal government. Your success in office is directly associated with the success of your cabinet-level agencies. Washington is filled with various bureaucrats who are capable of running the cabinet-level agencies, but the task is to find responsive managers and leaders who agree with your philosophy and can cut budgets and increase efficiency without risking a particular agency's operations.

Partisan politics will also factor into your decision because the Senate must confirm a cabinet appointment by at least a two-thirds plus one majority, and some senators will use this power for political motives. For instance, in 1986, Sen. William S Cohen (R-ME) blocked the nomination of a deputy secretary of agriculture in protest of the Reagan administration's treatment of potato farmers in Maine. The administration agreed to purchase 2.2 million pounds of Maine potatoes, and Senator Cohen removed his objection. Political bargaining and the use of pork to influence congressional votes to secure a confirmation may be hypocritical and inconsistent with your budget-cutting agenda.

Even though the Constitution does not provide for a presidential cabinet, every president, including George Washington, delegated enormous power to these individuals and their departments. When Washington was inaugurated in 1789, only three secretaries were appointed to the cabinet: Thomas Jefferson as the Secretary for Foreign Affairs (which later became the Secretary of State), Henry Knox as the Secretary of War, and Alexander Hamilton as the Secretary of the Treasury. As the United States grew, the number of cabinet posts slowly increased to serve important sectors of the economy and government. The Department of Agriculture was created in 1889 to aid depressed farmers. In 1903, the Department of Commerce and Labor was formed (it split into separate departments in 1913) to address the rising problems associated with unions and employers. From 1913 to 1947, a time encompassing the sweeping expansion of the government during the New Deal, the size of the Cabinet remained unchanged.

The eventual growth of the cabinet parallels the growth of the federal bureaucracy and the national debt. In 1948, when Harry Truman had eight secretaries in his cabinet, the federal government had an annual budget surplus of $11.7 billion. When George Bush and his 14 cabinet secretaries left office in 1992, the federal government was spending $290.2 billion more per year than was collected in revenue.

On this, your first day in office, you must begin the process of choosing the 14 cabinet members who will determine thousands of appointed positions and be responsible for multi-billion-dollar budgets in 14 distinct departments. Your success in cutting the deficit and maintaining the public's confidence will largely depend on how the 14 men and women who make up your cabinet manage their respective departments.

THE DEPARTMENT OF AGRICULTURE

The rural towns of agricultural America, typified by Norman Rockwell paintings of the 1930's, were once well-served by helpful federal employees and a supplemental agricultural extension service that taught undereducated farmers how to tend their fields and rotate crops. In the early 20th century, America's five million farms had one federal employee in the Department of Agriculture for every 1,800 farms. Due to technological advances, the nation's 2.1 million farms are now highly efficient. However, the Department of Agriculture did not change with the changes in the agricultural industry, and there is now approximately one bureaucrat for every 16 farms.

The Inauguration of President Ronald Reagan

The Department of Agriculture, created in 1889, still serves many significant functions, but the efficiency of modern farming has decreased the number of American farmers while increasing output. As a result, this department needs to be updated and reformed to service America's modern agricultural industry, which spans beyond the farm. The modern Department of Agriculture is responsible for the quality and content of the food we eat, as it makes its way from the farm or field through processing plants and distributors to your home and restaurants. As President, you must reform the system, hopefully, without alienating the rural voters, placing tens of thousands of people on unemployment or threatening the quality of the nation's food supply.

THE DEPARTMENT OF DEFENSE

As president, your power over the world's premier military force constantly places you in the forefront of the international arena. Every American citizen and millions of people around the world rely on the United States for protection. Your role, as the leader of the nation's armed forces, makes you ultimately responsible for the security of the United States, its protectorates, and democracies around the globe. In nominating your cabinet, perhaps no nomination will be as important and as widely scrutinized as your choice for secretary of defense.

Since the formation of the United States, when the War Department was formed to protect America's citizens and property, the Department of Defense has grown into the world's preeminent military force; a bureaucracy which spreads from the Pentagon, the world's largest office building, to bases around the world. In the post cold-war world, the United States has assumed the role of the only military superpower. International peacekeeping operations, under the auspices of the UN and NATO, rely on America's leadership. As a result, the secretary of defense will be one of your closest and most needed advisors.

DEPARTMENT OF EDUCATION

In 1979, President Jimmy Carter elevated the Department of Education from within the Department of Health, Education and Welfare. This department is constantly under fire as the American people believe their education system has declined, while the department's annual budget grew to over $31 billion. Your predecessors in the White House attempted to reform this system in various ways, and you promised to bring educational superiority back to the United States. However, many people are suspicious of federal mandates for education reform because education traditionally has been a local function where cities and states, for the most part, collect their own revenue and determine what is taught. In the process of administering or reforming this department, you cannot imperil the strength of higher education in the United States.

One of the department's most important responsibilities is the administration of the college loan program. A careful balancing act will be needed to maintain the status of America's universities and student loan programs, while improving the elementary and secondary schools. Your goal will be to instill confidence in the voters that our children and grandchildren will receive as good an education, or better, than your generation received.

DEPARTMENT OF TRANSPORTATION

The Department of Transportation oversees the nation's airports, highways, and rail system. Government regulations, formed by this department, affect private and commercial travel and transportation by regulating everything from speed limits on the highways to the routes airlines can fly. In the 1950's, the Federal Highway Administration, which in 1967 became a part of the newly formed Department of Transportation, managed the building of the nation's interstate highway system, the largest undertaking of its kind in the world. The interstate highways have long been complete, but the FHA remains one of the nation's major employers, constantly rebuilding old interstate highways and building new additions.

In 1970, Congress established Amtrak to run America's passenger rail service. Even though railways continue to be a major part of the nation's transportation system, Amtrak annually requires approximately $1 billion in government subsidies to operate. The Department of Transportation also raises and allocates funds to assist communities in building and modernizing the nation's airports. Because the department subsidizes airports and public transit operations, senators and congressmen will attempt to pressure the secretary of transportation to grant funds to their states and districts.

DEPARTMENT OF HOUSING
AND URBAN DEVELOPMENT

The Department of Housing and Urban Development (HUD) was formed in 1966 as a result of President Lyndon Johnson's Great Society programs. The department's duty was to create affordable housing for the urban poor. With its $26 billion annual budget and numerous sub agencies, HUD has created a massive and sometimes corrupt bureaucracy. Many of the presidents who served before you attempted to revamp HUD and make its programs more beneficial to the poor. Everything from private management of HUD housing projects to passing out vouchers for people to rent private housing has been tried in the past, but now your secretary of housing and urban development will attempt to house the poor as cost-efficiently as possible.

President Carter meets with his Cabinet

DEPARTMENT OF HEALTH
AND HUMAN SERVICES

In 1979, the Department of Health, Education, and Welfare split into the Department of Education and the Department of Health and Human Services (HHS). Every American is directly affected by the actions of the latter. From Social Security taxes and benefits, to welfare entitlements, to determining which drugs the Food and Drug Administration will allow a doctor to prescribe; this department runs some of the most expensive federal programs.

Your secretary of health and human services must be financially and politically wise. The money allocated to programs operated by this department are among the nation's largest expenditures and they are usually popular targets for budget cuts. According to various studies, welfare, and the numerous entitlements associated with it, is the nation's single largest budget item, surpassing defense spending and the interest on the federal debt. Annual federal and state spending on welfare exceeds $210 billion. Social Security, one of President Franklin Roosevelt's New Deal programs, has become more expensive as the nation's elderly population has risen to record levels. The political ramifications of cutting or altering Social Security and welfare can be disastrous, so you must be careful in administering or reforming this source of millions of people's livelihood.

DEPARTMENT OF ENERGY

The Department of Energy was created in response to the energy crisis during the 1970's. It determines policies regarding the nation's energy resources. The Department of Energy's most important responsibility is the supervision of the nation's nuclear facilities and the disposal of nuclear waste materials. Studies and processes involving nuclear-powered electric generators and weaponry are carried out and supervised by the Department of Energy.

DEPARTMENT OF COMMERCE

As President, you will often find yourself pressured by business and consumer groups who either want federal regulation to protect a trade (especially international), or prefer the government to release any controls it may hold on a market. By controlling export regulations and other trade-related activities, the Department of Commerce has a powerful grip on billions of dollars worth of US products and services. Other agencies, under the authority of this department, make it one of the most diverse. The Census Bureau, Patent and Trademark Office, and the National Oceanic and Atmospheric Administration all have vastly different functions that are often not related to the nation's commercial interests.

DEPARTMENT OF LABOR

The Department of Labor was formed in 1903, in large part to ensure workers' rights and help mediate the increasing number of labor strikes that were occurring. In the decades since its inception, the Department of Labor has been successful in ending the abuses that were once prevalent in mines, factories, and sweat shops. The current duties of the Department of Labor are not as controversial as they were in the past, but politically, many of the policies you will make regarding the US labor force influence a powerful voting segment. Workers-compensation, setting the minimum wage, and national employment standards are all functions that the Department of Labor administers. Practically every citizen and a large part of our economy is impacted by this department.

DEPARTMENT OF INTERIOR

The federal government owns almost one third of all the land in the United States. A large portion of the land under the federal government's control contains valuable natural resources. Many of these valuable resources are found in the nation's national parks, which are managed by the Department of Interior. Because these resources are both economically and naturally important, you will find yourself making decisions that will upset large groups of citizens. Modern presidents have to balance ecology with financial interests and national needs.

DEPARTMENT OF JUSTICE

Headed by the attorney general, the nation's top law enforcement officer, the Department of Justice houses attorneys and investigators who oversee a variety of federal laws and regulations. The largest and most well known agency, within the Department of Justice is the Federal Bureau of Investigation. The FBI is responsible for investigating federal crimes, and its intelligence-gathering duties include protecting the nation from acts of terrorism. The recent rise in illegal drugs and immigration have raised the public's awareness of the department's Drug Enforcement Agency (DEA) and Immigration and Naturalization Service (INS).

DEPARTMENT OF STATE

The duties of the secretary of state have been altered drastically since the time Thomas Jefferson held the position. Because of the complex global society and the conflicts associated with the post cold-war era, your secretary of state will be one of your most important advisors. Trade agreements, treaties, and foreign aid are negotiated by this department. The Department of State also frequently deals with international issues that do not directly affect the United States, as proven by the Camp David Accord when President Jimmy Carter acted as a mediator in the peace process between Egypt and Israel.

Another significant function of the Department of State is the network of US embassies, consulates, and state department officers stationed around the world. As our nation's new leader, you must now nominate the people who will represent the United States in countries all around the world. These ambassadorships are frequently given to friends and political allies because the position is sometimes viewed as ceremonial. However, your secretary and the department's support staff are extremely important in carrying out American policies and representing American interests abroad.

DEPARTMENT OF THE TREASURY

Another of the original cabinet-level agencies, the Department of the Treasury is constantly under public scrutiny. The department's largest, most important, and usually most unpopular agency is the Internal Revenue Service, which collects a majority of the money that the federal government spends. As President, your tax policies will be carried out by this massive, bureaucratic department, and many of your fiscal policies will need the full support of the secretary of the treasury. In addition to its financial duties, the department is also in charge of the Secret Service; the Bureau of Alcohol, Tobacco and Firearms; Customs; and Coast Guard. Over time, the Secret Service's main function of tracking down counterfeit money operations has grown to include the protection of the President — something you, as President, undoubtedly have a vested interest in.

DEPARTMENT OF VETERANS AFFAIRS

The most recent addition to the cabinet, the Department of Veterans Affairs operates 171 hospitals, 129 nursing homes, and 362 outpatient clinics for veterans of the armed services. The benefits and health care programs run by this department are constantly scrutinized for mismanagement and excess costs. Like so many other programs, changes in this department have a tremendous impact on an important segment of voters.

★ ★ ★ ★ ★

Overall, the corporate-like government that you are now in charge of has a total of 2.2 million employees. A flood of tens of thousands of resumes are pouring into the White House from people seeking one of the 9,000 federal jobs you are technically able to appoint. The transition from candidate to President, from one administration to another, has begun. Washington's realities, bureaucracy, and politics will bring success, defeat, and a variety of other experiences.

You have just concluded your first day as chief executive officer and, already, it is difficult for you to separate the demands of the bureaucracy and the ambitions of individuals or special interests from the true purpose of government: to establish justice, insure domestic tranquillity, provide for the common defense, promote the general welfare, and secure the blessings of liberty.

THE EXECUTIVE BRANCH

THE PRESIDENT

Executive Office of the President

White House Office
Office of Management and Budget
Council of Economic Advisors
National Security Council
Office of Policy Development
Office of the United States
  Trade Representative

National Critical Materials Council
Council on Environmental Quality
Office of Science and Technology Policy
Office of Administration
Office of National Drug Control Policy
National Space Council

THE VICE PRESIDENT

EXECUTIVE CABINET

DEPARTMENT OF STATE

DEPARTMENT OF JUSTICE

DEPARTMENT OF DEFENSE

DEPARTMENT OF LABOR

DEPARTMENT OF EDUCATION

DEPARTMENT OF HEALTH AND HUMAN SERVICES

DEPARTMENT OF THE TREASURY

DEPARTMENT OF COMMERCE

DEPARTMENT OF TRANSPORTATION

DEPARTMENT OF VETERANS AFFAIRS

DEPARTMENT OF THE INTERIOR

DEPARTMENT OF AGRICULTURE

DEPARTMENT OF ENERGY

DEPARTMENT OF HOUSING AND URBAN DEVELOPMENT

INDEPENDENT AGENCIES AND GOVERNMENT CORPORATIONS

ACTION
Administrative Conference of the US
African Development Foundation
American Battle Monuments Commission
Appalachian Regional Commission
Board for International Broadcasting
Central Intelligence Agency (CIA)
Commission on Civil Rights
Commission on Fine Arts
Commodity Futures Trading Commission
Consumer Product Safety Commission
Environmental Protection Agency (EPA)
Equal Employment Opportunity Commission
Export-Import Bank of the US
Farm Credit Administration

Federal Communications Commission (FCC)
Federal Deposit Insurance Corp. (FDIC)
Federal Election Commission (FEC)
Federal Emergency Management Agency
Federal Labor Relations Authority
Federal Maritime Commission
Federal mine Safety & Health Review Comm.
Federal Mediation and Conciliation Service
Federal Reserve System, Board of Governors
Federal Retirement Thrift Investment Board
Federal Trade Commission
General Services Administration
Inter-American Foundation
Interstate Commerce Commission
Merit Systems Protection Board

National Aeronautics & Space Administration- (NASA)
National Archives and Records Administration
National Capital Planning Commission
National Credit Union Administration
National Found. on the Arts & the Humanities
National Labor Relations Board
National Mediation Board
National Science Foundation
National Transportation Safety Board
Nuclear Regulatory Commission (NRC)
Occupational Safety & Health Review Comm.
Office of Personnel Management
Office of Special Counsel
Panama Canal Commission

Pennsylvania Ave. Development Corporation
Pension Benefit Guaranty Corporation
Peace Corps
Postal Rate Commission
Railroad Retirement Board
Securities and Exchange Commission (SEC)
Selective Service System
Small Business Administration
Tennessee Valley Authority
US Arms Control and Disarmament Agency
US Information Agency
US International Development Cooperation - Agency
US International Trade Commission
US Postal Service

THE REALITY OF GOVERNING

"Nothing is easier than spending the public money. It does not appear to belong to anybody. The temptation is overwhelming to bestow it on somebody."
— *Calvin Coolidge*

When George Washington and 38 other men drafted the Constitution of the United States of America, they designed three distinct branches of the government. In designating the legislative, executive, and judicial branches, the Constitution's framers wanted a system of checks and balances which would prevent any one branch from being more powerful than another. In the 200 years since the Constitution was signed, the three branches of government no longer have as many separate powers as they do *shared* powers.

As head of the executive branch, you will soon realize how power in Washington, DC, is shared. There will be a constant tug of war between the executive branch and Congress as politics and various interests influence the decision-making process. Rarely will the judicial branch interrupt the proceedings of the executive and legislative branches. The judicial branch, however, can step in if a congressional or presidential action is possibly unconstitutional. In the past, federal courts have interrupted disputes between the executive and legislative branches in order to promote the smooth functioning of the government.

As president, you have three exclusive powers: to nominate people for positions in your administration and the judiciary, to negotiate with foreign countries, and to pardon criminals. Except for the power to pardon criminals, you will need Congress' help in achieving the first two, since any major nomination or treaty with a foreign nation must be ratified by the legislative branch. Likewise, Congress is needed to pass legislation that will implement a majority of your most important policies and goals. You, your staff, and allies in Congress will form intricate and detailed pieces of legislation. Once legislative proposals are introduced to Congress as a bill, your legislation will be manipulated, altered, and amended to the point where the final version may be quite different from your original proposal.

THE FEDERAL BUDGET

Take, for example, the president's annual duty to present Congress with a budget plan. By January 20, you must prepare a complex budget, spelling out spending for thousands of federal programs. Ideally, you will attempt to spend no more than the federal government receives through taxes and other revenues. If you spend more, in any given year, than the federal government collects (which is referred to as deficit spending), you will be adding to the federal debt. One of your major campaign promises was to slash the budget deficit and attempt to balance the budget. Because of the diversity of the nation's interests at home and abroad and the spectrum of economic and political philosophies in your administration, this goal is difficult to attain. Streamlining and cutting costs in the federal bureaucracy can be your greatest challenge, but you do have some help, as you plan your financial strategies.

A major part of your budget and fiscal policy will be developed by the Department of the Treasury, the Office of Management and Budget, and the Council of Economic Advisors. These men and women will guide you through the budget process and create your administration's economic agenda. There are countless other agencies to help you, including the Internal Revenue Service, which collects taxes; the Federal Reserve Bank, whose input is needed to try to keep inflation at a minimum by setting interest rates; and the nonpartisan Congressional Budget Office, which will study your budget proposal for accuracy and any missing expenditures.

Once the proposal is complete, it will be presented to Congress where 100 senators and 435 representatives will attempt to cut programs they oppose and add their own pet projects. Various sections of the bill will be split up among the many committees and sub-committees in Congress. Even if you are a member of Congress' majority party, political bargaining will be needed to pass the budget. Most likely, the final version will only slightly resemble the original, so you and your staff must scramble to keep the bill's most important provisions intact. In doing so, the White House staff will spend countless hours lobbying congressional members and bargaining for their support.

There are many factors that will contribute to your success in dealing with Congress. In passing the budget, and any other piece of legislation, your relationship with lawmakers will depend, to a great extent, on how the White House approaches Capitol Hill. Congressional liaisons working for your administration have the sole duty of keeping track of what is happening in Congress. At times, these aides will be the most effective tool in planning a strategy for the passage of legislation. Your congressional liaisons will build important and valuable contacts on Capitol Hill, especially among congressional staff members, who have a lot of influence on a senator's or representative's vote or policy decision.

Obviously, political party affiliation will be a major factor. Even if the White House and Congress are headed by the same political party, you cannot automatically assume your political party's support for your programs. During his presidency, Lyndon Johnson's staff consulted with lawmakers and interest groups when forming legislation, because, as President Johnson explained, "When people have a hand in shaping projects, these projects are more likely to be successful than the ones simply handed down from the top." Like Johnson, President Jimmy Carter had a partisan, friendly Congress to deal with, but his style was in contrast to Johnson's style. Carter left much of his policy formation to his staff, which limited external input. Carter was able to present lawmakers with a bill containing the administration's objectives, leaving Congress and its committees to alter its contents.

Whatever your administration's style, Congress will play an important role during your presidency. Your budget plan will be one of your most important duties because money is a major factor in almost every facet of society, something that affects every individual. The most watched-after aspects of the budget will be your plan to raise revenue, which for the most part comes from personal income taxes. Tax breaks might be politically expedient, but they result in lost revenue, which either has to be collected from somewhere or someone else, or has to be borrowed. Eliminating specific programs is an easy way to cut spending, but it may also cut your popular support. Increasing funding for programs may win over hundreds, thousands, or even millions of votes, but you have the responsibility to impose a tax in order to raise the extra money. Added pressure will come from individuals, large organizations, and foreign nations who constantly voice their concerns and purported needs.

Since the national debt has now surpassed $4.6 trillion dollars, you are faced with the hard reality of having to cut back federal spending on social programs, which are referred to as entitlements. Entitlements account for nearly half of the nation's expenditures and include programs such as Medicare, social security and, welfare. These programs are possible opportunities for cutting expenditures. Previous presidents have cut federal spending on entitlements by passing additional costs on to states, a practice states object to, calling these costs unfunded federal mandates. These unfunded mandates, forced on the states, do nothing to solve the problems of waste and bureaucracy that impair federal programs. Your challenge is to cut the overall federal spending on entitlements without putting the people who rely on them in jeopardy. In other words, cut the administrative costs without cutting services to the truly needy. Since members of Congress rely on votes from people who rely on, or profit from, these entitlements, many of your cuts will be challenged and changed during the legislative process. Members of Congress now have control over your budget, and the legislative process can drastically alter its final form.

During the legislative process, the president has no direct control. Members of the administration will spend countless hours lobbying lawmakers to support your original plan, and often you will have to make concessions to gain votes in Congress. Even with intense lobbying efforts and political bargaining, the final legislation is likely to include amendments you completely oppose, and exclude major provisions you have promised to interest groups. It is also possible that an amendment was attached to the bill which is detrimental to the budget. Regardless, your fiscal plan has been passed by both houses of Congress and is now on its way back to your desk at the Oval Office for your signature of approval.

The president's most powerful legislative tool can now be used. If the budget bill, presented by Congress, does not meet your approval, you have the constitutional power to reject the bill by vetoing it within 10 days after it is presented to the White House. Once the bill has been vetoed, it is returned to Congress with the president's written objections attached. The bill, whether changed by Congress in order to meet the President's objections or kept intact by Congress, must be approved by two-thirds of the House and two-thirds of the Senate. If the bill is vetoed and fails to receive the needed two-thirds majority in each house, the budget does not become law. However, since this bill is the nation's annual financial plan, it eventually must be passed in some form.

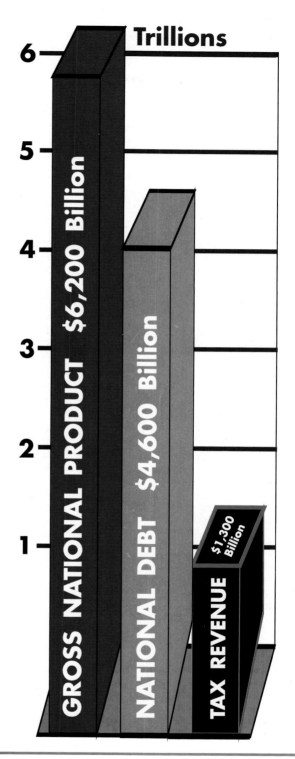

The "Gross National Product" column refers to the value of all final goods and services to be produced in the US in 1992.

The "National Debt" column refers to the total amount of money owed by the US government in 1992.

The "Tax Revenue" column refers to the total amount of money collected by the federal government in taxes and other revenues in 1992.

THE 1992 FEDERAL BUDGET

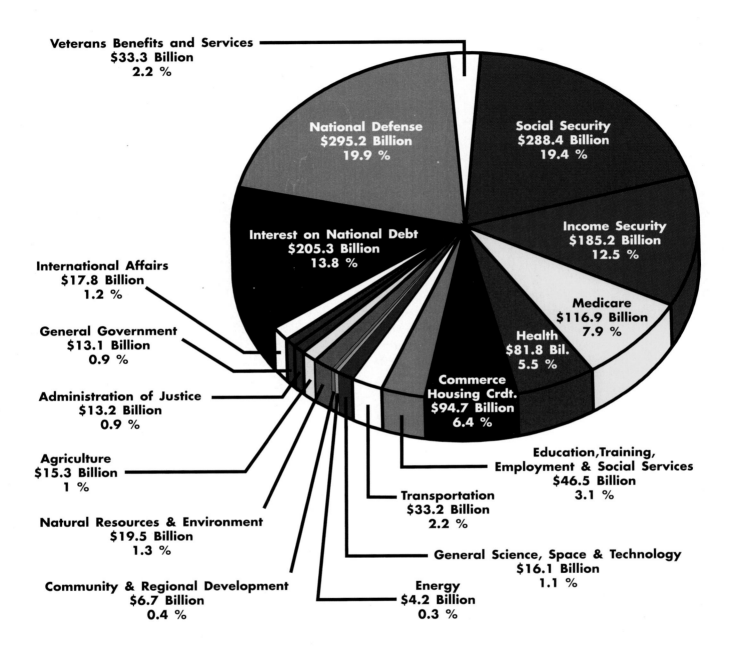

Veterans Benefits and Services
$33.3 Billion
2.2 %

National Defense
$295.2 Billion
19.9 %

Social Security
$288.4 Billion
19.4 %

Interest on National Debt
$205.3 Billion
13.8 %

Income Security
$185.2 Billion
12.5 %

International Affairs
$17.8 Billion
1.2 %

General Government
$13.1 Billion
0.9 %

Administration of Justice
$13.2 Billion
0.9 %

Agriculture
$15.3 Billion
1 %

Natural Resources & Environment
$19.5 Billion
1.3 %

Community & Regional Development
$6.7 Billion
0.4 %

Medicare
$116.9 Billion
7.9 %

Health
$81.8 Bil.
5.5 %

Commerce Housing Crdt.
$94.7 Billion
6.4 %

Education,Training, Employment & Social Services
$46.5 Billion
3.1 %

Transportation
$33.2 Billion
2.2 %

General Science, Space & Technology
$16.1 Billion
1.1 %

Energy
$4.2 Billion
0.3 %

Detailed breakdowns of each "outgoing" category can be found on pages 85 through 87.

1992 FEDERAL BUDGET BREAKDOWN

(dollar amounts in millions)

INTEREST ON NATIONAL DEBT

	Interest Received by Trust Funds	($77,165)
	Interest on Loans to Federal Financing Bank	($18,552)
	Other Interest Received	($4,687)
3	**Total Interest Recieved**	**($100,404)**
2	**Interest to be Paid on Refunds of Tax Collections**	**$2,248**
	Interest to be Paid on The Public Debt	$303,482
	Total Interest to be Paid	$305,730
1	**Difference – Interest Recieved & Interest Paid**	
		$205,326

NATIONAL DEFENSE

1	Military Personnel	$78,560
2	Operation and Maintenance	$86,427
3	Procurement	$74,488
4	Research, Development, Test & Evaluation	$35,386
5	Military Construction	$5,035
6	Family Housing	$3,272
7	Revolving & Management Funds	$1,192
	Offsetting Receipts and Rounding Adjustments	($754)
	Total National Defense	**$283,606**

VETERANS BENEFITS AND SERVICES

1	Income Security for Veterans	$17,290
2	Hospital & Medical Care for Veterans	$13,359
3	Veterans Housing	$1,182
4	Veterans Education, Training & Rehabilitation	$497
5	Other Veterans Benefits & Services	$930
	Total Veterans Benefits and Services	**$33,258**

SOCIAL SECURITY

1	Old-Age Survivors Insurance	$258,795
2	Disability Insurance	$29,594
	Total Social Security	**$288,389**

INCOME SECURITY

1	General Retirement & Disability Insurance	$5,617
2	Federal Employee Retirement & Disability	$59,225
3	Unemployment Compensation	$27,511
4	Housing Assistance	$19,768
5	Food & Nutrition Assistance	$30,116
6	Other Income Security	$42,921
	Total Income Security	**$185,158**

MEDICARE

1	Hospital Insurance	$77,711
2	Supplementary Medical Insurance	$52,188
	Medicare Premiums & Collections	($12,958)
	Total Medicare	**$116,941**

1992 FEDERAL BUDGET BREAKDOWN

(dollar amounts in millions)

HEALTH

1	Medicaid Grants	$59,899
2	Other Health Care Services	$6,800
3	Health Research	$9,132
4	Federal Employees Health Benefits	$3,010
5	Consumer and Occupational Health & Safety	$1,666
6	Education & Training of Health Care Work Force	$800
7	Health Insurance Tax Credit	$507
	Total Health	**$81,814**

COMMERCE and HOUSING-CREDIT

1	Federal Deposit Insurance (Resolution Trust & Other)	$88,053
2	Rural Housing Programs	$2,797
3	Mortgage Credit (FHA)	$1,495
4	Housing for the Elderly or Handicapped	$741
5	Small & Minority Business Assistance	$784
6	International Trade & Other	$835
7	Economic and Demographic Statistics	$448
8	Science & Technology	$304
	Recieved from Postal Service	($799)
	Total Commerce & Housing Credit	**$94,658**

EDUCATION, TRAINING, EMPLOYMENT & SOCIAL-SERVICES

1	Elementary, Secondary and Vocational Education	$12,965
2	Higher Education (Student Loans, Financial Assistance & Other)	$12,572
3	Training and Employment	$5,750
4	Other Labor Services	$890
5	Human Development Services	$3,538
6	Rehabilitation Services	$1,972
7	Grants to States for Foster Care, Adoption & Special Services	$2,963
8	Other Social Services	$2,999
9	Social Services Block Grant	$2,801
	Total Education, Training, Employment & Social Services	**$46,450**

TRANSPORTATION

1	Ground Transportation (Highways, Railroads, Mass Transit, etc.)	$20,856
2	Air Transportation	$8,733
3	Water Transportation	$3,393
4	Other Transportation	$256
	Transportation Total	**$33,238**

GENERAL SCIENCE, SPACE & TECHNOLOGY

1	General Science and Basic research	$3,348
2	Space Flight	$7,857
3	Space Science, Applications and Technology	$3,771
4	Supporting Space Activities	$1,173
	Total General Science, Space & Technology	**$16,149**

ENERGY

1	Energy Supply (R&D, Subsidies & Other)	$3,176
2	Energy Conservation	$442
3	Energy Information, Policy and Regulation	$343
4	Emergency Energy Preparedness	$246
	Total Energy	**$4,207**

1992 FEDERAL BUDGET BREAKDOWN

(dollar amounts in millions)

COMMUNITY & REGIONAL DEVELOPMENT

1	Community Development	$3,950
2	Area & Regional development	$2,521
3	Disaster Relief and Insurance	$200
	Total Community & Regional Development	**$6,671**

NATURAL RESOURCES & ENVIRONMENT

1	Water Resources	$4,522
2	Conservation & Land Management	$4,124
3	Recreational Resources	$2,498
4	Pollution Control & Abatement	$5,949
5	Other Natural Resources	$2,441
	Total Natural Resources & Environment	**$19,534**

AGRICULTURE

1	Farm Income Stabilization	$12,872
2	Agricultural Research and Services	$2,448
	Total Agriculture	**$15,320**

ADMINISTRATION OF JUSTICE

1	Federal Law Enforcement Activities	$5,799
2	Federal Litigative and Judicial Activities	$4,437
3	Federal Correctional Activities	$2,272
4	Criminal Justice Assistance	$698
	Total Administration of Justice	**$13,206**

GENERAL GOVERNMENT

1	Central Fiscal Operations	$6,572
2	Legislative Functions	$2,198
3	Executive Direction & Management	$281
4	General Property and Records Management	$878
5	Central Personnel Management	$165
6	Other General Government	$1,593
7	General Purpose Fiscal Assistance	$2,172
	Deductions for Offsetting Receipts	($725)
	Total General Government	**$13,134**

INTERNATIONAL AFFAIRS

1	International Security Assistance	$7,938
2	International Development and Humanitarian Assistance	$5,776
3	Conduct of Foreign Affairs	$3,391
4	Foreign Information and Exchange Activities	$1,375
	International Financial Programs	($668)
	Total International Affairs	**$17,812**

COMMANDER IN CHIEF

Congress wields a tremendous amount of power on domestic issues, since its members must ratify a majority of your initiatives affecting the nation. Turning to foreign affairs, however, Congress has considerably less control than the president. Congress' main power, regarding foreign affairs, is its power to ratify or reject any treaty the president negotiates. For example, any nuclear-reduction pact between the United States and Russia must be ratified by two-thirds of the Senate. For less important international pacts or agreements, the president can implement them without Senate approval, through an executive agreement. An executive agreement is only binding during your presidency and can be overridden by the Senate.

When dealing with other nations, your secretary of state will be your lead negotiator. The State Department plays an integral role in keeping the US involved and informed in world matters, and serves as your first line of defense in trying to avoid American military involvement. Since the United States is the world's remaining superpower, the secretary of state and the numerous assistant secretaries of state will often be called upon to negotiate for the US, or act as a mediator between quarreling nations. Often, the United Nations will attempt to do the same, and if military involvement is needed, a UN force, composed of various nations, may intervene. Since the United States is the major source of funding for the UN, the president's role in the UN is powerful.

Sometimes, intervention by the Department of State or the UN may not be enough. Various international situations can put America into a military conflict and, as commander in chief, it is your responsibility to head the nation's armed forces. Arguably, this makes you the world's most powerful individual. Of the three branches of government, the executive branch is the only one with the unilateral power to use the nation's military resources. As part of the government's system of checks and balances, Congress has the sole power to declare war, but history has proven this power is basically a formality. The Vietnam War was carried out by a succession of commanders in chief. As John Kennedy, Lyndon Johnson and Richard Nixon moved in and out of the White House, the war continued without a declaration of war ever being issued by Congress.

The legislative branch, however, is a vital ally in creating and maintaining consensus regarding military operations. Without Congress' support, military endeavors can be unpopular with the public. Additionally, Congress must ratify your annual budget, which sets military spending each year. If members of Congress are opposed to your use of the armed forces, they can use their legislative power to control spending for everything from troop levels to advanced weapons systems. An unfriendly Congress can also threaten your domestic agenda if its members are displeased by your foreign policies. Keeping this in mind, you must keep the legislative branch involved in your decision-making process, as you direct America's armed forces.

Through the efforts of four different Presidential administrations, the Palestinian Liberation Organization (PLO), and the nation of Israel, sign a peace treaty, in the White House Rose Garden, ending over 30 years of conflict between the two rivals.

Within the last few decades, legislative action has forced the president to share his power over the military with Congress. Wars, in places such as Vietnam and Korea, lasted years under the leadership of the president without a declaration ever being declared by the legislative branch. As a result, Congress attempted to reassert its constitutional role by passing the War Powers Act of 1973. This act restricted presidential action by giving Congress the power to withdraw troops. In most cases, the president has 90 days to unilaterally commit troops until congressional permission or a declaration of war is required. In 1983, the Supreme Court ruled in INS v. Chadha that major provisions of the War Powers Act were unconstitutional. Since this decision, the effect of the War Powers Act has been greatly diminished. For example, President George Bush kept Congress informed during the Gulf War, as a matter of respect, claiming that the War Powers Act was unconstitutional.

Because of the president's control over the military, none of your responsibilities are more awesome than your ability to control the US's nuclear arsenal and the lives of thousands of soldiers and sailors. Your secretary of state, national security advisor, chairman of the Joint Chiefs of Staff, and other advisors will present you with an overwhelming amount of information and various strategies if an armed conflict ever arises. Even with this large group of experts, the final decision regarding the use of the nation's military is yours.

DEALING WITH CONGRESS & THE PUBLIC

Whether you are guiding the nation's domestic agenda and annual budget, or negotiating with foreign nations, you have an enormous bureaucracy to control. Numerous advisors will present you with their views and will want to attempt to convince you that their plan should be your national policy. Throughout this process, you must keep in mind the political realities of Congress and the voters. If your domestic and foreign policies are successful, Congress will try to take the credit; if your decisions fail, that failure rests with you alone. As Ross Perot says, "No good deed will ever go unpunished."

When you were sworn in as president a year ago, your agenda was to change the Washington establishment. The federal government was not responding nor accountable

PRESIDENTS OF THE UNITED STATES

NAME	STATE	AGE ON TAKING OFFICE	POLITICAL PARTY	YEARS IN OFFICE
George Washington	Virginia	57	Federalist	1789 - 1797
John Adams	Massachusetts	61	Federalist	1797 - 1801
Thomas Jefferson	Virginia	57	Democratic-Republican	1801 - 1809
James Madison	Virginia	57	Democratic-Republican	1809 - 1817
James Monroe	Virginia	58	Democratic-Republican	1817 - 1825
John Quincy Adams	Massachusetts	57	Democratic-Republican	1825 - 1829
Andrew Jackson	Tennessee	61	Democratic	1829 - 1837
Martin Van Buren	New York	54	Democratic	1837 - 1841
William Henry Harrison	Ohio	68	Whig	1841
John Tyler	Virginia	51	Whig	1841 - 1845
James K. Polk	Tennessee	49	Democratic	1845 - 1849
Zachary Taylor	Louisiana	64	Whig	1849 - 1850
Millard Fillmore	New York	50	Whig	1850 - 1853
Franklin Pierce	New Hampshire	48	Democratic	1853 - 1857
James Buchanan	Pennsylvania	65	Democratic	1857 - 1861
Abraham Lincoln	Illinois	52	Republican	1861 - 1865
Andrew Jackson	Tennessee	56	Democratic	1865 - 1869
Ulysses S. Grant	Illinois	46	Republican	1869 - 1877
Rutherford B. Hayes	Ohio	54	Republican	1877 - 1881
James A. Garfield	Ohio	49	Republican	1881
Chester A. Arthur	New York	50	Republican	1881 - 1885
Grover Cleveland	New York	47	Democratic	1885 - 1889
Benjamin Harrison	Indiana	55	Republican	1889 - 1893
Grover Cleveland	New York	55	Democratic	1893 - 1897
William McKinley	Ohio	54	Republican	1897 - 1901
Theodore Roosevelt	New York	42	Republican	1901 - 1909
William Howard Taft	Ohio	51	Republican	1909 - 1913
Woodrow Wilson	New Jersey	56	Democratic	1913 - 1921
Warren G. Harding	Ohio	55	Republican	1921 - 1923
Calvin Coolidge	Massachusetts	51	Republican	1923 - 1929
Herbert Hoover	California	54	Republican	1929 - 1933
Franklin D. Roosevelt	New York	51	Democratic	1933 - 1945
Harry S. Truman	Missouri	60	Democratic	1945 - 1953
Dwight D. Eisenhower	New York	62	Republican	1953 - 1961
John F. Kennedy	Massachusetts	43	Democratic	1961 - 1963
Lyndon B. Johnson	Texas	55	Democratic	1963 - 1969
Richard M. Nixon	New York	55	Republican	1969 - 1974
Gerald R. Ford	Michigan	61	Republican	1974 - 1977
James A. Carter	Georgia	52	Democratic	1977 - 1981
Ronald W. Reagan	California	69	Republican	1981 - 1989
Goerge Bush	Texas	65	Republican	1989 - 1993
William J. Clinton	Arkansas	46	Democratic	1993 -

to its owners, and you set out to reclaim the system for the people. As it turned out, the White House is not the ideal place from where to lead such a revolt. Some progress is being made in stabilizing taxes, reducing the bureaucracy, and controlling the rapidly increasing federal debt and deficit. But a majority of these successes have been accomplished through an endless series of deals, compromises, and concessions. In addition, the press and opposing party have been a constant source of criticism, often aggravating a problem or crisis.

As your administration has progressed on its ambitious and difficult mission, mistakes, political infighting, media criticism, and public outcries have caused a number of changes to your original plans. In only a year, the composition of your administration has changed in order to better fight political battles with congressional foes and powerful special-interest lobbies. The result has been a lack of fresh, creative ideas that were supposed to change business as usual. Granted, you have been in office only a year, but in that time you have fully realized how difficult it is to form a cooperative working relationship with Congress and other members of the establishment. As Wes Gallagher, a former president of the Associated Press, said, "The Washington politician's view of what is going on in the United States has been substituted for what is actually happening in the country."

PARTY GAMES

At times, misperception or ignorance keeps Congress from realizing the nation's wants and needs. In addressing this problem you must bring Democrats and Republicans together to define the nation's concerns and formulate the appropriate answers. This will be one of your most difficult tasks, as partisan bickering does not always conclude with an answer to a problem. For example, during a majority of President Ronald Reagan's two terms, Senator Daniel Patrick Moynihan, a New York Democrat, gave speeches and wrote newspaper columns claiming that budget deficits were being created deliberately by the Reagan administration. By slashing taxes while doubling military spending, Moynihan said that Reagan intended to create a fiscal crisis in order to force the country into reducing social spending for years to come. However, for all but two of Reagan's eight years in office, Congress had a Democratic majority, which passed each of Reagan's eight annual budgets. Moynihan, a Democrat, and Reagan, a Republican, blamed their opposition party for the rising annual deficits and national debt. In the meantime, neither one did anything to alleviate the problem. Blame was more important than a sound financial policy.

In his farewell address, George Washington warned against the "baneful" effect of political parties. In a letter to John Adams in 1814, John Taylor shared a similar fear as he wrote, "All parties...degenerate into aristocracies of interest." The public, Taylor warned, had to be careful about where party "integrity ends and fraud begins." Party influence, on the executive branch ranges from recommending and ratifying major appointments, including the Cabinet, to favors for contributors. In the early 1970's, Lew Wasserman, the owner of the Music Corporation of America, saved the Democratic National Committee from bankruptcy. During a visit to Washington, Wasserman could not get a room at his favorite Washington hotel. After Democratic leaders failed to get Wasserman a room at this hotel, they were able to put him in the Lincoln Bedroom at the White House. For major contributors to the president's party, lodging at the White House is not an uncommon perk.

The power and influence that money brings to Washington is extensive and something you must deal with everyday. Special-interest lobbyists and political action committees play a decisive role in the legislation that is introduced in Congress, as well as how the members of Congress vote on the issues. Often, members of Congress are caught in the middle between your administration's stance and pressure from these special interests. The money that political action committees give to a senator's or representative's campaign fund can be more influential than anything a president has to offer. Between special interests and partisan politics, there will be all sorts of hurdles along your journey to reform Washington.

Your attempts to end partisan politics are resulting in a few successes. Slowly, senators and representatives are crossing party lines when voting for legislation, and you have been at the forefront of this bipartisan movement. Bills which make at least minor reforms on lobbying activities and campaign donations were passed because of public pressure, even though a majority of Congress personally opposed these measures. Other pieces of pending legislation will dramatically hinder your budget-cutting agenda, but the public overwhelmingly supports them. Members of the opposition party will take full advantage of this situation to gain concessions. You must then weigh the pros and cons of whether it is to your advantage to fight the legislation and upset millions of voters, or to support the legislation and worry about its monetary effects later.

Pressure from your own political party will also force you to rethink many of your administration's strategies. Even though one of your major goals has been to get Democrats and Republicans to work together and end gridlock along political party lines, you must face the reality that you are the party's leader. To many of your party colleagues, this role is just as important, if not more important, than your role as chief executive. Raising money and making appearances for your party's candidates for offices, nationwide, is a frequent duty. Again, this will create many difficult situations. If the members of your party in Congress are upset with your actions, they are likely to criticize you and your administration. For example, some of the earliest criticisms of the Carter administration came from members of his own party. Congressional Democrats, upset with some of President Carter's actions, described their disillusionment to the media, creating an even larger division between the legislative and executive branches.

MEDIA MADNESS

Besides Congress, your most important ally and potentially your worst antagonist is the press. During the presidential campaign, you learned the importance of the press in creating your public image. In the age of modern communications, great speeches, such as Lincoln's speech at Gettysburg, or Kennedy's inaugural address, are no longer as important as they once were in rallying the nation. Instead, soundbites — brief 10-and-15 second quotes or video clips — dominate the news. Full-time members of your staff have the sole responsibility for creating soundbites, making sure your image in the media is positive. For modern presidents, this concern with their public image has become an obsession.

Your political advisors will claim that the most important information you will receive in office are public opinion polls relating to your image, and they should be a prime consideration in every aspect of your presidency. These polls can dictate everything from the rhetoric you use to how you gain congressional votes on a piece of legislation. For instance, President Bill Clinton relied on polls more than any other president before him. In his first year in office, the Democratic National Committee spent $1.9 million for surveys, polls, and focus groups. As a comparison, the Republican National Committee paid pollsters $400,000 during George Bush's first year as president. Carrying his 1992 campaign successes into the White House, Clinton continued to use polls and focus groups to make sure his rhetoric paralleled what the public preferred to hear.

Still in your first term, you may also rely on pollsters to discover the American people's perceived wants and needs. Even as you try to change business as usual in Washington and attempt to portray yourself as a different kind of politician, you may succumb to the urge to campaign throughout your term, if you intend to seek reelection for an additional four years. Unfortunately, even if you do win the election for a second term, this campaigning probably will not cease. Perhaps your vice-president, a member of your cabinet, or a member of your party in Congress decides to succeed you as president. As your party's leader, you will be obligated to campaign for them to ensure your party's hold on the White House. Campaigning is the art of trying to be all things to all people. Governing is the art of making difficult choices in order to lead this great nation. A good campaigner is not necessarily a good chief executive.

No matter how successful you are in office or how high your public approval rating reaches, members of the media will still thrive on negative stories about you, your party, and your administration. For better or for worse, the media no longer differentiates between a public official's public or private life. Whether someone's allegation is factual or a lie, you must deftly deal with each and every matter and never underestimate the potential fallout that can result. Episodes such as the Watergate scandal, which forced Richard Nixon to resign, have increased the power of the press to the point where journalists are constantly looking for scandals.

Because scandals can easily interrupt a president's agenda and affect his popularity, Congress and your opposing party can make a small scandal into a headline story. By holding public congressional hearings or appointing a special prosecutor, Congress can make its own news and, to a certain extent, control the information the press receives. Congressional hearings, such as the ones held during the Watergate investigation, can be a public-relations nightmare for an administration, especially if televised nationwide.

The President's "Oval Office" in the White House

As Congress and the press attempt to extract as much information from your administration as possible, you will use the various powers of the presidency to keep what you deem to be selected information confidential. In the past, presidents have had a varying degree of success in keeping important information away from the press and public. Explaining that some information is better kept confidential for the nation's security or is subject to presidential privilege, you may attempt to keep a lot of information classified. The Constitution's first amendment guarantees freedom of the press, and the Freedom of Information Act has extended the ability of the press to obtain government information. The press, in its attempt to break a story, will not be concerned with the ramifications on you or your administration. As a result, you may find your administration in court defending the confidentiality of classified material, such as when the Nixon administration took *The New York Times* and *Washington Post* to court in an attempt to prevent the release of the secret military information contained in the *Pentagon Papers*.

★ ★ ★ ★ ★

The presidency has become overly complicated for one individual. You now realize that with every action and decision you make, there are numerous complications. Pleasing everyone is impossible. Now that you have a year of experience with Congress, the press, special interest groups, and an indefinite amount of other components of the American political system, your next three or seven years will only be more complex. From directing the military to vetoing a bill, you now know the spectrum of powers of the presidency. A few powers, such as your ability to pardon an individual, cannot be challenged by the legislative or judicial branches. But these powers are rare. The reality is that you must share your power; success in politics relies on your ability to lead and compromise.

CHAPTER 7

HOW THE SUPREME COURT WORKS

by Keith A. Fournier, Esq.
Executive Director – American Center for Law and Justice
with Bryan J. Brown

ACLJ

GLOSSARY

for How The Supreme Court Works

Appeal
1. The transfer of a case from a lower to a higher court for a new hearing.
2. A case so transferred.
3. A request for a new hearing.

Appellate/Appellee
1. Appellate: Having the power to hear appeals and to review court decisions.
2. Appallee: One against whom an appeal is taken.

Civil
1. Law. Relating to the rights of private individuals and legal proceedings concerning these rights as distinguished from criminal, military, or international regulations or proceedings.

Conspiracy
1. An agreement to perform together an illegal, wrongful, or subversive act.
2. An agreement between two or more persons to commit a crime or accomplish a legal purpose through illegal action.
3. A group of conspirators acting together, as if by sinister design

Constitutional
1. Consistent with, sanctioned by, or permissible according to a constitution: a law that was declared constitutional by the court; the constitutional right of free speech.

Contempt of Court
1. Interference with the functioning of a court, either direct (occurring before a judge) or constructive (actions obstructing justice, e.g., disobeying an INJUNCTION). Contempt is punished to enforce a party's rights (civil contempt) or to vindicate authority (criminal contempt). The court may impose a fine or imprisonment; in the case of direct contempt, no hearing is required.

Criminal
1. Of, involving, or having the nature of unlawful activity
2. Relating to the administration of penal law.

Deliberation
1. To think carefully and often slowly, as about a choice to be made.
2. To consult with another or others in a process of reaching a decision.
3. Discussion and consideration of all sides of an issue.

Docket
1. A calendar of the cases awaiting action in a court.
2. A brief entry of the court proceedings in a legal case.
3. The book containing such entries

Felony
1. One of several grave crimes, such as murder, rape, or burglary, punishable by a more stringent sentence than that given for a misdemeanor.

Hierarchy
1. a. Categorization of a group of people according to ability or status. b. The group so categorized.
2. A series in which each element is graded or ranked: put honesty first in her hierarchy of values.

Ideology/Ideologies
1. The body of ideas reflecting the social needs and aspirations of an individual, a group, a class, or a culture.
2. A set of doctrines or beliefs that form the basis of a political, economic, or other system.

Judicial
1. Of, relating to, or proper to courts of law or to the administration of justice: the judicial system.
2. Decreed by or proceeding from a court of justice: a judicial decision.
3. Belonging or appropriate to the office of a judge

Misdemeanor
1. A misdeed.
2. An offense less serious than a felony.

Naturalized
1. To be of foreign birth and granted full citizenship.

Preponderance
Superiority in weight, force, importance, or influence.

Prosecute/Prosecution
1. To initiate civil or criminal court action against; to seek to obtain or enforce by legal action.
2. A lawyer empowered to prosecute cases on behalf of a government and its people.

Recognizance
1. An obligation of record that is entered into before a court or magistrate, containing a condition to perform a particular act, such as making a court appearance.

Roman Empire
1. An empire that succeeded the Roman Republic during the time of Augustus, who ruled from 27 B.C. to A.D. 14. At its greatest extent it encompassed territories stretching from Britain and Germany to North Africa and the Persian Gulf. After 395 it was split into the Byzantine Empire and the Western Roman Empire, which rapidly sank into anarchy under the onslaught of barbarian invaders from the north and east. The last emperor of the West, Romulus Augustulus (born c. 461), was deposed by Goths in 476, the traditional date for the end of the empire.

HOW THE SUPREME COURT WORKS

Keith A. Fournier, Esq.

Executive Director - American Center for Law and Justice
with Bryan J. Brown

"Justice is the firm and continuous desire to render to everyone that which is his due."

— *Justinian*

The US Supreme Court is the nation's highest court and the court of last resort, in the administration of justice, in the United States. But before one can fully understand the Supreme Court, one must first understand the nature and background of the American judicial system, and the ideologies involved. Therefore, this chapter will walk you through the entire judicial process, from the basics of your local district court, through the hierarchy of state and federal courts, right up to the Supreme Court. Through real-life examples of these differing court systems, you will clearly understand the US system of justice. The "system" itself is merely a tool. The factor of most importance is the heart of the person using the tool to "make" and enforce the law. Bad judges tend to spawn bad law, good judges tend to render justice.

The US system of justice seems very complex, and in some ways, it is. But it can become much clearer by stepping back and looking at the big picture, rather than trying to study all the details up close. We will begin where most "outsiders" do, with a personal need for what the law can provide. Take the hypothetical case of Ms. Plaintiff:

THE PLIGHT OF MS. PLAINTIFF

Hurrying to get to the office for the closing of the most important contract in her life, Peggy Plaintiff steps out of the subway and onto a busy street. Fast paced and determined, she closes in on her destination. MCA executives await her arrival for the final audition and signing of a million-dollar recording contract. Her ship has finally arrived! Quickly boarding the elevator, she checks her watch, knowing that even a 10-minute delay could cost her this opportunity of a lifetime. All of the tabloids have been following the story because Peggy's competition, Debra Defendant, has publicly stated that she wants to edge

"the off-key Ms. Plaintiff" out of the picture. In the balance hangs the contract for the soundtrack to "Minnie Mouse sings the Courthouse Blues." Little does Peggy know that Debra has hired professional comedians with orders to keep her from this great hour. Suddenly the elevator stops mid-floor, and Peggy Plaintiff is trapped with Debra Defendant's hired bellhop, who's doing a very bad Jerry Lewis impersonation.

The bellhop feigns an attempt to call for help, all the while doing everything he can to unnerve Peggy and render her too upset to audition. Peggy had not noticed the Groucho Marx look-alike who had boarded the elevator behind her, but now she could not help but notice him. Lighting his cigar and waving it in her face, he launched into a non-stop and nonsensical monologue on religion. Having exhausted an overview of the subject, he landed on his own brand of Zen, and, edging Peggy into a corner of the elevator, he badgered her with a battery of questions: "What, really, is the sound of one hand clapping? How do blind cave fish know when it is daytime? Is it not possible that all religions are one and all roads lead to Cleveland?" Distressed and desperate, Peggy reaches around the comedians to ring and re-ring the elevator alarm. However, the hotel security guard has fallen asleep at his post and fails to respond to her rings and shouts. Hours go by. At noon, having given up on waiting for Ms. Plaintiff, MCA awards the recording contract to Debra Defendant.

The MCA contract now secured, the hotel security guard finally frees Peggy from the elevator. Running up 65 flights of stairs, the frazzled Peggy bursts into the MCA suite and learns that she has been beaten and tricked. Where does one in Peggy Plaintiff's situation go to get relief? In the United States, the answer is, as we hear so often, you take them to court! If you were Peggy's best friend, how would you advise her to get the wheels of justice turning?

CIVIL AND CRIMINAL LAW

Our judicial system makes a distinction, in its rules and its results, between a civil and a criminal case. From the perspective of the person being haled into court, the primary difference is one of penalties. A criminal case can result in a penalty of imprisonment, a civil case cannot. (Exceptions almost always exist in law. Anytime one stands before a judge, in a criminal or a civil trial, a contempt-of-court charge can result in jail time. Technically, this is not a penalty arising from the allegations of the case, but rather a penalty for violating the procedural law of the courthouse.) Fines can, and often do, result from both criminal and civil cases. Civil cases differ from criminal cases in terms of money awards, in that, in a civil case, the court often mandates the losing party to pay damages to the prevailing party, sometimes including court costs. In criminal cases the victim does not get a payment from the guilty party.

Another difference between criminal and civil cases is the question of who is pressing the case, that is, who is the party seeking a court judgment. The government, and only the government, can prosecute in criminal actions. The victim relates the crime to the police, who relate it to the prosecuting attorney's office. The local, state, or federal prosecutors then decide if the alleged event is illegal. If they determine that a law has been broken, the government then enters a criminal prosecution suit against the alleged victimizer. The victim's advocate is the government, the people, and the community. The person being prosecuted, (called the accused or defendant), can either hire an attorney, be self represented (pro-se), or, if the "defendant" is without the finances to hire an attorney, request a court-appointed attorney. The essential question in a criminal suit is whether the accused is guilty or not guilty, and the government has the burden of presenting evidence that overcomes the presumption that the person is innocent, unless the defendant pleads, "Guilty, your Honor." Many jurisdictions allow a third option in pleading, that being "nolo contendere." This literally means "I do not wish to contend," and differs from a plea of guilty only in that it cannot be used as an admission of responsibility for the act in any other litigation. The "nolo" plea is used most often by defendants who believe that they will be found guilty in a criminal trial, and so desire to insulate themselves from follow-up civil litigation. By constitutional mandate, all defendants entering pleas of "not guilty" to charges involving "serious" crimes, (crimes in which the defendant faces more than six months possible incarceration), must be given the option of a jury trial.

According to a textbook on the law, a number of policies differ between civil and criminal cases. The following policies are specific to criminal litigation only: "The policy of placing the individual's interest ahead of the state's; the policy that presumes that it is better to protect one innocent person from punishment than to punish many persons for crimes they did commit; the policy of protecting the guilty as well as the innocent against unreasonable harassment by the state, by being required to defend against criminal charges that have little chance of being proved in court; and the policy of requiring the police and other representatives of the state to perform their duties in a lawful manner, even though this may, at times, require letting guilty persons go free." [1] These policies, setting criminal trials apart from civil trials, are supported by the provisions of the Fourth, Fifth, Sixth, Eighth, and Fourteenth Amendments to the US Constitution. Our Founding Fathers had experienced the horrors of police-state trial practices in Europe, and so built powerful hedges around the law in the American Experiment.

Trial by a jury of your peers is allowed, be it a criminal or civil case. This right is very old, coming from the Magna Carta of 13th century England. The Seventh Amendment of the US Constitution states, "In suits at common law, where the value in controversy shall exceed twenty dollars, the right of trial by jury shall be preserved...." As designed, the jury is supposed to weigh the facts of the case, and the judge is supposed to apply the law to the facts that the jury deems true. This right to a jury trial can be waived. In a criminal trial, it is a choice made by the defendant. If the questions in the case are mostly the application of law to facts that, while being grievous or socially repugnant, are likely not, by the letter of the law, illegal, then conventional courthouse wisdom holds that the defendant would probably do well to waive the jury and present his case directly to the judge.

This century's breakdown in the social consensus has resulted in a great upsurge in criminal prosecutions. To seat a jury in all criminal cases would create a very high social burden. Three procedural "adaptations" have arisen to treat this problem. Adaptation number one: The Supreme Court has ruled that only in criminal sentences exceeding six months need a jury be involved in the fact-finding. (State constitutions often guarantee broader rights to jury trial.) Adaptation number two: If the "crime" is not one that was around in 1791, a jury trial is not to be guaranteed. (This is why many trials before government agencies are conducted as "bench trials," that is, with only a judge weighing both the facts of the case and the law to be applied to the facts.) Adaptation number three is the "de novo appeal." In most cities, lower courts sit without a jury, and all cases tried are granted an automatic appeal and re-trial before a court of record, if the parties feel that justice was not done.

The latter adaptation, essentially, functions on the local court level as a plea-bargaining system. Plea bargaining is a creature of the criminal law. Its corollary in civil law would be "settling out of court," and like settling out, the result is that the court docket is significantly lightened. Statistics reveal that approximately 90 percent of all criminal cases are finalized at the pleading stage, with the defendant pleading guilty. In many cases, the guilty plea is to a lighter charge than the main charge against the defendant. This is not done to make the defendant's life more enjoyable or as a general act of compassion and forgiveness on the part of the prosecution. According to an obviously biased Texas defense attorney, "The prosecutor negotiates on plea-bargaining terms with the defense counselor in the prison market place for pieces of the human being's life and/or money from the human being and/or other confessions from the human being and/or evidence which could hurt other people and/or anything else which the prosecutor believes that he needs.[2] The game is 'Let's make a deal.' Innocence or guilt is frequently irrelevant and often ignored throughout the negotiations. If it is considered at all, it is just one of many variables. The possibility, or probability, of a lengthy sentence is likely to be the primary topics on the conversational agenda between prosecutor and defense attorney."

Burdens of proof differ greatly between a criminal trial and a civil trial. The state must prove, beyond a reasonable doubt, that a person has committed a crime. In the case of serious crimes, the state must also prove that the defendant purposed or understood his or her conduct to be criminal, or at least likely hurtful. The burden of proof, in a civil case, is much less — a mere "preponderance of the evidence." In other words, the plaintiff need only prove that his or her theory on the case is more likely to be true than the defendant's theory. It is much easier to obtain a verdict against a defendant in a civil trial than in a criminal trial.

In a civil action, the person bringing the suit (the plaintiff or petitioner) submits a pleading to the court that sets forth a non-criminal complaint against the party being sued (the defendant or respondent). Such claims are based upon the alleged violation of the rights of the plaintiff. Torts (harm done to persons or property), contract violations, divorces, wills, and trusts are only a few of the possible areas of civil litigation. In criminal proceedings, the complaint is the allegation that the defendant broke a law.

Parties seeking injunctions or restraining orders are also involved in civil litigation. In these "equity law" actions, the court acts, before any harm can occur, in an attempt to make the occurrence of the harm less likely. Defendants are restricted in their activities upon proof that they will likely, if not so restricted, do harm to another's person or property.

The primary question in civil litigation is conflict resolution through the application of law. The person bringing the suit (plaintiff or petitioner), has the burden of "making their case." The verdict is not a question of innocence or guilt, but rather of prevailing or "being prevailed upon." To put it in plain language, either the court rules as the plaintiff requests (against the wishes of the defendant) or the court sends the plaintiff away without the desired ruling.

Those who are "prevailed upon" are usually unhappy with the ruling. In most situations, the initial court judgment can be appealed to a higher court, although that does not necessarily mean that the appellate court will re-open or even review the case. If the verdict is appealed, the party appealing to the higher court may be either the plaintiff/petitioner or the defendant/respondent. In either case, it will almost always be the party who lost on the trial level. The appealing party, upon entering the appellate court, becomes the appellant. The party involuntarily brought into the appeal is the appellee.

PRIMARY SOURCES OF AMERICAN LAW

Constitutions

The US Constitution is the foremost authority in the nation. In the Constitution is embodied the skeleton for the American system of government, including the federal court system, congressional powers, executive powers and the rights of states to govern within their borders. State constitutions are also primary sources of authority, but they are limited in their application to the state borders.

Statutes

Rules, written by a legislature, are, also, a primary source of law. Congress is given the power, by the constitution, to draft statutes, binding upon all Americans. State statutes are binding law upon those individuals who reside or do business within the borders of the state. All statutes must comply with the Constitutions, under which, they operate. The courts have the function of determining if statutes pass constitutional muster.

Regulations

Administrative agencies, appointed by presidents, governors and congresses, also draft binding law. These agencies are created by legislative acts and subject to judicial controls. The body of regulations, mandated by these agencies, is referred to as administrative law, and is the fastest growing source of authority in our present legal bureaucracy.

Case Rulings

"Judge made law" is the fourth, but not least, primary source of law. The doctrine of stare decisis states that legal precedent is binding: today's decision should be in keeping with yesterday's. This doctrine was, for the most part, strictly adhered to in the courts of America until the latter half of the twentieth century. However, the modern courts have often sailed into uncharted waters, making novel rulings that break with the past and significantly weaken the doctrine of stare decisis. Judicial activism is the term, often used, to describe this breaking with preceding (precedent) case law.

Constitutions, statutes, regulations and case rulings must be applied to specific situations by judges, in courts of law. It is, in this context, that two "schools of thought", in the current legal debate emerge. Liberal schools of interpretation stress the "spirit of the writings" and the need for courts to draw from the latest understandings and ideologies to solve current social problems. Unchained from the actual wording of the law, these judges set themselves free to apply their own theories in shaping a ruling. Judges, who so rule, are often referred to as judicial activists. On the other side of the continuum, we find the judicial restraintists. These conservative judges stress the need to strictly interpret the language of the Constitution and other sources. They tend to favor a limited, rather than activist, role for courts, and purposely attempt to restrict their own theoretical social biases from entering into the law.

MS. PLAINTIFF SEEKING JUSTICE

Applying the civil or criminal question to our fictional conflict between Peggy and Debra, we find Ms. Plaintiff seeking criminal prosecution against Ms. Defendant and her cohorts. The state prosecuting attorney, after hearing the facts of the case, has decided that there is enough evidence to charge the comedians with false imprisonment. The prosecutor does not, however, believe that Peggy's allegations of conspiracy against the hotel security guard and Ms. Defendant can be worked up into a criminal case. She advises Peggy that her case against the hotel and Debra are probably best pursued in a civil case, where the burden of proof is lower.

A police detective gets information from Peggy and, using his skills, tracks down "Groucho" and young "Jerry" at a local hang out for aspiring stand-up comics. They are arrested, taken to the jail, and "booked," and have their first appearance before a judge the following morning. The judge sets bond, after determining the gravity of the charged offense and the likelihood that, if released to await trial, the accused will conduct themselves with civility and return to court for trial. The bond is money put in escrow, to be forfeited if the accused do not return for trial. Bail is a percentage of bond, often 10%, which is a fee paid to a bail bondsman who guarantees to pay the full bond if the accused fails to return to court for trial. While a posted bond is refundable, once the trial is completed, bail money is paying the bail bondsman to promise to cover the bond, and so it is not refundable. Since the civil courts have no power to incarcerate, it has no corollary to the bonding system.

"Jerry" is released on his own recognizance since he had no prior criminal convictions, but "Groucho" did not get off as easily. He had many priors, all of them misdemeanors and none that resulted in a sentence longer than six months. Furthermore, the judge did not find his courtroom slapstick entertaining. (They usually don't.) His bond was set at $10,000. A call to a bail bondsman whom he knew resulted in a discount rate, and for $300, "Groucho" was back on the street.

A few months or more pass and both are on trial, in which "Jerry" and "Groucho" are the defendants and the state the prosecutor. Acting on behalf of Ms. Plaintiff, the prosecuting attorney will attempt to prove that the comedians' actions were against the law. In this case, the law that was allegedly violated is section 212.3 of the Model Penal Code: false imprisonment. The prosecutor must prove, beyond a reasonable doubt, that the defendant "knowingly restrained Ms. Peggy Plaintiff, unlawfully, so as to interfere, substantially, with her liberty." The prosecutor will call as its primary witness, the victim, Peggy Plaintiff.

Down the hall, Peggy is testifying in the civil trial that she began against the hotel security guard. Unlike the comedians, the security guard did not "knowingly restrain Ms. Plaintiff." He, rather, was negligent, sleeping on the job and not hearing her cries for help. Since the government does not prosecute persons for this activity, Peggy brought a civil suit against the security guard. Ms. Plaintiff is alleging that the defendant owed her a duty of care, and failed to act in a reasonable manner to carry out that duty. Peggy requests a judicial ruling to right this wrong, claiming the security guard's breach of his duty caused her great suffering, pain, and a lost recording contract. The court does not appoint attorneys in civil cases, so it is very likely that both are represented by attorneys whom they are paying. In order to make the suit, the plaintiff must prove, with a preponderance of evidence, that she was wronged by the defendant and that the court can order a remedy that will make the situation more bearable. In this case, Ms. Plaintiff has requested a very large sum of money from the security guard. The security guard's attorney has cross-filed against other "blamable" parties, pulling the hotel and the insurance company that bonds the security guard into the suit as well.

Since these actions were begun in the state courts, let's get an overview of how the system works. Please review the diagrams included in this chapter while reading the following material, and note the different courts available within the state and federal legal systems.

THE STATE COURT SYSTEM

America is a nation of law, and thus, a nation of courts. We enjoy the liberty of having 51 separate court systems; the federal courts, as described above, and 50 independent state court systems, all operating under differing state constitutions, criminal codes and procedural laws. Due to this tremendous diversity, presentation of the state court system must be broad.

Like the US Federal system and all western-law-tradition systems, the state court system has a pyramid-like distribution of authority. Each state has a single court of highest authority, usually called the state supreme court (New York is the exception, calling their highest court the Court of Appeals). Below this highest court sit the courts of intermediate appeal. At the bottom, but not nearly as uniform or simple as the federal system, are the trial courts. Forty-nine states have built their judicial system on the "common law" model inherited from England, Louisiana being the exception in using the Continental "civil law" model from France. (Quebec, Central America, and South America, are also based in the civil law tradition.)

The term, "civil law" refers to the court system that is descended from the Roman Empire, on the continent of Europe. The primary difference between the common law and civil law is the emphasis and importance placed upon case law. In a civil-law nation, the specific case decisions are not nearly as important sources of law as they are in the common-law nations. The courts of civil law nations rule primarily from the statutes passed by their governments, without attempting to build a body of case "common law."

YOUR LOCAL SPECIALTY COURT OF LAW

Beginning at the local and lowest level, in the typical state court system, one encounters a division of judicial authority between various courts of law. The "blue pages" of the phone book, The County Courthouse Book[3] or the reference librarian at the public library will likely be helpful in understanding how this system functions in your area.

Local courts sit under the authority of the state constitution, and thus are rightly thought of as state law courts, rather than city or county courts. The district or circuit court has delegated, to these specialty courts, the duty to rule in specific cases. As the "lowest" courts on the ladder, however, they often lack the jurisdiction to rule on matters of great weight, being limited in dollar amounts, geographical area, and severity of criminal charges. These courts also usually lack a jury or court recorder; the magistrate or judge handles all cases with "judicial discretion." Typically, these courts are named for the types of cases that they are authorized to handle.

Small claims courts: These courts handle civil cases involving controversies up to a set amount, usually not over a few thousand dollars. It is common for these courts to exclude lawyers, requiring all cases to proceed "pro se," that is, with the plaintiff and defendant being self-represented.

Domestic Relations courts: These family-law courts are involved in divorce and child custody\support cases.

Juvenile courts: Interfacing with the state social services, this court is involved in criminal law involving underage defendants. Juvenile law tends to differ greatly from the criminal law binding on adults, especially in terms of punishment.

Probate courts: A direct descendant of the medieval church courts, probate judges settle administrative matters arising from wills, estates, and (often) orphaned children.

Traffic courts: These courts serve as a good example of the lack of formality and trappings in the local state courts. Even without the usual pomp and circumstance of the other court systems, a traffic court judge can suspend your license with one blow of the gavel.

Other courts can be created, as needed, to deal with pressing social issues. Some localities still retain a court of chancery that deals only with equity law. In most state courts, however, common law, statutory law, and equity law are not singled out for different treatment.

YOUR LOCAL GENERAL COURT OF LAW

Sitting alongside all of these "specialty courts" is the court of general jurisdiction. West of the Mississippi, these courts are usually referred to as district courts (of the county in which they sit), and east of the Mississippi, circuit courts. All cases brought in the state court system that do not fall into the jurisdiction of the specialty courts, come before the general courts. Larger cities usually further divide their general court into civil and criminal courts. (Specific information as to the breakdown between specialty and general courts in your area can usually be gained by visiting the clerk of the court's office.)

Being pyramid-like in structure, the state courts have a system of appeals to higher courts. At the base of the pyramid, the lowest courts often sit without record and without juries; to make up for this deficiency in constitutional trial guarantees, all who appear before these courts are granted a de novo trial upon request. (A de novo trial is a retrial without any weight being given to the previous trial.)

APPEALING THE DECISION

State courts of intermediate appeal, above the actual trial-of-record courts, but below the state supreme courts, are not all the same. Some shadow the federal courts in organization, resembling a "three-tiered system" with many appellate courts of regional jurisdiction. Other states have only one appellate court, a "clearing house" for the supreme court, seated above it in the chain of command. Still other states do not have a court of intermediate appeals at all; appeals go directly to the state supreme court. In the states that do have courts of intermediate appeals, the judges often sit in "en banc," usually in groups of three, to review the application of the law to the facts of the case. This is not a de novo appeal, and the facts are not to be re-weighed in the scales of justice. The role of the intermediate appellate court is only to determine if the lower court used the correct rules of law to judge the facts of the case.

INTO THE STATE SUPREME COURT

All states have a court of last resort, a court sitting in the highest judicial authority. With one exception, such a state court is referred to as the state supreme court. (New York uses the title Court of Appeals for its highest court and Supreme court for its trial courts.)

The procedural rules for gaining a hearing in the state supreme court vary greatly across the nation; some require the granting of an appeal, others hear any and all cases as a matter of right.

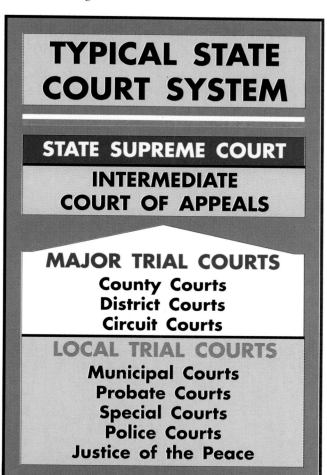

TYPICAL STATE COURT SYSTEM

STATE SUPREME COURT

INTERMEDIATE COURT OF APPEALS

MAJOR TRIAL COURTS
County Courts
District Courts
Circuit Courts

LOCAL TRIAL COURTS
Municipal Courts
Probate Courts
Special Courts
Police Courts
Justice of the Peace

All state supreme courts have multiple justices, ranging from three in Delaware to nine in many other states. Rules governing court procedures such as how lawyers are to enter the paperwork for cases to be reviewed, the length of oral arguments, and how cases are deliberated among the justices, also vary widely from state to state. As Northwestern law professor Herbert Jacob observes, "Cases are decided by majority vote of the justices. Those who disagree with the majority may simply note their dissent at the end of the case. They may also write a dissenting opinion in which they specify their reasons. Although the right to dissent is unquestioned in both the state and federal appellate courts, dissents are much less frequent on state supreme courts than on the federal Supreme Court." [4]

MS. PLAINTIFF'S DAY IN COURT

Meanwhile, back to Ms. Peggy Plaintiff's cases. The criminal prosecution hit a roadblock early on as that the defense attorney for the Jerry Lewis look-alike "dropped a bombshell," revealing that his client was only 16 years old and therefore was not under the jurisdiction of the court. The action was moved by the judge into the juvenile system, which sentenced the defendant to attend acting lessons and complete 30 hours of community service as a golf caddie for the judge. Case closed.

"Groucho's" attorney met with the prosecutor and outlined his plans to claim a constitutional "religious freedom" defense. The prosecutor attempted to dissuade the defense attorney, calling it a "cheap shot" and attempted "end-run of responsibility." The defense attorney stood his ground, and suggested that his client probably would plead guilty to the charge of loitering, smoking in a no-smoking area, or possibly even verbal assault, as long as no jail time would result. The prosecutor refused to entertain a plea bargain, and advised the defense attorney to prepare his client for a loss and a long vacation from the stage.

"Groucho," on his attorney's advice, waived his right to jury trial. His attorney felt that the public would likely be much more sympathetic to Peggy Plaintiff than to "Groucho," and would let their emotions override the legal issues involved. Before the judge, in a bench trial, "Groucho" asserted the sincerity of his new-found faith. He testified that he came to a heartfelt dedication to his own brand of Zen-like New Age Sufism, with a mixture of Tantrism and Zoroastrianism thrown in, for good measure, by way of an angelic vision he had on the morning of the fateful elevator experience. In his unrestrained zeal to share his new found faith, he admitted that he over-stepped the boundaries of good taste, but meant Ms. Plaintiff no harm or ill will. He also admitted that he did indeed purposely corner her, but that he was doing it for what he sincerely believed was her own good and, hopefully, her very enlightenment. "Groucho" denied that he was working with the lad or Ms. Defendant, stating that all of his actions were directed toward the higher good of spreading his newly-created religion of peace and thrills. He then attempted to demonstrate for the judge, by way of deep meditation and levitation, his esoteric perspectives on religion. The honorable judge, in turn, shared with the Groucho look-alike his ability to throw defendants who attempt to frustrate criminal proceedings into jail for contempt of court.

At the close of the defendant's case, the judge, without a pause, announced his verdict: "Guilty as charged!" Obviously annoyed with "Groucho," the judge then "threw the book at him": a maximum sentence of three years. Shocked, the comedian turned to his lawyer for counsel. He was told, "first off, with the state's new 'two for one' rule, you will get double credit for each day served. That gets you down to a mere year and a half. Given the prison over-crowding problems and the fact that you will likely be a model prisoner, we will stand a good chance of an early release, probably after one year." The comedian was still not relieved. His attorney came up with plan two: "The religion defense is not strong, but this state does have a very broadly written constitutional amendment on the subject. If you can raise the money, we can appeal this decision."

The money is raised and the appeal is entered. By posting an appeal bond, "Groucho" is allowed to delay serving his sentence until the case is decided in the higher courts. Constitutional issues often bypass all intermediate state courts of appeal and go directly to the state Supreme Court. A year later, the case is brought before the panel of five state supreme court justices. The oral arguments are followed by much deliberation and heated debate in chambers. Finally, a majority position is reached — a position in keeping with the broad freedoms granted by the mostly Quaker drafters of the 200-year-old state constitution. "Groucho" is innocent, his freedom of religion defense found to be within the scope of the constitutional protections.

Fearing a landslide of religion defenses and a choking of the court system, the state prosecutor immediately files for an appeal to the US Supreme Court. The High Court realizes the stakes involved and agrees to hear the case. Due to the Fifth Amendment's provision against "double jeopardy," that is, trying a person twice for the same crime, "Groucho's" freedom will not be affected by the appeal to the Supreme Court. A significant policy issue does, however, hang in the balance.

The civil case against the security guard has also become quite interesting. The judge had ruled on a similar case a few years earlier: A Ferris wheel operator had wandered away from his job during the County fair, leaving 30 people stranded and circling for over three hours. All sued for general damages, and one person sued for the specific damage that he was, because of the lengthy ride, kept from buying a lottery ticket. He argued that the lottery, that very night, was won by his neighbor, and it was a record-breaking jackpot. The judge ruled that the Ferris wheel operator was negligent and that all general damages for pain, discomfort, lost time, and emotional harm were justified. The specific damages of missing the lottery were not, however, recoverable.

In keeping with precedent case law, his Honor thus ruled, in the case of *Ms. Plaintiff vs. The Hotel Security Guard*, that the guard was negligent and would have to pay for all of Peggy's psychiatrist bills arising from her feelings of being trapped and abandoned in the elevator, as well as all missed wages from her job at the bank due to the psychological fallout. As to her million dollar claim, arising from the missed contract: no award.

PHILOSOPHIES OF AMERICAN LAW

"Jurisprudence" is a term used to introduce the concept of legal philosophy. What is law and why is it authoritative? Who has the right to make and enforce laws? What are the differences between law, power, and morality? These and a myriad of other questions are struggled with, in discussions of jurisprudence. "Schools" of jurisprudence are the major theoretical "camps" on the subject of legal philosophy, not an actual classroom environment or educational institution. The major "schools" are natural law, positivism, historical, and social-philosophical.

Natural Law

The medieval philosopher and theologian Thomas Aquinas is credited as being the greatest proponent of natural law. His system arises from the assumptions that God exists and has revealed truth to us through the created order, prophets, and Jesus Christ. The thoughts of Bracton, Blackstone, and the Founding Fathers of the United States are also part and parcel of the natural law model. Classical natural law stresses inherent rights given to individuals by the laws of Nature and of Nature's God: that human government derives its authority to rule from Nature's God, and that the whims of the king are not necessarily the "natural" way things ought to be, or the way "God" wants them to be. You may recall that in the Congressional hearings that rejected nominee Robert Bork and seated Justice Clarence Thomas, the concept of natural law was often brought up as a "stumbling stone" in the area of philosophy of law by Senators Biden and Kennedy.

Positivism

Supreme Court Justice Oliver Wendell Holmes was a vocal opponent of the natural law school, stating that he rejected the concept of a "brooding omnipresence in the sky." For Holmes and the school of positivists, law is merely power. Law is what the government commands. While this school of law made great advances in the late 19th and early 20th centuries, especially in its attempts to discredit natural law theory, it suffered a major setback in the concentration camps of Hitler's Germany and the Nuremberg trials that followed. How could a positivist punish German officers who were merely carrying out the orders of their government?

Historical School

Stressing the need for continuity with what has gone before, this conservative school relies upon a cultural stare decisis doctrine. (Stare decisis is the legal doctrine that future rulings should be in keeping with past rulings.) Given the rich natural law roots to American jurisprudence, this school tends to reflect natural law values, albeit without an allegiance to the natural Lawgiver. Tradition becomes a kind of surrogate deity. The "law above the law" is legal precedent, not revealed divine law or a Supreme Law-giver.

Socio-Pragmatic School

Also known as the Social Philosophical School, this is the dominant jurisprudence today. In the centuries past, theology was hailed as the "queen of the sciences." Natural law reflected this by building law upon the foundation of theology. "Enlightenment thought" of the 17th and 18th centuries, managed to eventually topple theology from the university citadel, replacing it with the "social sciences." Positivism then plowed through the law schools and legal institutions, rooting out much of natural law theory. Eventually positivism fell out of fashion, and pragmatism took its place. This "whatever theory works best for society" school of jurisprudence, now, has the playing field. A current legal textbook states that the socio-pragmatic school is "in one sense, an outgrowth of the natural law school, but instead of predicating rules on the concept of a divine lawgiver, it substitutes for that branches of knowledge outside of the law such as economics, sociology, psychology, politics, and history. Law ideally should be declared with a view to the needs not only of today, but also of tomorrow, and this can best be done in the light of the knowledge given by disciplines outside the law."[5]

Judicial Restraintists

Judicial Restraintists tend to come from the schools of natural law and historical law, stressing an adherence to precedents and legal absolutes. Restraintists also stress the need to evaluate current law against the standard of a higher law revealed in the halls of history.

Judicial Activists

Judicial Activists, on the other hand, tend to arise out of the schools of positivism and social-pragmatic law. They often appeal to the need to use the law as a tool for shaping and defining society, believing they have a duty to aid in our cultural evolution and judge current law against the ever changing standards of government or social desires.

Peggy's attorney immediately briefed her on the possibilities of appeal. "Winners" usually do not appeal, but in this case a very real and very expensive question hangs in the balance. The attorney was careful to tell her that the judge's ruling was in keeping with almost all previous state district court rulings on the "recoverable damages" subject, including one state supreme court ruling. He had told her from the beginning that the case did not look strong. On the question of appealing, he stated that only if the appellate court wanted to break with the past and set new policy could she expect a different ruling on the contract-damages question, and that if that happened the case would be appealed by the defendant to the Supreme Court, where it would quite possibly be reversed. It looked as if the case was dead-ended.

At this point, the young comedian stumbled into the courtroom, late for his court-ordered task of caddying for the judge. Upon seeing Ms. Plaintiff, he tearfully broke down and confessed to her that he was acting on the orders of Debra Defendant and under the supervision of the Groucho clone. Filled with guilt and remorse, the lad now wants to do all he can to help Peggy Plaintiff recover damages against Ms. Defendant and "Groucho."

Debra Defendant now lives clear across the continent and "Groucho" has joined a commune in Guam. What is Peggy to do? Shall she sue in civil court, file criminal charges, or do both? Should she go to the state court system or the federal system? If she chooses the state court system, should it be the state she lives in, the state Ms. Defendant lives in, the territory "Groucho" has re-located to, or the state in which the elevator incident took place? How will she ever get all of the parties together again for a trial?

BALANCING THE POWERS

While state supreme courts have great power and discretion over their states, they do not create binding case law outside of their jurisdiction. California is not bound to grant contract rights that the Massachusetts Supreme Court finds to be just and right. This is because the state supreme courts sit under the flag and constitution of their state; thus, they are sovereign only within that state. However, once the state supreme court ventures into the waters of federal law or US Constitutional provisions, an appeal to the Supreme Court of the United States is a possibility.

States' rights, over and against federal rights, is a field of law all to itself, as well as a very rich history that includes, within it the bloodiest war ever fought on US soil—the Civil War. Our system of independent state constitutions under a federal constitution mandates a delicate balancing act between the governmental powers, a balancing act that all realize has shifted dramatically in the past 94 years. This shifting of power from state to federal control has been quite evident in the US Supreme Court, as revealed in mandates from the Highest Bench that are carried out through the agents of the federal and state judicial systems.

BALANCING THE JURISDICTIONS

The relationship of authority and case allocation between state and federal courts is largely misunderstood. Due to the existence of both a system of state courts and federal courts, a balancing of interests must be undertaken. The federal courts are restricted in the cases they may hear. Congress and the Constitution (Article III) have set the limits, keeping the federal dockets clear. Some areas of the law are deemed to be solely the function of the federal courts; bankruptcy, patent rights, and cases involving the IRS are examples. Other cases are never allowed in the federal system under any circumstances, mainly family issues like divorce and child custody. In situations that cover subjects that can be entered as civil suits, in either the state or federal system, allocation of the case load is primarily undertaken by restricting access to the federal courts. Federal law requires that a civil suit entering the local US district court, involve either citizenship diversity in a controversy exceeding $50,000 or a "federal law" question. In other words, a civil suit must be between parties who are citizens of differing states and are seeking damages greater than $50,000, or the suit must center on the denial of federally guaranteed legal rights.

Criminal cases, in the federal system are also restricted. A federal prosecutor is limited to pressing a case only on federal law violations. Kidnapping and transportation of stolen goods across state lines are two such federal crimes.

Keeping the jurisdictional lines clear and deciding which law applies among the 51 independent court systems can be difficult at times. Authority problems are, at times, apparent, but the primary "pecking order" was established long ago. Professor Herbert Jacob writes:

"The relationship between state and federal courts was complex from the beginning. The Constitution provided that the state judges should swear allegiance to its provisions and obey them, regardless of the constitution or laws of their own state. Section 25, of the Judiciary Act of 1789, gave the United States Supreme Court authority to review state court decisions that had ruled against a claim based on the federal constitution, a treaty or a federal statute. Moreover, the Supreme Court held that state courts were bound by Court decisions on these matters. This ruling meant that state courts were bound by the federal interpretation of state laws, when the constitutionality of those laws was questioned." [6]

Furthermore, the US Constitution's Full Faith and Credit clause (Article IV) mandates that state courts respect and enforce judgments originating in other judicial systems that rule under the authority of the US Constitution. Thus, order and balance is maintained between the Federal Supreme Court and the state systems, as well as between states.

MS. PLAINTIFF SUES MS. DEFENDANT

One should easily see that the case of *Ms. Plaintiff vs. Ms. Defendant and "Groucho"* will meet the test to make it into the federal district court. The plaintiff and defendants are citizens of differing states, and the controversy is over a million-dollar contract. According to the federal rules, the case will have to be entered in the district court system in which one of the defendants live, or in which the event giving rise to the claim happened. The pleading that Peggy files to begin the case against Debra and "Groucho" includes many allegations: Tortious interference with a business contract, conspiracy, racketeering, and the tort of false imprisonment. The case looks good, and will likely, with the young comedian's testimony, result in a very large judgment against the defendants.

Debra Defendant's day has, most certainly, been ruined, because under these facts the federal prosecutor may also enter criminal charges against her. Criminal RICO (Racketeer Influenced and Corrupt Organization Act) could top the list, in that she has been charged with conspiring with another toward the goal of engaging in a criminal activity to further a business interest. RICO, however, requires a pattern of criminal activities, and so probably could not be proved against Ms. Defendant, unless other facts came to light. It is more likely that the state court in the county in which the elevator incident took place would charge her, after Ms. Plaintiff swore out a complaint alleging conspiracy toward the goal of false imprisonment.

Likewise, "Groucho" faces imminent criminal prosecution on both state and federal charges. He cannot be tried again on the false imprisonment, due to the Fifth Amendment's double jeopardy policy, but he can be tried for conspiracy and aiding to the delinquency of a minor. He also will likely end up owing much money to his attorney and Ms. Plaintiff, after the civil litigation, due to the fact that the burden of proof is lower than in the criminal trial. His freedom of religion defense is much less helpful, and "Jerry's" testimony is very damaging. The federal wheels of justice appear to have caught up with both Debra and "Groucho," to be followed by yet another pass from the state wheels.

THE FEDERAL COURT SYSTEM

The US Constitution provides for a federal court in Article III, section 1: "The judicial power of the United States shall be vested in one Supreme Court, and in such inferior courts as the Congress may, from time to time, ordain and establish." From such humble beginnings, a massive system of courts and procedures has arisen. With a few constitutional exceptions, all federal court cases must begin with a trial in the "inferior courts," that is, the lowest level of the judicial hierarchy. As noted on the diagrams on page 104, the federal court system is made up of three tiers: the district courts, the appellate courts, and the Supreme Court.

Ms. Plaintiff seeks justice in a court of law

GOING TO TRIAL

The district courts are the federal trial courts. District court judges, like those on the higher levels in the federal system, are appointed for life by the President of the United States. Presidents can, and do, greatly affect the shaping of our national laws by such judicial appointments. (President Jimmy Carter, for example, made over 100 appointments to the federal bench.)

The 94 federal district courts are scattered across the nation, which is divided into 11 judicial districts. Consult the US government section, of your phone directory to contact the federal district court in your area. The court reporter's office has packets of information detailing procedure and policies, including how to file your own federal case. (This is not, however, a recommended activity. The rules governing federal court procedure are complex and judges are often not favorably disposed to pro se litigants. Under the revised Civil Practice Rule 11 a federal judge has the ability to, at his discretion, jail a pro se litigant for misuse of the judicial system).

Both civil and criminal cases are heard in the same federal district courts. In the case of an especially urgent and important matter, an ad hoc tribunal can be formed in this court system. Three judges make up this tribunal, one of them being a judge of the court of appeals. The ruling of a tribunal, if appealed, bypasses the intermediate court of appeals and goes directly to the US Supreme Court. This is the fastest case-law path to the highest court in our nation.

APPEALING THE DECISION

Most federal cases are resolved at the trial level. However, either party does have the right to one appeal. Each district court system may be made up of courts sitting in many major cities or states, with the sizes of the districts roughly correlating to the population density of the nation. Over each district is seated a branch of the United States Court of Appeals, usually in the largest city in the district (Chicago, Denver, Boston, New York, San Francisco, and so forth). The percentage of cases appealed is small.

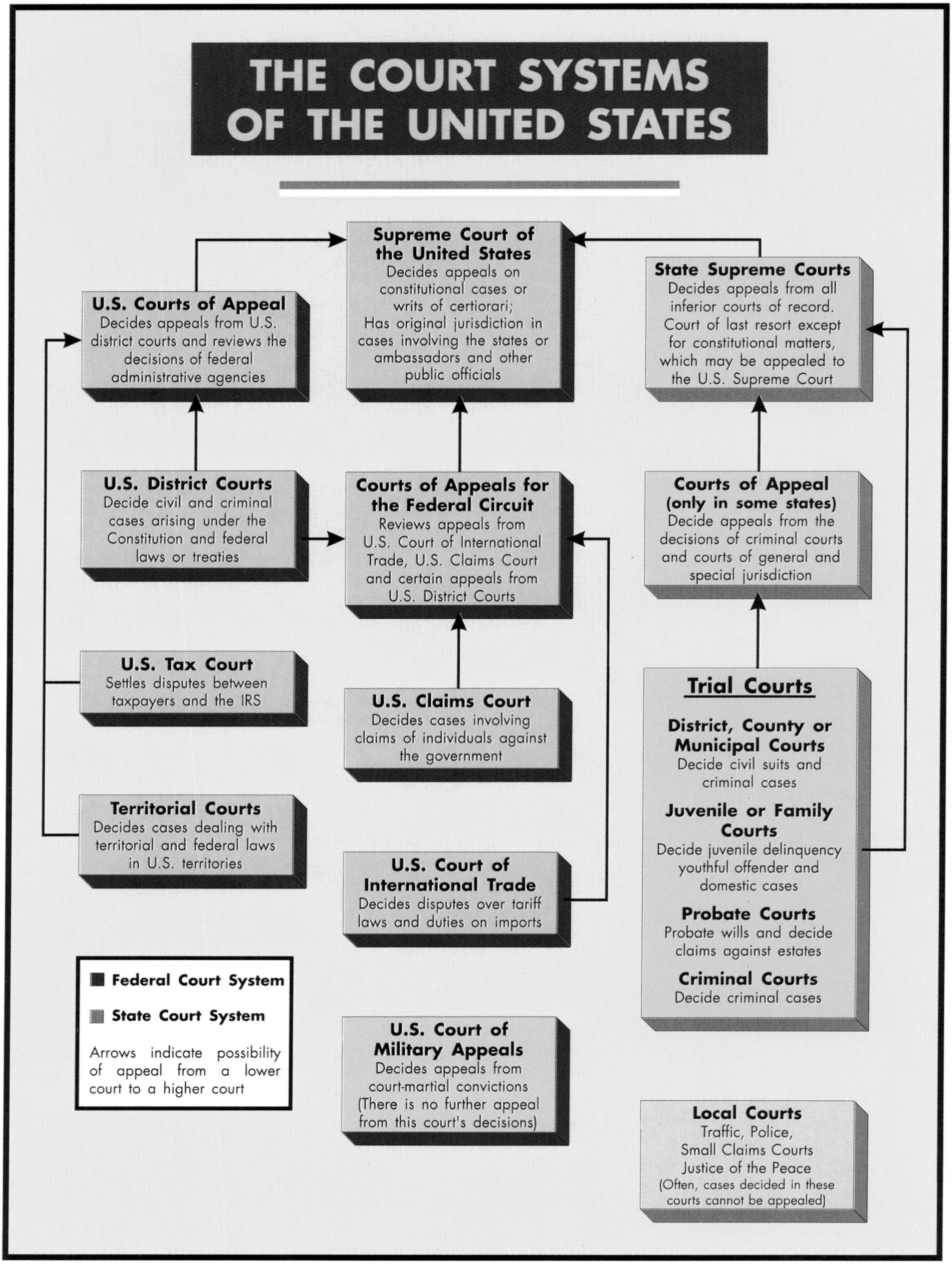

THE COURT SYSTEMS OF THE UNITED STATES

Supreme Court of the United States
Decides appeals on constitutional cases or writs of certiorari; Has original jurisdiction in cases involving the states or ambassadors and other public officials

U.S. Courts of Appeal
Decides appeals from U.S. district courts and reviews the decisions of federal administrative agencies

State Supreme Courts
Decides appeals from all inferior courts of record. Court of last resort except for constitutional matters, which may be appealed to the U.S. Supreme Court

U.S. District Courts
Decide civil and criminal cases arising under the Constitution and federal laws or treaties

Courts of Appeals for the Federal Circuit
Reviews appeals from U.S. Court of International Trade, U.S. Claims Court and certain appeals from U.S. District Courts

Courts of Appeal (only in some states)
Decide appeals from the decisions of criminal courts and courts of general and special jurisdiction

U.S. Tax Court
Settles disputes between taxpayers and the IRS

U.S. Claims Court
Decides cases involving claims of individuals against the government

Trial Courts

District, County or Municipal Courts
Decide civil suits and criminal cases

Juvenile or Family Courts
Decide juvenile delinquency youthful offender and domestic cases

Probate Courts
Probate wills and decide claims against estates

Criminal Courts
Decide criminal cases

Territorial Courts
Decides cases dealing with territorial and federal laws in U.S. territories

U.S. Court of International Trade
Decides disputes over tariff laws and duties on imports

■ **Federal Court System**

■ **State Court System**

Arrows indicate possibility of appeal from a lower court to a higher court

U.S. Court of Military Appeals
Decides appeals from court-martial convictions (There is no further appeal from this court's decisions)

Local Courts
Traffic, Police, Small Claims Courts Justice of the Peace (Often, cases decided in these courts cannot be appealed)

Upon appeal, the case is reviewed by a panel of three judges pouring over the written trial transcripts, searching for "reversible errors." If it is found that the district court erred in its application of law in the case, the Court of Appeals can order a new trial (remand) or reverse the judgment of the trial court. If the court finds no error, then the ruling of the district court is upheld.

Unlike the trial courts, appellate courts often "hand down" their rulings in written format. These cases then become a source for law, preserving the rulings as binding precedent upon future litigation. Previous rulings have a binding effect upon federal courts in the same district, with a persuasive, but not binding, effect upon state courts and federal courts outside of the district.

INTO THE HIGHEST COURT

If one of the parties is yet unsatisfied with the justice rendered, the case can be appealed to the US Supreme Court. However, unlike the appeal to the US Court of Appeals, being heard by the Supreme Court is not a right. An appeal to the US Supreme Court is automatic only if the case involves a conflict between the US Constitution and government statutes or agencies; otherwise, the party must petition the Supreme Court for a hearing, referred to as seeking a Writ of Certiorari. The US Supreme Court receives four to five thousand such requests a year, and usually grants, at their discretion, less than 150. Court time is limited, and thus, is guarded "judiciously."

The US Supreme Court is not in session year-round. Federal law sets its term as beginning on the first Monday in October and continuing until June or July, depending upon the caseload. The decision to hear a case must be reviewed by at least six of the nine sitting Supreme Court Justices, who then vote on the merits of pulling the case into the Court for deliberation. Four justices must vote yea for the case to appear on the annual docket of the Supreme Court. Once on the docket the case is scheduled for a hearing, often months in advance.

Once the justices decide to grant Certiorari, the case is slated for oral argument before the seated panel of justices. Normally, the Court's calendar is set to hear oral arguments on a rotating schedule — two weeks hearing the arguments, followed by two weeks of deliberation and opinion drafting. The cases themselves are often accompanied with a great depth of court records and briefs (a brief is a written legal argument that seeks to apply established rules of law to the facts of a particular case and so argue for the most lawful solution to the problem). The oral arguments are given from opposing sides of the issue, and are limited to one hour (30 minutes for the plaintiff's and defendant's attorney to each put forth the most important points of their case). Weeks before the day of oral argumentation, the justices acquaint themselves with the case, reading lower court rulings, briefs from the opposing counsels, and briefs submitted by parties outside the case. These "outsider" briefs are called amicus curiæ, or "friend of the court" briefs, and are written with the goal of advising the Supreme Court of the law and social ramifications of a pending case. Just as politics make strange bedfellows, so too are strange alliances often found on the pages of the amicus briefs.

When the day of oral argumentation arrives, the spotlight is on the lead counsels for the plaintiff and defendant. Rarely, however, are these attorneys allowed the opportunity to, in unbroken soliloquy, present their case. Usually the Supreme Court Justices vigorously question the attorneys, posing hypotheticals based upon the application of the law to the facts of the case, critically questioning the logic of the precedent law cited, and generally attempting to uncover the weaknesses of the arguments.

After the hour of oral argument has passed, the period of deliberation begins. The justices must, through their legal assistants (assisting attorneys are referred to as clerks), do the research needed to arrive at a judicial decision on the case at bar. During this process of reflection and research, the deliberations are ongoing between the Supreme Court justices. Rough drafts and written decisions are passed back and forth, as the law is reviewed, and often formed, in the chambers of the justices. Clerks research the finer points of law and a "majority position" is arrived at through consensus.

This decision is expected to be in keeping with previously decided law (the doctrine of stare decisis), but is not written in a cultural vacuum. The Supreme Court, especially in the past century, is expected to understand American culture and cultural needs, and rise to meet the occasion. (Pursuant to our previous discussion of judicial activism versus judicial restraint, this "rising to meet the occasion" is not likely to be agreed upon, particularly as to the reasons and goals, between the two schools of thought.)

After the initial discussions, the Chief Justice assigns a justice the task of writing the majority "opinion," that is, a carefully reasoned legal argument defending the collective and agreed upon decision reached by the majority of the justices. For this reason, the Court is designed to have an odd-number of sitting justices. An even number could, too often, result in a "split court" and no majority decision.

Highly controversial or debatable cases often result in a divided court. In fact, due to the diverse political and ideological rifts in the Court, the justices are sometimes extremely divergent in their views on the case under review. When this happens, a majority decision will almost always be accompanied by a minority decision, perhaps numerous minority decisions, referred to as dissenting opinions. If a justice sides with the majority, yet wants to set forth his or her own logic and case analysis, he or she will author a concurring (with the majority) opinion.

The majority opinion rendered by the US Supreme Court becomes binding case law in the nation, law to which all other courts (federal, state or local) must comply. The dissenting and concurring opinions are not authoritative, but are often a source of commentary on the legal reasoning and social impact of the majority position.

So as not to leave our highly speculative (and not very probable) hypothetical hanging, a few years after the elevator incident, "Groucho's" freedom of religion defense makes it to the US Supreme Court. "Groucho" does not, because he is serving out a sentence for conspiracy, aiding and abetting the delinquency of a minor, and smoking in a no-smoking area.

The Court is asked to weigh the issue of "private religious belief" against criminal conduct, in light of the very broadly worded and subjectively weighed state constitutional protections. The Court builds upon its previous rulings, holding that "while freedom to believe is absolute, freedom to act, pursuant to one's religion, cannot be." Furthermore, the Court rules that while the state's broad constitutional definition of religion was adequate for the functioning of a culturally monolithic culture of 200 years ago, we simply cannot allow such a "loose" definition of religion, given all of the socially deviant and even criminal practices that can be justified in the name of "faith," in the religiously diverse modern age. Therefore, a "culturally valid" test for determining if a religion is to be taken seriously by the courts is updated, and the very private religion of "Groucho" is weighed in the scales of justice and found to be wanting. The Court instructs the states to use this "balancing of social interests" test in determining if a religion is to be given social standing, prior to applying the protections of the various constitutions to the practice of the religion. (Dissenting and concurring opinions are generated.)

LEADING SUPREME COURT RULINGS

The all-pervasive power of the US Supreme Court has had a tremendous impact upon the shaping of our culture. The following are but a few of the myriad of cases in which the highest court has reached out and touched life in these United States.

Condoning Slavery and Prejudice

In *Dred Scott v. Sandford* (1857), the Supreme Court decided by a 7-2 vote to, in effect, continue slavery in most of the United States. Many consider this to be the most ill-considered decision of the US Supreme Court. Congress, the court declared, did not have the authority to encumber the holding of chattel property rights anywhere in the nation, without due process of law. Therefore, a slave owner would not lose ownership rights merely because his slave was in the northern states. The Court majority also held that blacks were not, and could not become, citizens of the United States, and therefore were not entitled to its privileges and immunities. After the Civil War, the US Congress gutted the Dred Scott decision by ratifying the 14th Amendment in 1868. This powerful constitutional amendment granted (or rather recognized) that state citizens are also citizens of the United States. Therefore, all natural born or naturalized citizens, regardless of race, are guaranteed protections as granted under the US Bill of Rights. These rights include equality under the law and due process of the law.

The Civil War may have brought an end to slavery, but it was not until 1954 that the tide began to turn on the institutionalized racism of the ante-bellum era. *Brown v. Board of Education of Topeka* (1954) stands out as a historical desegregation case. In a unanimous decision, the Supreme Court decided that separate but equal schools for black and white students were inherently unequal. State-sanctioned segregation in public schools, therefore, violated the equal protection guarantee of the 14th Amendment. The Court, in this case, specifically overruled the "separate but equal" doctrine that it had declared to be constitutional in *Plessy v. Ferguson* (1896).

The *Plessy* ruling, which made a great distinction between political equality and social equality, had for decades "blessed" the Jim Crow laws of the Southern states. (The Jim Crow laws were drafted to enforce the separation of blacks and whites, mandating such practices as separate drinking fountains, separate schools, segregated areas in public transportation, and the like). Much to his credit, Supreme Court Justice Harlan had dissented in *Plessy*, stating that "our Constitution is color-blind, and neither knows nor tolerates classes among citizens." The Brown ruling led to the end of state-sponsored segregation in all other public facilities.

Policing the Media

Public outcries of blasphemy against a movie entitled "The Miracle" moved the City of New York to attempt to end its public showing. The debate came to a head in the 1952 case of *Burstyn v. Wilson*. The Supreme Court held, in a unanimous ruling, that the First Amendment permitted no media censorship based upon religious preference or offense. This decision opened the floodgates. Past laws that had punished speech considered to be blasphemous, as expressions of treason, had already been deemed unconstitutional. The decision rendered in *Burstyn v. Wilson* further lifted the restraints of responsibility from the shoulders of the media. In a few short years, the standards "evolved" to a condition that shocked many communities.

With the battle over blasphemy lost, many citizens sought to protect their communities from an increasing outpouring of obscenity. One of these cases, *Miller v. California* (1973) ended up in the US Supreme Court. In a five to four split decision, Chief Justice Burger wrote the majority opinion. The Court ruled that states have the power, without violating the First Amendment, to regulate material that is obscene in its depiction or description of sexual conduct. Material is obscene if the average person, applying contemporary local community standards, would find that it appeals to the prurient interest, and if it depicts in a patently offensive way sexual conduct specifically defined by the applicable state law, and if the work, taken as a whole, lacks serious literary, artistic, political, or scientific value. This definition of obscenity replaced the previously embraced, and too vague to use, "utterly without redeeming social value" test.

Finding the Right to Privacy

The issue before the Court in *Griswold v. Connecticut* (1965), was whether a constitutionality protected privacy right exists in the marital relationship. In a very clear example of judicial activism, the High Court did not allow an absence of specific language in the Constitution to deter it from finding a privacy right in the Ninth Amendment. The Amendment in question reads, "The enumeration in the Constitution, of certain rights, shall not be construed to deny or disparage others, retained by the people." Quoting from the majority opinion, "specific guarantees, in the Bill of Rights, have penumbras, formed by emanations from those guarantees that help to give them life and substance...the right of privacy, which presses for recognition here, is a legitimate one. The present case, then, concerns a relationship lying within the zone of

Justices of the US Supreme Court pose for a group photograph.

Front Row:
Justice Antonin Scalia
Justice John P. Stevens
Chief Justice William H. Rehnquist
Justice Sandra Day O'Connor
Justice Anthony M. Kennedy

Back Row:
Justice Ruth Bader Ginsburg
Justice David H. Souter
Justice Clarence Thomas
Justice Stephen G. Breyer

privacy created by several constitutional guarantees...We deal with a right of privacy, older than the Bill of Rights." The Court found that Connecticut law interfered with personal privacy in the marriage relationship when it prohibited anyone, including married couples, from using contraceptives. Rather than allowing the state legislature of Connecticut to determine this issue, the Court struck down the law as being against the "spirit" of the Constitution. Esteemed law professors Paul Bartholomew and Joseph Menez comment, "The Constitution does not mention any right of privacy, but the Court concludes it is one of the penumbras of the Bill of Rights. It virtually became the cornerstone of the abortion decision in Roe vs. Wade." 7

In another case, however, the alleged right to privacy did not compel the Court to overrule community sensitivities. In Bowers v. Hardwick (1986), the plaintiff brought suit in federal court challenging the constitutionality of a Georgia sodomy statute criminalizing sexual acts between consenting adults. Bowers claimed that the statute placed him, as a practicing homosexual, in constant fear of arrest. The Court, by a narrow vote, found the Georgia statute constitutional. The slim majority refused to extend the "right of privacy" to cover consensual sodomy in the home. They found no fundamental right was involved, and ruled that the presumed belief by society that certain sex acts are immoral and unacceptable is a rational basis for the statute. This was a close case. "Consenting adults behind closed doors" has long been a rallying cry for those who wish to see all such laws against "unnatural acts" deemed unconstitutional.

Privacy Leads to Abortion on Demand

Consider Roe v. Wade (1973) as an extension of Griswold. Roe addressed the new found 'right to privacy' as it related to a woman's right to terminate her pregnancy. The plaintiff sought the right to have an abortion in Texas, a state with legislation forbidding abortion. The defendant, in this case the State of Texas, countered that the unborn child was a person within the meaning of the Fourteenth Amendment, and as such, was entitled to both a right to life and state protection.

The case moved from the Texas court system into the US Supreme Court.

At the Supreme Court level, the majority ruled that the state does have a legitimate interest in preserving the health of a pregnant woman, as well as in protecting "potential life." They acknowledged that the Constitution does not explicitly mention a right to abortion, but by building upon the right to privacy, previously discovered in Griswold, the Court discovered a "penumbra" broad enough to cover abortion.

In his attempt to balance the state's rights against the privacy interest of the mother, Justice Blackmun, writing for the court's majority, arbitrarily created a trimester analysis. Blackmun ruled that the state's interests increase as the pregnancy progresses. Specifically, the Justice mandated that, during the first trimester of pregnancy the decision to have an abortion should be left entirely to a woman and her physician. From the first day of the fourth month to the last day of the sixth month of the pregnancy, the state may regulate the abortion procedure in ways reasonably related to maternal health. On the first day of the seventh month, the unborn child enters into a court created rite of passage, a point called viability by Blackmun. On this day, the unborn child gains even more contingent rights as an individual, since it could survive outside of the mother. (The medical definition of viability has, now been pushed back to the fifth month, but Blackmun never recanted his views as a result.) The court granted that the state may, if it wishes, forbid all third trimester abortions except those necessary to protect the life of the mother. This liberalization of abortion law struck down existing state laws nationwide. Later Supreme Court decisions on the restricting abortions issue added mental health and even the economic well-being of the mother as factors to be weighed, allowing abortion, with few limitations, in the third trimester.

A slim majority on the court recently reaffirmed Roe in a Pennsylvania case called Planned Parenthood v. Casey (1992). Casey threw out the unscientific trimester test and replaced it with an "undue burden" standard, continuing to support abortion on demand, literally up to the moment of natural birth.

Regulating "Free Speech" at School

In *Tinker v. Des Moines Independent Community School District* (1969), the majority ruled that students have the right to engage in peaceful, non-disruptive protest. The Court recognized that the First Amendment guarantee of freedom of speech protects symbolic as well as oral and written speech. Seven justices determined that students wearing black armbands in protest of the Vietnam War was a protected activity, well within the First Amendment framework. Therefore, a public school ban on this form of protest (which did not disrupt the school's work or unreasonably offend the rights of others) violated students' rights. Justice Abe Fortas wrote, "It can hardly be argued that either students or teachers shed their constitutional rights to freedom of speech or expression at the schoolhouse gate." Students involved in prayer, the wearing of religious garments, or the propagation of political thought have often used the *Tinker* case to defend their freedom-of-expression rights.

However, the Court's guarantee of free speech liberties in the public schools has proven to be quite limited in scope. Using the "separation of church and state" argument, the court removed Bibles and prayer from the schools in the sixties, the Ten Commandments in 1980 and, most recently, moved to limit the practice of graduation prayer. The battle between judicial activists and judicial restraintists has become open and hostile in these cases. Dissenting in *Wallace v Jaffree* (1985), Chief Justice Rehnquist has warned that the Court is ignoring the "stare decisis" of history. He asserts that "history must judge whether it was the father of this country in 1789, or a majority of the Court today, which has strayed from the meaning of the Establishment Clause." Chief Justice Rehnquist reminded the Court that the "separation clause" is not found in the Constitution, and that the founding fathers prayed often and prayed fervently. After a brilliant review of national history and case law on the subject, Rehnquist concludes, "The 'wall of separation between church and state' is a metaphor based on bad history, a metaphor which has proved useless as a guide to judging. It should be frankly and explicitly abandoned."

By refusing to heed the Chief Justice's warnings or take notice of his lessons in history, the Court has wandered down a difficult to predict path in the interpretation of free expression, especially when it involves religion at school. In an 8-1 decision, the High Court granted Bible and Prayer clubs the same rights in the public school as any other service-type club. The majority in *Westside Community Schools v. Mergens* (1990) determined that, "If a state refused to let religious groups use facilities open to others, then it would demonstrate not neutrality, but hostility toward religion." According to the attorney, who argued Mergens before the Supreme Court, ACLJ lead counsel Jay Sekulow, "With the decision in *Mergens*, the Supreme Court has sent a clear message to the school systems of America. No longer will religious discrimination be tolerated under the guise of 'separation of church and state.'" [8]

Teachers and administrators have not fared as well however; the Supreme Court expelled officially supervised graduation from public high schools in *Lee v. Weisman* (1992). The majority voted to deny school officials the right to facilitate even completely non-denominational prayers, of these public ceremonies, due to their concerns over "separation of church and state." Spontaneous student-initiated prayers, however, is allowed; student-originated and student led religious speech is fully protected in school, at graduation, and in the classroom. However, "official" school prayers are illegal. Teachers and administrators are not allowed to be involved in the process of sponsoring graduation prayer. Justice Scalia authored a bitter dissent that reveals the great dichotomy between the activists and the restraintists on the court. After once again pointing out the very strong historical case for maintaining prayer at public functions, Scalia chastises the majority for their blatant rewriting of history and culture. He refers to judicial activism as "the bulldozer of social engineering" and states, "Today's opinion shows, more forcefully than volumes of argumentation, why our Nation's protection, that fortress which is our Constitution, cannot possibly rest upon the changeable philosophical predilections of the Justices of this Court, but must have deep foundations in the historic practices of our people."

IN CONCLUSION

These are but a few of the Supreme Court cases that demonstrate the ability of courts to shape our society. Given the great power of the courts to define the law and "re-define" the intent of the framers of our constitutions, one can easily understand how important judicial appointments, especially Supreme Court appointments, become.

Soviet dissident Aleksandr Solzhenitsyn once stood before the United States Congress and proclaimed: "Very soon, only too soon, your country will stand in need of not just exceptional men, but of great men. Find them in your souls. Find them in your hearts. Find them in the depth of your country." [9] Fine women and men are currently being trained in law by dedicated professors (a handful of whom are God-fearing and still holding to the natural law model in a few select law schools in our nation). These schools, professors, and students are national treasures. We must guard this heritage and fan the flames of its promise. By encouraging our children, grandchildren, spouses, and selves to become involved in the law, in legal education, in the courts, and in the political system, we can and will make a difference.

Where will the future local, state, and federal judges, representatives, governors, and presidents come from? The responsibility falls upon us to raise them up. The task will not come easy, but it must come if we are to preserve the heritage that this great nation was built upon. Just as our founding parents sacrificed to build the system of law and culture called America, so we must sacrifice to reclaim it. We must, together as the voting public, do all we can to ensure that men and women of integrity inhabit the White House and Congressional committees that make appointments to the benches of our nation. We must do all we can to identify and elect good persons to local, state, and then federal offices. Only with persons, of high moral and intellectual caliber in the elected government and the judiciary are the foundations of our Republic truly secure.

Thanks to ACLJ Research Analyst Reggie Ecarma for legal research on this project.

SIGNIFICANT SUPREME COURT CASES

Marbury vs. Madison (1803)	A section of the Judiciary Act of 1789 declared unconstitutional; set a precedent for the doctrine of judicial review.
Fletcher vs. Peck (1810)	Georgia violated the constitution in not honoring a contract; this was the first case where the Court declared a state law unconstitutional.
McCulloch vs. Maryland (1819)	The national government could establish a Bank of the United States; Maryland could not tax it; established the principal of national supremacy and the doctrine of implied powers.
Gibbons vs. Ogden (1824)	The state of New York could not grant exclusive navigation rights; the Court ruled that interstate commerce includes navigation (Congress regulates interstate commerce).
Dred Scott vs. Sanford (1857)	Black people were not citizens of the U.S.; Congress could not ban slavery in the territories; strengthened the abolitionist cause and made the civil war almost inevitable.
Plessy vs. Ferguson (1896)	A state could require racial segregation in public transportation if the facilities were equal; strengthened segregation for almost 60 years.
Schenck vs. United States (1919)	Freedom of speech can be restricted in wartime; established the "clear and present danger" formula; a nation has a right to protect itself.
Brown vs. Topeka Board of Education (1954)	Racial segregation in public schools is a violation of the equal protection clause of the Fourteenth Amendment; gave impetus to the civil rights movement.
Miranda vs. Arizona (1966)	Criminal suspects must be informed of their right to remain silent before any questioning begins.
In re Gault (1967)	Juveniles are entitled to due process of the law the same as adults; the state of Arizona denied due process to 15 year-old Gerald Gault.
United States vs. Nixon (1974)	The rule of law prevails over executive privilege; President Nixon must release his journal tapes for Watergate trials.
Regents of the University of Cal. vs. Allen Bakke (1978)	The Court ruled that Bakke should be admitted to medical school; the Court compromised on the use of affirmative action programs.
United States vs. Leon (1984)	Evidence seized by police under a warrant that was later found to be invalid could still be used in court if the officers acted in objective good faith, believing the warrant to be valid.

FOOTNOTES

1. Cataldo, Kempin, Stockton and Weber, Introduction to Law and the Legal Process, (Nwe York: John Wiley & Sons, 1980), 27
2. Minns, Michael L., The Underground Lawyer, (Katy, Tx., Gopher Publications, 1989, 219
3. Elizabeth Petty Bentley, The County Courthouse Book, (General Publishing, 1990)
4. Herbert Jacob, Justice in America, (Boston: Little Brown and Company, 1984), 238
5. Cataldo, Kempin, Stockton and Weber, Introduction to Law and the Legal Process, (Nwe York: John Wiley & Sons, 1980), 276
6. Herbert Jacob, Justice in America, (Boston: Little Brown and Company, 1984), 162
7. Paul C. Bartholomew and Joseph F. Menez, Summaries of Leading Cases on the Constitution, (Towata, N.J.: Rowman & Allanheld, 1983), 257
8. Jay Alan Sekulow, Knowing Your Rights, (Virginia Beach, Va.: CBN, 1993), 20
9. Aleksandr Solzhenitsyn, Warning to the West, (New York: Farrar, Straus and Giroux, 1976), 96

CHAPTER 8

HOW STATE GOVERNMENT WORKS

by   Hon. Cheryl Lau – NV Secretary of State
and Hon. Bill Diamond – ME Secretary of State
Chair & Vice-Chair of NASS Project Democracy

**Project
Democracy**
*National Association of
Secretaries of State*

GLOSSARY
for How State Government Works

Blue Laws
1. A law designed to regulate Sunday activities, such as shopping in retail stores.
2. One of a body of laws in colonial New England designed to enforce certain moral standards.

Bureaucracy
1. Administration of a government chiefly through bureaus or departments staffed with nonelected officials.
2. The departments and their officials as a group.
3. Management or administration marked by diffusion of authority among numerous offices and adherence to inflexible rules of operation.
4. An administrative system in which the need or inclination to follow complex procedures impedes effective action: innovative ideas that get bogged down in red tape and bureaucracy.

Complaisence
1. The inclination to comply willingly with the wishes of others.

Deficit
1. The amount by which a sum of money falls short of the required or expected amount; a shortage: large budget deficits

Executive
1. A person or group having administrative or managerial authority in an organization.
2. The chief officer of a government, state, or political division.
3. The branch of government charged with putting into effect a country's laws and the administering of its functions.

Felony
1. One of several grave crimes, such as murder, rape, or burglary, punishable by a more stringent sentence than that given for a misdemeanor.

Fortune 500
1. The five hundred most successful corporations in a given year, as determined by Fortune magazine (founded in 1936 by Henry Luce as a business monthly).

Gubernatorial
1. Of or relating to a governor.

Initiative
1. The power or right to introduce a new legislative measure.
2. The right and procedure by which citizens can propose a law by petition and ensure its submission to the electorate.

Jeffersonian
1. Of, relating to, or characteristic of Thomas Jefferson or his political attitudes and theories about limiting the role of federal government.

Judicial
1. Of, relating to, or proper to courts of law or to the administration of justice: the judicial system.
2. Decreed by or proceeding from a court of justice.
3. Belonging or appropriate to the office of a judge

Jurisdiction
1. The territorial range of authority or control.
2. Law. The right and power to interpret and apply the law: courts having jurisdiction in this district.
3. a. Authority or control: islands under U.S. jurisdiction; a bureau with jurisdiction over Native American affairs. b. The extent of authority or control: a family matter beyond the school's jurisdiction.

Legislative/Legislation
1. The act or process of legislating; lawmaking.
2. A proposed or enacted law or group of laws.

Lobbying/Lobbyist
1. To try to, or one who tries to, influence the thinking of legislators or other public officials

Old Boy's Network
1. An informal, exclusive system of mutual assistance and friendship through which men belonging to a particular group, such as the alumni of a school, exchange favors and connections, as in politics or business.

Policy
1. A plan or course of action, as of a government, political party, or business, intended to influence and determine decisions, actions, and other matters.

Precinct
1. a. A subdivision or district of a city or town under the jurisdiction of or patrolled by a specific unit of its police force.
2. An election district of a city or town.

Ratify/Ratification
1. To approve and give formal sanction to; confirm.
2. The act of ratifying or the condition of being ratified.

Referendum
1. The submission of a proposed public measure or actual statute to a direct popular vote.
2. Such a vote.

Sovereign
1. Self-governing; independent: a sovereign state.

Special Interests
1. A person, a group, or an organization attempting to influence legislators in favor of one particular interest or issue.

Tocqueville, Alexis Charles Henri Clérel de
1. French politician, traveler, and historian (1805-1859). After touring the United States (1831-1832), he wrote Democracy in America (1835), a widely influential study of American institutions.

Unicameral
1. Having or consisting of a single legislative chamber.

Ward
1. A division of a city or town, especially an electoral district, for administrative and representative purposes.

HOW STATE GOVERNMENT WORKS

Hon. Cheryl Lau - NV Secretary of State
Hon. Bill Diamond - ME Secretary of State
Chair & Vice-Chair of NASS Project Democracy

"You can't run a government solely on a business basis...Government should be human. It should have a heart."
— *Herbert Henry Lehman*

"Why do I like living here? Well, 'cause there's not every stinking law telling me what I can and can't do, that's why. And there's no stupid income tax." — "Sure sounds good to me," the Las Vegas cabby's fare responded. The visitor had just been lambasting the state of Connecticut for a $300 speeding ticket he had received there during a business trip. Not that he planned to pay a cent of it. The citation was for a "mere" 65 miles per hour, the legal speed on Nevada's expansive desert highways, where most people drove even faster, with few citations. "I won't be back in Connecticut anytime soon, if ever," the visitor chuckled. "So what are they going to do?" — "Nothing. Stick it to them!" the cabby barked approvingly, his white beard and hair standing out against his tanned, rugged face.

That the two men were describing one of the most unique things about these United States of America, never entered their minds. Like separate nations, some states are tax havens, others have high taxation. Commit anything but a felony in one state, and it's possible to evade prosecution by "hiding" in another. It was just one of the many truly astonishing accomplishments of the Founding Fathers: that the Constitution greatly expanded the powers of the new central government, yet did not seriously threaten the independence of the states. Critics of centralization, at that time and ever since, have predicted the imminent disappearance of the states as sovereign bodies. But despite a definite trend toward centralization (not to mention all the fast-food chains, department stores, and interstate highways that have likened our nation's culture), the states remain powerful political organizations and absolutely sovereign in many areas of government. These issues (which were so pivotal in the passage of the US Constitution) regarding the sovereignty of the individual states and the rights of the individual, have seemed to remain secure through the years, as the discussion in the cab clearly showed.

Today, Presidential action is a daily staple of media news coverage. Yet, for the average citizens, the most important news is usually happening in their own states. And it is on that level that they can, and do, get most involved. As Alexis de Tocqueville noted, in his famous journal on America in the 1830s, "No sooner do you set foot upon American ground than you are stunned by a kind of tumult; a confused clamor is heard on every side, and a thousand simultaneous voices demand the satisfaction of their social wants. Everything is in motion around you." — "The people," de Tocqueville added, "reign in the American political world as the Deity does in the universe." Yet, for all this grass-roots activity, when it comes to the ballot box, the majority of the electorate, by far, shows its greatest interest during federal, and particularly Presidential, elections. That is curious, considering that while members of the US House of Representatives and the Senate maintain state and local offices, they are normally in Washington. Also, although these national politicians are committed to serving the best interests of the districts and states they represent, they tend to be more nationalistic in their agendas, which compels them to look at the "big picture" when debating matters of national interest. By contrast, all state legislators must continually wrestle with the needs of their districts, as opposed to the general welfare of the state.

In contrast to these federal lawmakers, the average citizen has far greater control over state, and particularly local, government, because those public officials are more accessibile. Indeed, in smaller communities, some members of local and even state government can be reached simply by picking up the phone. Thus, it is often easy for concerned citizens to not only make their voices heard, but to shape and mold the communities in which they live. And those communities fall under the direct jurisdiction of their respective states. When viewed from a broad perspective, states provide citizens with order and organization, as well as guidance and protection. In as much as the federal Constitution allows, there are state laws on issues like the death penalty, health care, the sale of alcohol, or the curriculum in public schools. To enhance their administrative effectiveness, states exercise their greatest power, creating supplementary local governments. All states are empowered to create individual self-sufficient governing bodies, such as cities, towns, and counties. Federal and state government are actually two sides of the same coin, neither can exist without the other. Local government, on the other hand, exists entirely at the will of the state. Local government is an instrument, used by the states, to effectively meet the needs of their citizens.

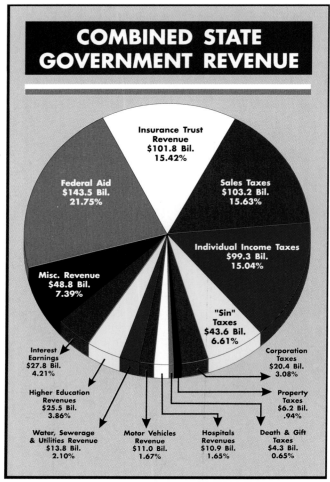

COMBINED STATE GOVERNMENT REVENUE

Insurance Trust Revenue $101.8 Bil. 15.42%

Federal Aid $143.5 Bil. 21.75%

Sales Taxes $103.2 Bil. 15.63%

Individual Income Taxes $99.3 Bil. 15.04%

Misc. Revenue $48.8 Bil. 7.39%

"Sin" Taxes $43.6 Bil. 6.61%

Interest Earnings $27.8 Bil. 4.21%

Corporation Taxes $20.4 Bil. 3.08%

Higher Education Revenues $25.5 Bil. 3.86%

Property Taxes $6.2 Bil. .94%

Water, Sewerage & Utilities Revenue $13.8 Bil. 2.10%

Motor Vehicles Revenue $11.0 Bil. 1.67%

Hospitals Revenues $10.9 Bil. 1.65%

Death & Gift Taxes $4.3 Bil. 0.65%

anti-discrimination actions of some type. The federal agency handling that area is likely to threaten the state with a cutoff of all such funding. In most areas, most notably highways, such a cutoff would be devastating. In recent years, given the federal budget problems, Congress and the agencies have been known increasingly to require the states to undertake projects, without providing them with any federal assistance. These mandates have often been blamed for forcing state and local tax levies higher. If the state government refuses to comply with the federal requirement, funds can again be cut off, and state officials could even go to prison. So the federal-state partnership can often be an uneasy one. Even so, the overall revenue-generating process places 28 states financially equal to or greater than the nation's top 100 companies in the "Fortune 500" listing. In fact, 17 states rank with the top 50 of these businesses.

Here's how the funding system works: The federal government normally contributes funding for specific projects, such as highway construction or low income housing. All states set aside special funds, which are collected from various insurance and retirement programs. State insurance revenue is collected from payments made to various funds such as unemployment insurance and workman's compensation. Insurance funds do not go into the general fund. Rather, they are placed in special accounts and used to support the programs for which they were collected. State governments also raise revenue by conducting business activities. In general, states collect user fees from a variety of sources such as toll roads, public parks, and tuition at state colleges and universities. Roughly one half of the 50 states receive revenue from state-run lotteries. In recent years, this has become a popular source of income. To have a lottery or not, to have an income tax or not, is a political decision that, theoretically in a democracy, should be based on the people's wishes. Following, in detail, are the structures of that political machinery, beginning with the state political parties.

Even as President Clinton has dismantled much of the Reagan legacy, the former administration's efforts to lessen the role of the federal government, along with the huge budget deficits that have preoccupied federal lawmakers, have left an expanded role for states to supply political and policy leadership for the country. It is in the states, that health-care efforts were first begun, where the concept of turning welfare into "workfare" (where able-bodied recipients must work for their assistance) was launched. Some political scholars now argue that state governments have become the most responsive, innovative, and effective level of government in the American political system. Others argue that the increased role of the states has brought problems ranging from corporate bribes of state politicians to bureaucratic waste. In this chapter we shall dissect the system of state government, so you can decide for yourself.

THE FEDERAL PARTNERSHIP

Since the 1960's, each state has received some form of federal revenue. Since Lyndon Johnson's block grants programs of the 1960's, Richard Nixon's state and local revenue sharing of the 1970's and extending to Ronald Reagan's new federalism, each state has received some form of federal revenue. The collective result has been an ever-increasing federal-state partnership. The aid, however, is not without strings attached. Say, for example, that a state or locality fails to construct a sewage treatment or water facility or take

THE PARTIES

It is difficult to overstate the pervasiveness of political parties in state politics. All of the 50 state governors are either Democrats or Republicans. The other statewide elected officials are unanimously adherent to one of the two major parties. All of the 7,461 state legislators are Democrats or Republicans, except for the members of Nebraska's unicameral legislature and a handful of independents. This situation is rather interesting when one considers that the largest group of Americans is neither Democrat nor Republican. According to the National Elections Center at the University of Michigan, 37 percent of Americans label themselves as independents, while only 36 percent are Democrats and 29 percent are Republicans. However, state and local rules drawn up by the two major parties, effectively keep most independents off the ballots. In fact, many state parties have tremendous control over who the citizens will eventually get to vote for in their own party. In Connecticut, for example, a citizen cannot even become a candidate for statewide or federal office in his or her own party without the approval of a percentage of delegates at the party convention.

State parties are organized in a remarkably similar fashion, with leaders and committees. It is an effective, time-honored system that helps get the electorate's feelings to the candidates, who then campaign accordingly. On the other hand, the strong party discipline in this system can weaken the power of elected officials, as they are often forced to go against the wishes of their constituents. Structurally, each party has a governing committee, presided over by the state party chairperson. This Democratic or Republican State Central Committee is made up of party activists who oversee party efforts at the same level. The state party chairs, elected by the state committees in three-fourths of the states and by the state party conventions in the rest, provide leadership and management for their state organizations. These state chairs may be the state's principal political leaders, or they may be agents of, and perhaps even hand-picked by, the governor.

The smallest political unit in the state is the precinct. It is there that the grass-roots party leaders (the precinct committee members) reside. Between this precinct leadership and the main party committee there is a range of party committees typically established in congressional districts, state legislative districts, towns, cities, and wards.

THE LEGISLATIVE BRANCH

State government mirrors the federal system in many ways. Originally the states developed and organized America's federal system, ultimately providing federal and state constitutions with several common governmental components. The establishment of legislative, judicial, and executive branches of government (known as the separation of powers, or the system of checks and balances) is indeed a key element of both state and federal governments. Federal and state constitutions also reflect the shared political philosophies of popular sovereignty, the belief that it is the people who ultimately hold the highest political power, limiting the power of government, and the belief that public officials can only exercise powers which have been expressly granted to them by law. The original thirteen states wrote these concepts into their own state constitutions and further insisted they be written into the Federal Constitution. In addition, the states demanded that the Federal Constitution include a Bill of Rights, to protect both individuals and states from the central government assuming too much power. Today, the Bill of Rights guarantees that powers not delegated to the United States by the Constitution, nor prohibited by it to the states, are reserved to the states respectively, or to the people. Although America is a sovereign nation, each of the fifty states conduct their governments under the shared umbrella of the federal system. While the US Constitution is rarely amended, it is the status of a state constitution that is fluid and ever changing.

The process of changing a state constitution to repeal outdated and puritanical "blue laws" is both difficult and cumbersome. Nevertheless, state constitutions are constantly altered, in response to popular support as well as modifications in socio-economic conditions. Amending a state constitution is a process involving two distinct steps: proposal and ratification. In most states, it is the members of the House and Senate who propose constitutional change.

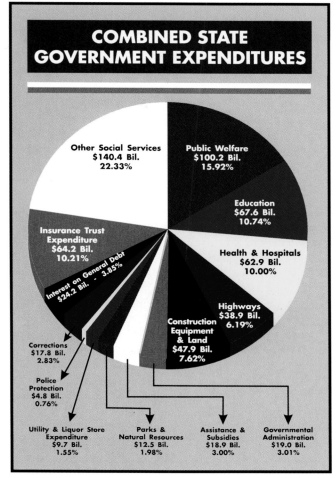

COMBINED STATE GOVERNMENT EXPENDITURES

Other Social Services $140.4 Bil. 22.33%
Public Welfare $100.2 Bil. 15.92%
Education $67.6 Bil. 10.74%
Health & Hospitals $62.9 Bil. 10.00%
Insurance Trust Expenditure $64.2 Bil. 10.21%
Interest on General Debt $24.2 Bil. - 3.85%
Highways $38.9 Bil. 6.19%
Construction Equipment & Land $47.9 Bil. 7.62%
Corrections $17.8 Bil. 2.83%
Police Protection $4.8 Bil. 0.76%
Utility & Liquor Store Expenditure $9.7 Bil. 1.55%
Parks & Natural Resources $12.5 Bil. 1.98%
Assistance & Subsidies $18.9 Bil. 3.00%
Governmental Administration $19.0 Bil. 3.01%

However, in twenty four states, citizens can bypass the legislature by instituting a constitutional initiative. It is no accident that the voters' growing resentment and distrust of government has led to an extraordinary increase in the filing of initiative and referendum petitions. Through the petitions process, a group of citizens can, in fact, modify state laws or the constitution itself by collecting the number of signatures required to place such a modification or "question" on the ballot for final approval from the electorate. Moreover, the petitions process often provides public officials with valuable insight into the mood of the electorate as it pertains to particular issues. Another method by which a state constitution can be modified is to initiate a constitutional convention. Upon the need to amend or effect a re-write, such a constitutional convention can be called by the legislature, or the voters themselves. Once change has been proposed, it must be ratified. It is interesting to note that in every state, except Delaware, it is necessary for a majority of the voters to accept the proposed change, making it the direct responsibility of the people to accept or reject the laws under which they shall live.

All states share certain prerogatives or rights. States are entirely responsible for creating local governments, directing and supervising elections, establishing educational systems, and providing police protection for their citizenry. From requiring pre-school measles shots to enforcing speed limits, states are permitted to take measures that ensure the safety and health of the population. States also regulate banking, corporations, and even marriage and divorce. Be it laws regarding public smoking or laws that affect life itself, such as health care and the death penalty, state government has a tremendous impact on the lives of all its citizens.

In all states, the legislatures are "bicameral" (have two houses), except for Nebraska, which only has one. The upper house is the Senate and the lower house is usually called the House of Representatives or Assembly. In general, the districts for both houses are divided or apportioned into districts by population. State legislatures are responsible for apportionments or ensuring that all voting districts, both state and federal, are divided fairly, according to population. Nevada, like several states, has biennial (occurring every other year) legislative sessions that convene in mid-to-late January of every odd numbered year. The primary function of the legislative body, is to introduce, debate, and pass or reject bills which become law upon approval. Of course the passage of such legislation is quite involved, in the sense that legislators must weigh the issues, as well as public opinion. State senators and representatives are empowered to enact law they possess legislative powers as well as limited executive powers. This executive power usually takes the form of approving appointments to state agencies, the governor's cabinet, and, in some cases, judgeships. It is interesting to note that state legislators also have limited judicial powers, with impeachment being the most common judicial power granted to the state legislature. With the exception of Oregon, legislative bodies in all states, are empowered to remove the governor, as well as other state leaders, from office. In most cases, the lower house decides by vote whether or not to accuse a state official of criminal activity. The senate then presides over hearings and determines the guilt or innocence of the accused state official. If found guilty, the official may be impeached.

Each legislative session includes the debate or consideration of a large number of bills. They cover many diverse topics, from designating a state flower to crime and enforcement. Nonetheless, issues concerning the state's tax base and the manner in which public funds are managed and allocated tend to dominate most legislative sessions, due to the fact that state legislatures are empowered to impose taxes. In addition, in all fifty states, budgets are submitted, by the governor to the legislature for approval. Because state senators and representatives must act on a tremendous volume of bills each session, the legislative bodies in all states employ legislative committees to help process the work load. Legislative committees are small groups of ten or twelve members, with the average legislator serving on two or more committees at one time. Since legislative committees are open to the public, voters are able to directly monitor the competence and effectiveness of their legislators, and may publicly speak, either in favor of or against a piece of impending legislation. The vast majority of legislative measures that are debated before the legislature go through the committee process. Many bills never make it out of the committees. For example, a proposed bill that violates the state or Federal Constitution, would be terminated at the committee level. Bills move through the committee system and into the house or senate

for further action. Although the various states have procedural differences, the process used to propose and adopt bills into law is fundamentally the same in all states.

THE EXECUTIVE BRANCH

The executive branch of government is composed of several elected and appointed officers, led by the state's chief executive, the governor. Together, the governor and executive staff are responsible for carrying out the laws and mandates of the state legislature, in addition to acting as a state's chief administrators. Subsequently, governors are policy leaders. They identify problems and propose programs or legislation to enact change, while using political and party loyalties to sway legislation. The governors are frequently a state's official spokesperson and ceremonial leader. Like the President, the governor of a state is also considered leader of the political party that he or she represents.

The executive branch has expanded powers, simply because it is their duty to enact and enforce all laws passed by the legislature. In all but five states, it is also the responsibility of the governor to submit a state budget to the legislature. Control over the state budget gives a governor tremendous political and legislative authority. In fact, such a budget can influence the direction of every issue or project that desires state funding. Governors, also like the President, are the commanders in chief of the state's military, or National Guard. The executive branch also has limited legislative powers. In addition to the state budget, governors in all states, except North Carolina, are empowered to veto bills passed by the state legislature. In all but seven states, governors are provided with a line item veto. In other words, they may reject either a provision, section, or line, of a bill. Although governors are allowed line item vetoes in forty-three states, several states limit the use of this veto exclusively to bills that involve the appropriation of funds. As a state's chief executive officer, the governor directs the activities of the cabinet, as well as administrative boards and departments. Interestingly enough, in forty-seven states, some members of the governor's cabinet are elected by popular vote. The remaining members are usually appointed by the governor and, occasionally, the state legislature.

The executive branch also has the responsibility of collecting the state's taxes. Taxes account for roughly one half of most state revenue. In most cases, tax dollars go directly into the general fund and eventually are used to pay operating expenses. There are several types of taxes, and all states have a variety of tax programs. A general sales tax is collected in forty-five states. Because sales taxes are popular, easy to collect, and ensure a steady source of revenue, they are the largest single source of revenue in thirty states. Many states also receive revenues from an assessment known as an excise tax. The excise tax is a tax placed on the sale of specific or limited items, such as tobacco or alcohol or gasoline. Moreover, some states collect an income tax based on what an individual or corporation earns. Many states also have other common taxes that often take the form of fees for permits and licenses.

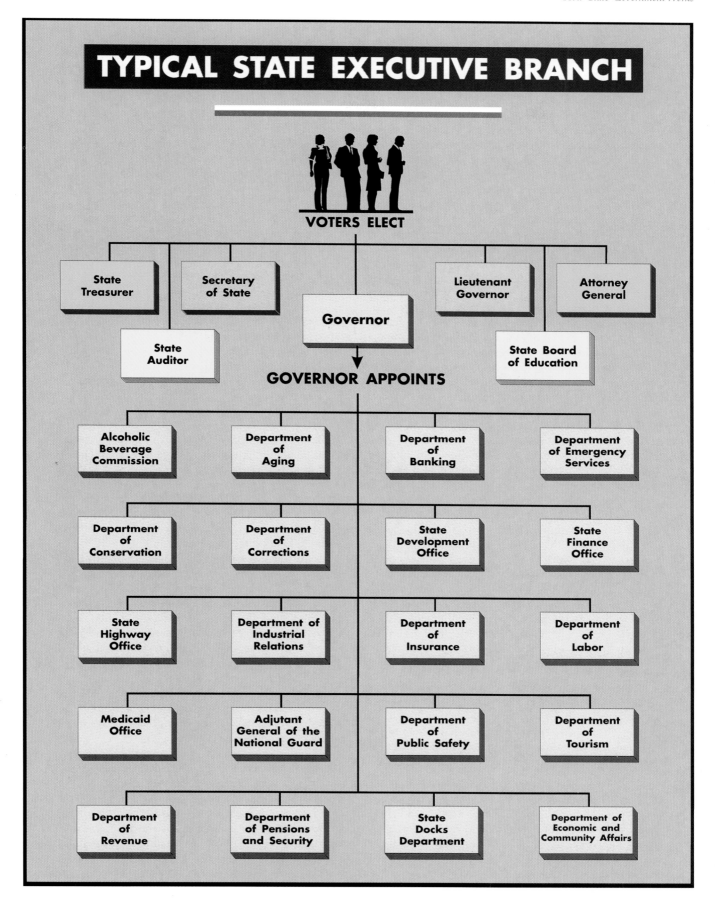

TYPICAL STATE EXECUTIVE BRANCH

VOTERS ELECT

- State Treasurer
- Secretary of State
- **Governor**
- Lieutenant Governor
- Attorney General

- State Auditor
- State Board of Education

GOVERNOR APPOINTS

- Alcoholic Beverage Commission
- Department of Aging
- Department of Banking
- Department of Emergency Services

- Department of Conservation
- Department of Corrections
- State Development Office
- State Finance Office

- State Highway Office
- Department of Industrial Relations
- Department of Insurance
- Department of Labor

- Medicaid Office
- Adjutant General of the National Guard
- Department of Public Safety
- Department of Tourism

- Department of Revenue
- Department of Pensions and Security
- State Docks Department
- Department of Economic and Community Affairs

CENTRALIZATION OF POWER

In 1936, a Gallup poll found that 56 percent of those polled favored federal over state government. Following the Democrats' "New Deal," after the Great Depression, the federal government became the center of the universe for Americans, administering everything from social security to welfare. However, as federal programs grew increasingly ponderous, public satisfaction waned. When Gallup asked the "government preference" question again in 1981, 64 percent preferred the states. The respondents got what they desired, then, with the "New Federalism" ushered in by the Reagan era, which transferred financial and programmatic responsibilities from the national capital to the state capitals. Washington's increasing fiscal belt-tightening has caused the states to shoulder more of the domestic policy burden, while the federal government copes with the national debt and defense.

As the states' responsibilities increase, so do the power and importance of their governors, legislatures, bureaucracies, and courts. Interest groups, lobbies, political action committees, legislative staff, and the media, as well, have become more prominent players in the states. "In an age when the federal government is retrenching, both the national government and the localities are looking to the states, as never before, for leadership," observed government scholar Larry J. Sabato, several years ago. "State governments are facing unprecedented challenges, and we need to be more attentive than ever to their agendas." After reviewing the situation in the states, Richard Nathan of Princeton University and Martha Dethick of the University of Virginia reported, "State governments are on a roll ... they are reforming education and health systems, trying to convert welfare to workfare and building new roads and bridges and other public works."

Dynamic happenings in the states are often happening from two very different directions: the old-fashioned political machine, and the growing concept of citizen-introduced initiative, which bypasses the state legislature and even the veto of the governor. As with the US Congress, but sometimes even more so, state legislative leaderships wield tremendous power. For example, in Massachusetts, the Senate president, William ("Billy") Bulger, is considered more powerful than the governor, due to his tight control of the state senate democratic majority. State Senate presidents and Assembly speakers attain this kind of power through three mechanisms:

1) Instead of the entire legislative body voting for who will sit on the specific committees, as is done in the federal Congress, the committee chairs and the committee members of state legislatures are *appointed* by the legislative leaders, such as a Senate's president. The state's committee appointees are then, as a result, indebted to the person who put them there, thus creating an "old boys network."

2) These same legislative leaders, of course, also appoint members of the senate and assembly party campaign committees. Through favors owed, as mentioned in #1, the legislative leader can influence who gets what amount of campaign financing from the campaign committee. Since most candidates receive 60 percent to 80 percent of their campaign finance from this source, the legislative leader is in a position to amass yet more favors from the elected members of the legislature.

3) The legislative leaders themselves, and members of their "old boy network," also have control of party "soft money" (unrestricted campaign donations made to a political party that are often appropriated to benefit "selected" party candidates) through the various party organizations on the county level. In NY, for instance, Clarence Norman is a Brooklyn assemblyman and the King's county democratic chair and Denny Farell is a Manhattan assemblyman and the NY County Democratic chair. This network can provide a helping hand in those tight election races to those who know "how to play ball."

With so many favors owed, state legislative leaders have a great deal of influence over what legislation is introduced on the floor for debate in the first place, since all legislation must first be released by the committees, who owe the leader favors (see #1 above). If a piece of legislation is released by a "renegade" committee, the legislative leader can still influence how the bill is voted on by the many members of the legislature who owe the leader favors (see #2 and #3 above). This is how the legislative leadership's power is amassed. Some argue that this type of centralization of power in the legislature is a good thing because it's more professional and creates an organized system that can effectively stand up to a powerful governor, providing for a sort of "checks and balances" system. Others argue that this is how the legislative process is often corrupted, to the point where freshman "citizen" representatives, or even the governor, are rendered virtually powerless against this type of entrenched political machine.

STATE INITIATIVES

On the opposite end of the spectrum is the initiative process, where any citizen can bring an issue to a public vote, provided he or she has the "initiative" to prove that there is some "initial" public support for the cause. This is done by obtaining the minimum number of signatures on a formal petition to meet the requirements of the state's initiative process. Twenty three states have the initiative process, the use of which has grown dramatically in the 1970's and has held steady in the 1980's. The exception is California, where ballots became more crowded with each election. The initiative "opens up the political process, as well as the rest of society, to new ideas and approaches," claims David Schmidt, director of the Initiative Resource Center in Berkeley, California.

Activist author Martin Gross, whose most recent book vilifies the entrenched two-party system, likens initiatives to the nation's political salvation, saying they must be implemented in the other 26 states that don't currently allow the process. "All voters have to do is sign a petition that they want a specific law, say to hold all state and local taxes down to one percent of the state's GDP (gross domestic product), and it is automatically placed on the next ballot," explains Gross. "If the voters win, no one, neither the legislature nor the governor, can tamper with it. It is the will of the people and the law, until the people decide to change their mind with another initiative." However, US voting-trends expert Curtis Gans argues that the initiative "bypasses or discharges the legislature from, what should be, its responsibilities under a representative government."

Gans concedes that professional lawmakers can write poor laws, but says "with a reasonable hearing and legal review...with legislatures, you're likely to come out with more carefully considered laws that deal with the complexities and nuances of public policy. And there's someone to hold accountable....But, an initiative often places a complex issue into a few paragraphs that voters are expected to decide on." Gans cites what he calls, "the descent of the California public school system, from one of the best in the nation to one in the lowest quarter of the nation," as an example of the damage citizens can cause through initiative. Yet, many states without the initiative process are no better off. So Gans proposes this: "No initiative ought to pass without a 60 percent popular vote, and no popular referendum should pass without a 55 percent vote." Through the referendum, which is usually found only on the local level, voters endorse or reject the legislation that is passed by their representatives. Referendums are common in Europe, where nations such as France and Denmark have voted on whether to remain in the European economic union. Gross sees a day when citizens would have the right to approve entire state and federal government budgets. "Then," says Gross, "citizens would have only themselves to blame, if the tax burden was too high."

LOBBYIST ASSOCIATIONS

As a young State House reporter, Harvey Fisher of the *New Jersey Reporter*, would watch in fascination as lobbyists would "just sit" outside the offices of the "big shots in the legislature," or "park themselves near the offices of the governor's most powerful advisers." It was "curious," he would think, that nobody ever told them to leave, "even though the general public gets shooed away." After sixteen years in the job, Fisher admitted in 1989 that he had never successfully defined exactly what a lobbyist is. Which is why, he assumed, that lobbyists are so successful. His best stab at explaining what they do: "Kill, maim, promote, create, or sometimes just tinker a little to satisfy their clients."

These days, lobbyists are usually mentioned scornfully on the federal level. In fact, however, at least since the mid-1970's, there has been a widespread conviction that lobbyists have a freer reign in state legislatures than they do in Congress. Thus, bribery of state legislators by lobbyists is considered prevalent. Kickbacks from highway contractors, or other firms doing business with the state, are exposed often enough to strengthen these claims. One of the most notorious examples was when Vice President Spiro Agnew was forced to resign because of kickback payoffs that came to him when he was governor of Maryland.

While high profile resignations for governors and other state leaders are rare, reports of influence-buying surface constantly. In Massachusetts in 1994, the Republican Party was slapped with the largest fine for a campaign-finance violation ever levied against a state political party - $50,000 - after GOP officials agreed they broke the law by promising business officials access to Republican Gov. William Weld, in exchange for donations. In closing an investigation that embarrassed both the governor, who had become something of a national figure, and his party, the state

A Typical State House of Representatives

Attorney General required the Republicans to pay another $6,446 for illegally collecting corporate donations as part of the same scheme.

Even in the midst of such incidents, however, state lobbying has become such a viable and successful practice for well-heeled corporations that now there exists "Lobbyist Associations" from which a special-interest group can access the right lobbyist for the right job. Each member of the Lobbyist Association gets friendly with a specific legislator, gaining access and influence. When a "Client" (usually a special interest group) wants to push or defeat specific legislation, the Lobbyist Association can employ their "guns for hire" to influence the legislators with whom they have become "friends." Through this process, individual lobbyists don't represent any specific interest, but any interest that they are hired to represent at a given time. The top lobby firms who head the Lobbyist Association will organize these "prostitutes" for a given client, offering "one-stop shopping" for those who would like to buy legislative influence. As New Jersey's Harvey Fisher put it, mockingly, "Lobbyists are generous, especially in taking people to lunch or the Caribbean. They are extremely fair-minded, and willing to teach things to legislators and other public officials. They readily explain three, even four, reasons why a policy they oppose might be a good thing. Then they offer 300 reasons why it is not."

The lobbyist "association" phenomenon is more prevalent on the state level, because state campaigns are much less expensive to "buy." As state legislatures trend away from "citizen candidates" and more toward "professional politicians," this type of practice is becoming more prevalent. These "friendly lobbyists" (usually outnumbering legislators by 2 or 3 times) are often involved in fundraising for the politicians' campaigns, as well as helping to form "strategic planning" or "platforms" for governors' and legislative campaigns. Through this process, allegiances between lobbyists and their "legislative friends" are also much more pronounced. The bottom line is that there are many more lobbyists today than there have ever been before, which is a telling indication that they are effective in influencing legislation. This is a reasonable assumption, since business people will seldom expand a program, unless they are getting results.

FAVORED CONTRACTS

As was evident from the recent Massachusetts incident, the executive branch of state government is often in a position to grant state contracts to corporations that have been "helpful" in financing a gubernatorial campaign. While some states, such as New York, have strict contract regulations that would make this practice impossible, other states do not. For example, federal EPA regulations and provisions of the federal Clean Air Act require the states to set up centralized environmental-emissions testing sites for automobile inspections. The state of Connecticut sought bids for the construction and management of these testing sites from independent contractors. The Connecticut Motor Vehicle Department recommended that the firm ESP Inc. win the approx. $150 million contract because it is a native corporation with the lowest bid. But, Governor Weiker granted the contract to Envirotest, Inc., an out-of-state corporation with a higher bid. Investigation by the *Hartford Courant* found that the governor's chief of staff was on the incorporation papers for the lobby firm (John Doyle Corp.) that represents Envirotest. Furthermore, when the director of the Connecticut Motor Vehicle Department protested the governor's choice, he was fired. Envirotest took out full-page ads that slammed ESP, Inc., and supported the governor's decision. Investigations were launched by the state attorney general, the legislature, and the governor's own office.

CITIZEN INVOLVEMENT
MAKES THE DIFFERENCE

As the state of Maine grew in population and industrial strength, it experienced many of the political problems found in larger states such as New York, Illinois or California. Professional politicians, powerful lobbyists, and a complacent public made an entrenched political machine a distinct possibility for the state of Maine. By 1991, the Assembly speaker, John Martin, had held his position for 20 years, and the senate president, Charley Prey, had held his position for nearly as many. It was not until a deadlock over a workman's compensation reform bill, which caused the governor to reject the state budget, that the public realized how entrenched the political machine had become. As a result of the deadlock between the governor and the powerful legislative leaders, the state had no budget and therefore had to shut down all state agencies and services (except "essential services"). Since the governor campaigned for reelection in '90 on a "no recession or budget problems" platform, and now the state government was shut down because of a political power struggle, the state's electorate became enraged. The public's rage was seen in the '92 elections, where Martin was forced to step down and Prey was defeated.

Today, most of the members of the "part-time" state legislature are working citizens, devoting their time to the Jeffersonian ideal of citizen government, with only 8 percent of the legislature made-up of lawyers or wealthy people. The new Senate president is a school teacher and the new Speaker of the House is a hotel manager.

Two-thirds of the lobbyists in Maine are also working people who represent the particular profession they work in, with only one-third representing professional lobbyist groups or law firms. While many state legislatures will pass ethics rules for the executive branch and exempt themselves from such regulations, Maine's "citizen legislature" has no problem passing strict reporting regulations that compel *both* branches of government to disclose to the public how much time lobbyists spend working on a certain issue, and all gifts over $25 that are accepted. The new legislature also passed term limits on legislative leadership, policy reforms regarding committee makeup, and passed a balanced budget from a recession-strained revenue base. It may have taken a government shutdown to usher in these reforms, but, in Maine, citizen involvement makes the difference.

CHAPTER 9

HOW
LOCAL GOVERNMENT
WORKS

by Mr. John Parr
President – National Civic League

NATIONAL
CIVIC
LEAGUE

GLOSSARY

for How Local Government Works

Aggregate
1. Constituting or amounting to a whole; total: aggregate sales in that market.

Bureaucracy
1. Administration of a government chiefly through bureaus or departments staffed with nonelected officials.
2. The departments and their officials as a group.
3. Management or administration marked by diffusion of authority among numerous offices and adherence to inflexible rules of operation.
4. An administrative system in which the need or inclination to follow complex procedures impedes effective action: innovative ideas that get bogged down in red tape and bureaucracy.

Charter
1. A document issued by a sovereign, legislature, or other authority, creating a public or private corporation, such as a city, college, or bank, and defining its privileges and purposes.

Coffers
1. Financial resources; funds.
2. A treasury: stole money from the union coffers.

Colonial Era
1. Of or relating to the colonial period in the United States (the time of the American colonies - just before and during the Revolution).

Cosmopolitan
1. Having constituent elements from all over the world or from many different parts of the world: the ancient and cosmopolitan societies of Syria and Egypt.

Governance
1. The act, process, or power of governing.

Incorporation
1. To cause to form into a legal corporation:
2. To form a body that is granted a charter legally recognizing it as a separate legal entity having its own rights, privileges, and liabilities distinct from those of its members.

Infrastructure
1. An underlying base or foundation especially for an organization or a system.
2. The basic facilities, services, and installations needed for the functioning of a community or society, such as transportation and communications systems, water and power lines, and public institutions including schools, post offices, and prisons.

Jurisdiction
1. The territorial range of authority or control.
2. Law. The right and power to interpret and apply the law: courts having jurisdiction in this district.
3. a. Authority or control: islands under U.S. jurisdiction; a bureau with jurisdiction over Native American affairs. b. The extent of authority or control: a family matter beyond the school's jurisdiction.

Lowest Common Denominator
1. That which is understood, believed, or accepted by a majority of people or the least educated of a specific group.

Metropolitan
1. Of, relating to, or characteristic of a major city.
2. Of or constituting a large city or urbanized area, including adjacent suburbs and towns: the Dallas-Fort Worth metropolitan area.

Municipal Bond
1. An often tax-exempt certificate of debt guaranteeing payment of the original investment plus interest by a specified future date, issued by a city, county, state, or other government for the financing of public projects.

Municipalities
1. A political unit, such as a city or town, incorporated for local self-government.

Quid pro quo
1. An equal exchange or substitution.

Recall
1. The procedure by which a public official may be removed from office by popular vote.
2. The right to employ this procedure.

Reciprocity
1. A mutual or cooperative interchange of favors or privileges, especially the exchange of rights or privileges of trade between nations.

Status Quo
1. The existing condition or state of affairs.

Statutes/Statutory
1. A law enacted by a legislature.
2. Enacted, regulated, or authorized by statute.

Think Tank
1. A group or an institution organized for intensive research and solving of problems, especially in the areas of technology, social or political strategy, or armament.

Urban
1. Of, relating to, or located in a city.
2. Characteristic of the city or city life.

Variance
License to engage in an act contrary to a usual rule: a zoning variance.

HOW LOCAL GOVERNMENT WORKS

Mr. John Parr
President – National Civic League

"All free governments are managed by the combined wisdom and folly of the people"

— *James A. Garfield*

To most Americans, the word "home" means more than a house, it also means a community. From large cities like New York or Los Angeles to tiny towns like Sweet Gum Head, Alabama, local communities are an important part of each individual's identity. Local governments, or jurisdictions, come in a variety of sizes and configurations. They may be designated by one of a number of titles. The most common are cities, towns and townships, counties, and special districts.

Metropolitan areas, which consist of central cities and their surrounding suburbs, are geographic units established by the US Census Bureau for purposes of collecting demographic and other data. These urbanized regions, while they may include numerous local governments, are not governed by any single jurisdiction. Certain functions, however, such as mass transportation or the management of sports stadiums, may be assigned to a single, regional agency. Such agencies are authorized by the state legislature or the voters residing in the affected metropolitan region.

Municipalities are, typically, responsible for repairing roads, assisting the poor, conducting elections, and, of course, imposing the taxes. Local government is, quite often, more efficient than state government in delivering public-safety services, such as police and fire protection. Both emergency and non-emergency medical treatment is routinely furnished, very effectively, by community hospitals. Local government is, often charged with the responsibility of executing programs mandated by the state constitution or state statutes. Public education, for example, is administered at the local level in all states, most typically by local school districts, which are public institutions independent of city and county government. It is at the local level that people interact most directly with "government." This daily, sometimes almost intimate, contact renders local government relatively responsive to the wishes of voters and politically active citizens.

Combined, the 50 states have established roughly 83,000 local governments, with new cities and special districts established annually. In some places, two or more local jurisdictions may be consolidated to achieve greater economy. The trend, however, is towards more local governments. As a whole, local government is one of the nation's largest employers, having grown dramatically during the Reagan years. It now involves roughly nine million employees, an increase that has meant a rise in local tax rates. On the other hand, because the job performance of these public servants is subject to close public scrutiny, local government is often very responsive to criticism from the general public.

COUNTY GOVERNMENT

Throughout the United States, there are slightly more than 3,000 counties, or boroughs, as they are called in Alaska. Dating back to America's colonial era, counties were intended to govern large, sparsely populated rural areas. Critics, like author Martin Gross, say county government today is "a carry-over from the squiredom of old England and is outmoded." They say that all states should follow Connecticut's lead in eliminating counties (Connecticut's neighbor, Rhode Island, also has no counties).

Historically, the northern colonies generally did not assign substantial administrative power to county government. But precisely the opposite was true in the southern colonies. That pattern continues to this day, except where significant reform has taken place.

The **county seat**, or center of government, usually is located in a geographically central city or town. It is difficult to generalize about counties because they vary widely. Counties such as San Bernardino, Calif., which covers over 20,000 square miles, are extremely large. On the other hand, New York County, NY (Manhattan Island), is a tiny 22 square miles.

While county government retains an overwhelmingly "rural" image, Denver County, in Colorado, is a single city, and Los Angeles County, in California, is one of the nation's largest metropolitan areas. Counties, in general, do not have a single chief executive. Instead, they are governed by a board of commissioners, which usually selects a chairperson. Most county boards meet once a month. The commissioners may represent individual districts within the county, (often corresponding to cities, towns, and townships), or they may be elected by the voters of the county at large. County boards tend to have fewer than ten members, but some are much larger, particularly those of urban counties. As administrative agents of state government, counties ordinarily are structured uniformly within states, with county commissioners (or supervisors, as they are called in some states) serving for terms of two to four years. There are many exceptions to this general rule, but the graphic on page 126 offers a generic model of the governmental structure of many counties throughout the United States.

MUNICIPAL GOVERNMENT

Throughout the colonial era and much of the 19th century, county government was the principal local governing institution in the United States. Following the Civil War, however, the city-based industrial and technological revolutions — coupled with huge waves of immigration and the population explosion of the 20th century — resulted in a population shift from the rural countryside to the more densely populated and cosmopolitan city. As existing cities became more crowded, the excess population spilled over into other portions of surrounding counties, resulting in the establishment or "incorporation" of new cities and towns, which effectively were suburbs.

Today, clusters of population in excess of 2,500 people are designated by the Census Bureau as **urban areas**. When these populations possess their own local governing institutions, they are considered **municipalities**, although they formally may be known as cities, towns, townships, or boroughs. Currently, there are nearly 19,000 municipalities in the United States. Large cities (often called central cities), together with their smaller, surrounding suburbs, are called **metropolitan areas**. The residents of suburban municipalities often commute to the central city for employment, linking the economic health of suburbs closely to that of the central city. Nearly 80 percent of the US population lives in metropolitan areas.

While counties are established by state governments to serve the administrative needs of the state, municipalities are established in response to the needs of their local populations by the process of **incorporation**. The incorporation of a new municipality ordinarily is achieved in one of two ways. A municipality may receive its charter from the state, making it a "statutory" or "general law" municipality, or it may draft and adopt its own charter by majority vote, making it a **home rule** municipality. Home rule is an excellent example of citizen mastery of public affairs. However, irrespective of whether a municipal charter is state-issued or adopted locally, it must conform to requirements, limits, and guidelines established by the state constitution and/or the state legislature. Some states provide similar procedures whereby counties may adopt home rule charters.

Depending upon its charter, a municipality will have one of three forms of government. The oldest and most widely used is the **mayor-council** plan. This method of municipal organization provides for a directly elected mayor and law-making body, usually known as the city council, town board, board of trustees, or board of aldermen. Under this plan, the mayor possesses administrative (executive) and policy (law-making, or legislative) roles. The mayor may propose legislation for council approval, particularly the annual budget bill, as well as veto, or reject, local ordinances formulated and passed by the council. It is also the mayor's responsibility to enforce and execute city ordinances through a structure of administrative departments and officials who are typically answerable to the mayor.

This version of the mayor-council plan, often known as the "strong mayor-council plan," became popular in the early 20th century. It replaced the "weak mayor-council plan" of the 19th century, in which the executive authority of the mayor was often undermined by an abundance of separately elected administrative officials, such as chief of police or public works director, who could operate independently of the mayor. Cities operating under this system often had bicameral, or two-house, city councils patterned after the federal government's House of Representatives and Senate. In summary, the "strong mayor-council plan" was designed to counter the fragmentation and confused accountability of the "weak mayor-council" system.

The second most common form of local government is the **council-manager** plan, in which voters elect a council, which in turn hires a city manager to administer the day-to-day activities of the municipality. Operating under the guidance of the popularly elected council, city managers frequently hold advanced degrees in public administration. Council-manager cities also have mayors who serve as voting members of the city council. Lacking both administrative responsibility and the veto power, mayors in council-manager cities nonetheless supply important policy leadership, presiding over city council meetings and serving as a focal point for citizen involvement in municipal affairs. Representing the city in intergovernmental and ceremonial matters, the mayor may be directly elected, serve in rotation with other council members, or be selected to preside over the council for a fixed term by majority vote of the council. The council-manager plan was pioneered in the early 1900's, as part of a reform movement intended to minimize partisan politics and the corruption of big-city party machines. It is modeled after the corporate structure found in most large, successful companies, and continues to gain popularity because of its record of effectiveness.

The least popular form of local government organization is the **commission plan**, in which both legislative and executive powers are combined in a group of popularly elected commissioners. Lacking a focal point for leadership and accountability, the commission plan has fallen out of use. While over 500 communities have experimented with it, today fewer than 200 municipalities subscribe to it.

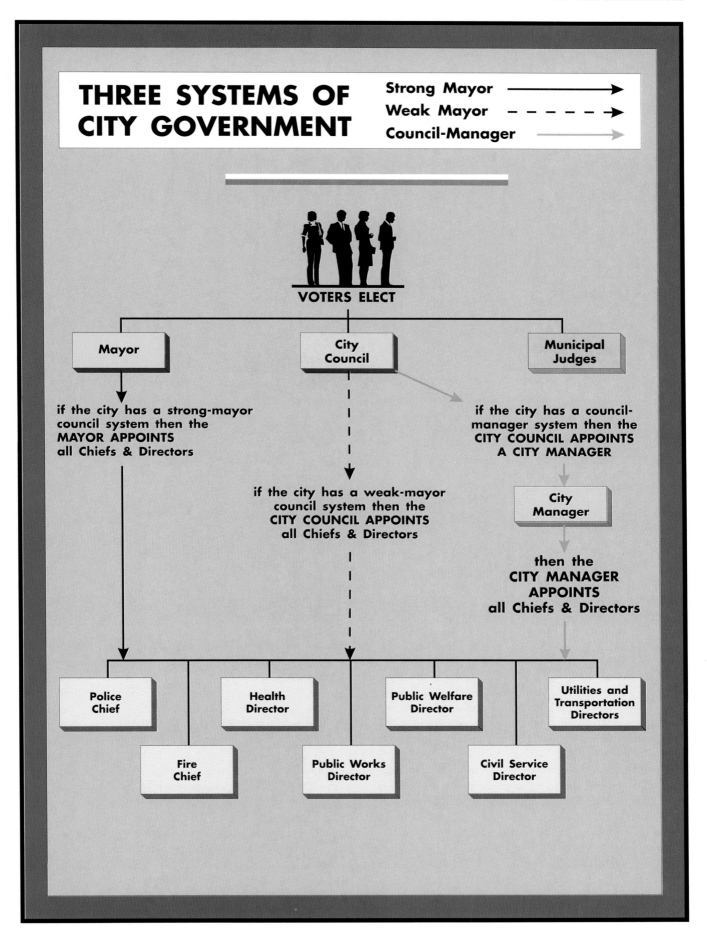

THREE SYSTEMS OF CITY GOVERNMENT

Strong Mayor ——————→

Weak Mayor – – – – – →

Council-Manager ——————→

VOTERS ELECT

Mayor

City Council

Municipal Judges

if the city has a strong-mayor council system then the **MAYOR APPOINTS** all Chiefs & Directors

if the city has a weak-mayor council system then the **CITY COUNCIL APPOINTS** all Chiefs & Directors

if the city has a council-manager system then the **CITY COUNCIL APPOINTS A CITY MANAGER**

City Manager

then the **CITY MANAGER APPOINTS** all Chiefs & Directors

Police Chief

Fire Chief

Health Director

Public Works Director

Public Welfare Director

Civil Service Director

Utilities and Transportation Directors

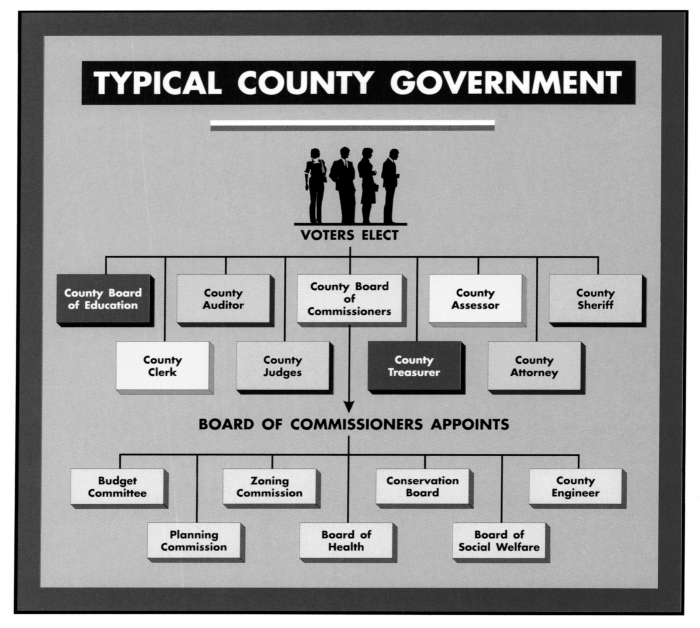

TYPICAL COUNTY GOVERNMENT

VOTERS ELECT

County Board of Education | County Auditor | County Board of Commissioners | County Assessor | County Sheriff

County Clerk | County Judges | County Treasurer | County Attorney

BOARD OF COMMISSIONERS APPOINTS

Budget Committee | Zoning Commission | Conservation Board | County Engineer

Planning Commission | Board of Health | Board of Social Welfare

OTHER LOCAL GOVERNMENTS

Apart from the relatively conventional and familiar forms of government presented above, the 50 states authorize several other plans for local government organization. Perhaps the best known of these is the **New England Town**, which epitomizes the ideal of American participatory democracy. Holding a state charter and delivering the range of municipal services, New England communities with this form of government convene an annual meeting open to all eligible voters of the town. At these meetings, which may be convened for several consecutive days, participants approve annual budgets, set rates of taxation, and elect officials to manage town business over the course of the year. These "selectmen" and "selectwomen" also aid in daily administration of town government. In light of population growth and increased complexity of municipal affairs, many New-England communities have been forced to abandon the town-meeting form, in part because public buildings capable of accommodating the entire voting-eligible population are not available.

In many places throughout the northeastern United States, **townships** have been established as a compromise between the full-blown, bureaucratic municipality and the more romantic town-meeting form. Typical of, but not limited to rural areas, townships are administered by elected officials called supervisors — originally "road" supervisors — or trustees. In some highly urbanized areas, the "township" characterization persists in name only, with the local government organization delivering or contracting for a full range of "big-city" municipal services.

Despite the high visibility of general purpose city and county governments, they are vastly outnumbered by **special districts**. Constituting over 85 percent of all local governments, special districts are established to fulfill a single function, such as water supply, sewage treatment, or public education.

School districts are the most common type of special district. State constitutions and supplementary state laws set the limits within which special districts may operate. The services and enforcement functions we demand of local government are not furnished free of charge. Approximately one-third of local government revenues consist of local taxes. Real property taxes contribute 75 percent to this sum. Additionally, some local governments are authorized by state law to impose sales and income taxes.

Education is the largest single expense for most communities. Education, together with utility bills for public buildings, street lights, and salaries and fees for social services, environmental enforcement and housing, constitute 78 percent of local government expenditures. Like the states, most local governments budget their money annually. To finance major capital improvements, such as roads and buildings, local governments are authorized to borrow money by selling **municipal bonds**.

Although central cities historically have been viewed as industrial centers, since the 1960's, many companies have expanded to the suburbs. While suburban communities have welcomed this trend because it alleviates some of the heavy property-tax burden shouldered by local residents, they nonetheless, have taken steps to manage commercial and industrial development. To this end, most municipalities have instituted **city and town planning boards**. It is the responsibility of these bodies to forecast population growth and develop a **master plan** to guide residential and business development.

Zoning is used to ensure that a community can accommodate the expected changes in a fashion that prevents the mixing of incompatible land uses and fosters attractive, healthy development. This practice involves the establishment of geographic districts, in which the uses of property are limited. There are four major types of zones: industrial, commercial, residential, and recreational. Some communities also establish agricultural zones. **Zoning ordinances** are laws that regulate the use of land and buildings. A master plan is implemented, principally through the enactment and enforcement of zoning ordinances. Communities occasionally relax the restrictions of zoning ordinances by granting **variances**, to permit, for example, the construction of a shopping center in an otherwise residential district.

THE REAL WORLD OF LOCAL GOVERNMENT

Many plans look better on paper than they turn out to be in practice. The cost of local, along with state, government has risen 350 percent, in real dollars, since 1960. With the advent of what political scientists regularly term Ronald Reagan's "New Federalism" — a heightened "partnership" between the federal, state and, local governments has been formed. Nonfederal employees have increased by 3.5 million people, a major cause of rising state and local taxes. In 1960, the cost of running cities, towns, counties, villages, and so on, took four percent of the gross domestic product index. Today, they take nine percent.

Given these issues, observers are increasingly calling for reforms to preserve participatory democracy, while ensuring effective and responsive administration.

METROPOLITAN GROWTH

In 1790, barely five percent of the nation's people lived in urban areas. At that time, America was an agricultural nation of independent rural farmers. By 1900, 39.7 percent of the nation's population lived in cities and towns, attracted by jobs, as well as services, that were not available in rural areas. Today, the United States is a heavily industrialized world power, with over three-quarters of Americans living in metropolitan areas. The number is expected to exceed 85 percent by the turn of the century. As metropolitan areas grow in size, however, most of the nation's central cities are experiencing population and job loss, principally because suburban cities attract both residents and businesses from the central cities. But the people leaving the central cities are those with the resources and social mobility to purchase expensive suburban housing and qualify for the high-tech occupations located at the urban fringe. Thus, those left behind in the central cities are increasingly poor and low-skilled.

URBAN SOCIAL PROBLEMS

Statistics indicate a correlation between crime and high concentrations of inner-city poverty and unemployment. Once a neighborhood acquires a reputation for crime and poverty, its decline may be hastened as middle-class residents and business owners choose to move or locate elsewhere. Poverty breeds other social ills such as broken families and teen pregnancy out of wedlock. The exodus of middle class Americans to the suburbs has driven up the cost of housing. With starter homes in the northeast and on the west coast costing in excess of $150,000, many Americans now, fear they may never be able to purchase a home. Both in big cities and their surrounding suburbs, the cost of housing for purchase and rental has placed decent shelter beyond the reach of many working Americans, forcing them to live on the streets. The ranks of the nation's homeless, are growing at an alarming rate. Some estimates claim that half the nation's homeless are former patients from mental institutions. Poverty, in effect, has become a way of life for many of our most vulnerable citizens — children and the elderly. A statistic that dramatizes this trend is the fact that of the 34 million Americans classified as impoverished or poor, more than half are children. These problems are most apparent in our nation's big cities, but recent research reveals that the economic and social health of suburbs is closely linked to that of their central cities. Urban problems, consequently, are metropolitan-wide problems, and all Americans will have to participate in solving them.

THE FALLACY OF PRESCRIBED ROLES

Cities with Strong Mayors

Introduced early in the progressive reform era, the strong mayor-council form of municipal government (the executive form in county government) was intended to install effective executive leadership capable of designing and implementing a coherent, rational, and accountable program of local governance. With broad power to draft budgets, appoint and dismiss heads of major municipal departments, and veto ordinances drafted by council, the strong mayor would embody the community's

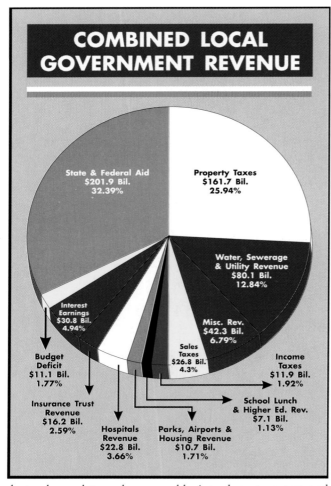

COMBINED LOCAL GOVERNMENT REVENUE

State & Federal Aid
$201.9 Bil.
32.39%

Property Taxes
$161.7 Bil.
25.94%

Water, Sewerage & Utility Revenue
$80.1 Bil.
12.84%

Interest Earnings
$30.8 Bil.
4.94%

Misc. Rev.
$42.3 Bil.
6.79%

Sales Taxes
$26.8 Bil.
4.3%

Income Taxes
$11.9 Bil.
1.92%

Budget Deficit
$11.1 Bil.
1.77%

Insurance Trust Revenue
$16.2 Bil.
2.59%

Hospitals Revenue
$22.8 Bil.
3.66%

Parks, Airports & Housing Revenue
$10.7 Bil.
1.71%

School Lunch & Higher Ed. Rev.
$7.1 Bil.
1.13%

Council-Manager Cities

Proposed and promoted at the height of the progressive movement, the council-manager plan was intended to correct the concentration of powers inherent in the strong mayor-council plan, by locating community-leadership and policy-formulation responsibilities in a popularly elected city council. Rather than fragmenting authority by vesting executive power in a separately elected mayor, the council-manager plan eschews the separation-of-powers principle by assigning administrative responsibilities to a city manager appointed by and accountable to the council. Theoretically, the council-manager plan reinforces the connection between citizen-electors and policy, while detaching policy from administration.

Developments of the last three decades in the political climate of localities, however, have operated to distort the original vision of the 'council-manager plan' and how it operates. The council-manager plan, it must be understood, was adopted as one element of a package of structural reforms calculated to increase popular participation in local government while weakening the influence of corrupt political parties and machines. But even where the council-manager plan functions smoothly, critics and observers are often distressed by what they perceive as inordinate involvement of the manager in policy formulation. Where the plan envisions the manager as a key advisor and consultant to the council in matters of policy, outsiders may regard such involvement as a violation of the premise of separation of political and administrative roles. The opposite phenomenon can also undermine the council-manager plan: In some communities, council members, wishing to curry favor with constituents, may bypass the manager by referring citizen complaints and other matters directly to administrative department heads, rather than acting through the manager. In either case, the effect is to increase tension between council and manager and diminish both the morale of municipal employees and the confidence of citizens.

CHALLENGES TO REPRESENTATIVE GOVERNMENT

Two fundamental contradictions characterize the development and conduct of democratic governance in the United States, particularly at the local level: On the one hand, we elect representatives to steward our public affairs for us, but insist on direct involvement in a range of critical and controversial issues; on the other, we demand strong leadership at the top of our public institutions, but fear executive authority.

Competing Special Interests

Today, these contradictions are dramatized by the movement toward political pluralism which has enabled numerous groups and interests to pressure elected leaders. In electoral politics, it may not matter that a candidate and a particular interest group agree on a variety of critical issues, if they are at odds on a single, "pet" issue.

electoral mandate and, presumably, introduce programs and policies reflecting the popular will. In many ways the strong mayor-council plan emulates the US presidency, with broad executive powers counter-balanced by the legislature's claim to popular representation.

In practice, executive mayors in American cities (distinguished from the non-executive mayors of council-manager cities), despite the high expectations their electorates may have of them, are severely limited in their authority to shape and guide the administrative branch of municipal government. Many municipal charters require councilman review of mayoral appointments. The ever-present threat of popular recall (available at the local level in at least 36 states), discourages courageous acts of reform. In cities with large municipal bureaucracies, important elements of administrative procedure are the province of career civil servants. Moreover, state and federal requirements may preempt creativity and flexibility on the part of the mayor.

For its part, the council, envisioned to represent the popular will of the community, is, often neither invited nor authorized to participate in or monitor critical decision-making processes of the executive staff. Some city charters adhere so closely to the principles of strong mayor-council government that the city council has no realistic power to revise or amend the annual budget as submitted by the mayor.

Direct Democracy

In many communities, this passion for popular control can extend past election day, with the direct democratic tools of initiative and recall serving as a constant reminder to elected officials that the deliberative institution of a legislature may be held hostage to majority whim at any time. The possibility of a citizen initiative or a petition drive to recall a council member often dissuades elected officials from taking courageous positions on controversial issues. Consequently, the fact is that extreme opinions held by small but vocal pressure groups carry a lot of weight due to the threat of the initiative process. And this can prompt city councils to adopt watered-down, "lowest-common-denominator" policies, when more activist solutions are more appropriate.

Term Limitations

One of the most popularly appealing political movements of the last decade has been to limit the number of consecutive terms in office of elected officials. Term limits on executive office holders (e.g., governors, mayors), are well founded in US history; the twist, in recent years, concerns popular dissatisfaction with <u>legislative</u> officials, expressed through ballot initiatives (and in some cases ballot referenda) to limit the number of terms that city council members and county commissioners may serve. Rejecting the traditional notion that regular elections constitute the primary means by which citizens may register satisfaction with their representatives, electorates have taken steps to ensure the rotation in office of policy makers, apparently convinced that incumbency constitutes guaranteed re-election for council members seeking another term. Citing the relative ease with which initiated ordinances and charter amendments may be placed on the local ballot, vis-a-vis the state ballot, some observers claim the term-limits movement reflects popular frustration with the conduct of state and federal politics (i.e., voters are registering their dissatisfaction at the most immediately effective level). Whatever the motivation, citizens are sending the clear message that if their elected officials are unable to act, their inertia will not be tolerated for long.

CITIZEN PARTICIPATION IN CONSTRUCTIVE SELF-GOVERNANCE

A successful petition drive to initiate an ordinance or recall a local official, paradoxically, may signal a breakdown in the democratic process, rather than its triumph. The need to resort to the initiative or the recall suggests that the relationship between citizens and their governing institutions and elected officials is distant and dysfunctional. It may also indicate that citizens' expectations of elected officials are too high, and that they acknowledge no personal responsibility for community progress and improvement.

Examples abound of well governed communities, in which citizens, businesses, voluntary service organizations, and government, have joined together to identify pressing local issues. Increasingly, local elected officials are opening the decision-making process to broader community interests — not in submission to relentless pressure, but in recognition of the creativity and energy of non-governmental community resources. Communities where this practice has become

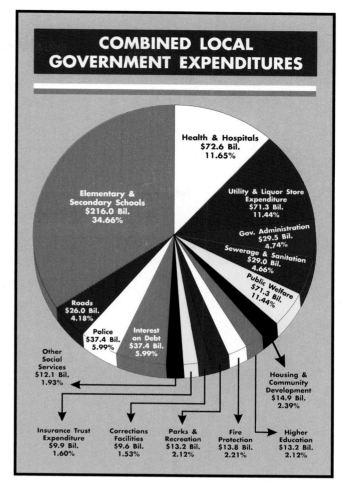

COMBINED LOCAL GOVERNMENT EXPENDITURES

Health & Hospitals $72.6 Bil. 11.65%

Utility & Liquor Store Expenditure $71.3 Bil. 11.44%

Gov. Administration $29.5 Bil. 4.74%

Sewerage & Sanitation $29.0 Bil. 4.66%

Public Welfare $71.3 Bil. 11.44%

Elementary & Secondary Schools $216.0 Bil. 34.66%

Roads $26.0 Bil. 4.18%

Police $37.4 Bil. 5.99%

Interest on Debt $37.4 Bil. 5.99%

Other Social Services $12.1 Bil. 1.93%

Housing & Community Development $14.9 Bil. 2.39%

Insurance Trust Expenditure $9.9 Bil. 1.60%

Corrections Facilities $9.6 Bil. 1.53%

Parks & Recreation $13.2 Bil. 2.12%

Fire Protection $13.8 Bil. 2.21%

Higher Education $13.2 Bil. 2.12%

institutionalized are said to possess a strong "civic culture" described as the networks and norms of trust, reciprocity, and civic engagement, through which issues are addressed and decisions made.

Some relationships between local government and the private sector are familiar and increasingly conventional, such as the contracting of public services to non-governmental vendors (commonly referred to as "privatization"). Others are so common that we hardly notice them, such as the critical role played by the nonprofit sector in human services delivery. Governmental support of nonprofit service providers amounts to approximately one-tenth of all public expenditures for human services. Increasingly important are the so-called "public-private partnerships" that have emerged in cities across the country, most visibly for economic revitalization and downtown redevelopment.

UNFUNDED MANDATES

These days, however, the USA's home towns are disgruntled, unhappy, and certainly feeling forgotten. With the poor state of the national budget, federal revenue sharing and grants to municipalities have been shrinking for years. Yet federal orders (mandates) for communities to undertake expensive projects on their own have been rising, leaving municipalities with their own budget crises and the inevitable tax questions.

A city council meets and plans in full public view

In the mid-1960's, the federal government discovered a convenient, low-cost means of implementing national policy: preemption of local government's authority through mandated action. State governments soon followed suit. While local government has always been subject to requirements imposed by senior levels, the state and federal governments, until relatively recently, restrained themselves from establishing such structures. This new wave of regulation began innocuously with the imposition of minimum standards for municipal water supplies and the prohibition of local government intervention in bankruptcy proceedings. At first mandates implied no great burden, since most local governments were either in compliance with the new standards or uninterested in entering an additional regulatory arena. Early mandates often were accompanied by funds for implementation.

With the passage of time and the ballooning of budget deficits at the national and state levels, mandates have become more burdensome for units of local government, particularly those that are not accompanied by additional funding for implementation. In recent years, the expense of compliance with unfunded mandates has grown so burdensome that legislation has been passed in fifteen states to restrain the enactment of any unfunded state mandates on local government. In general, however, state mandates do not approach those imposed by the federal government in either expense or administrative complexity. One measure of the increasing coerciveness of the US intergovernmental system is the fact that the aggregate cost of federal environmental mandates on local governments, has risen from $27.3 billion in 1981 to $32.8 in 1987. These costs (mainly incurred to meet environmental requirements for sewage sludge disposal, drinking water safety, air quality, and solid waste management) are estimated to exceed $48 billion annually by the close of the 1990's. In cash-strapped central cities, these expensive and wide-ranging requirements have severely curtailed the ability of local governments to respond to priorities in infrastructure maintenance, economic development, and the delivery of human services. Local jurisdictions, after all, do not have the luxury of running large budget deficits or borrowing to fund general operating expenses.

Local leaders face the tough balancing act of giving citizens the services they expect, without the high taxes they won't accept. The unfunded federal mandates present a particular dilemma because ignoring them is impossible. The federal government can cut funds in related areas and even put local leaders in prison.

In the best-selling book "A Call for Revolution," activist author, Martin Gross, blasted the unfunded mandates, and called for an end of duplicated services by local, state, and federal governments.

Since local and state governments have come to imitate the federal model through most of the country, this duplication occurs in 'fours.' For example, affluent White Plains, NY has a Department of Public Works. But so does its equally affluent county, Westchester, and so does the state of New York. Washington has the Federal Highway Administration, which built the interstate highway system and now continues operating by "studying" roads and related areas. The same pattern can be found in much less affluent areas. In industrialized New Kensington, PA., a city just outside Pittsburgh, there is a public works department. But Westmoreland County also has the same service, as does the state. All told, the nation had, as of the end of 1993, 86,743 local governments with 3,043 counties, 19,296 municipalities, 16,666 townships, 33,131 special districts, and 16,044 school and related districts. As a result, the overlap of service duplication is several thousandfold.

Localities pay mainly by imposing property taxes on residents. Washington provides $225 billion in programs that the localities and states can apply for. But most of the time there are strings attached: in addition to following federal guidelines, virtually without exception, the locals have to match the federal funds. According to the Cato Institute, a Washington think tank, there is an almost one-to-one relationship between rising local and state taxes and federal aid in the last forty years.

CONFRONTING THE METROPOLITAN AREAS

Except in the most isolated rural jurisdictions, problems such as environmental quality, transportation, economic development, housing, and social equity, can not be effectively solved by any single unit of local government. Liberal incorporation laws, federal policies favoring suburbanization, and the widely held view that public satisfaction is most readily ensured through small local governments close to the people, have encouraged growth in the number of local governments within metropolitan areas. Single-purpose governments, commonly called special districts, outnumber general-purpose local governments (e.g., cities and counties) by a ratio of nearly four-to-one. The resulting patchwork, however duplicative and wasteful, works to the apparent satisfaction of suburbanites, who fear inter-local agreements and the establishment of regional institutions as first steps toward income redistribution in support of ailing central cities.

Only a few metropolitan regions have addressed this prevailing fragmentation through the strengthening of county government, city-county consolidation, or the establishment of special multi-county structures of regional governance. Councils of government, with their voluntary membership and strictly advisory status, have, generally, been restricted to the role of regional planning. While recent transportation legislation enacted at the federal level will empower such regional agencies to shape transit decision making - job development, housing, and public-safety issues remain the province of numerous local governments acting in the interests of their immediate constituencies. In the absence of voluntary measures to coordinate land use and the location of employment opportunities, political fragmentation within metropolitan areas likely will continue to undermine the environmental and traffic-congestion objectives of federal policies. For central cities, the consequences of unbridled metropolitan expansion will include continued urban depopulation, concentration of poverty and crime, and loss of tax base.

THE DARK SIDE OF LOCAL GOVERNMENT

The term "bureaucracy" appeared around 1818. Its definition was not pretty: a system of administration marked by officialdom, red tape, and proliferation. Today, there is a new era of bureaucracy; what "systems simplification" expert Sid Taylor of the National Taxpayers Union calls "the new space age bureaucrat — or computercrat." This individual "no longer sits at a desk, but rather a computer console, fax machine, space-satellite, telephone, or television network node." The result, says Taylor, is that "we now have instant red tape and a global electronic bureaucracy." What Taylor does not mention is that much of this "improvement" was the effect of reform. Civil service reform, for example, professionalized government, but enshrined inert bureaucracy.

It can be convincingly argued that the reform movements of this century have been magnificently successful in improving the efficiency and responsiveness of local government bureaucracies, empowering traditionally under-represented minorities, and reducing the incidence of blatant corruption. But governing institutions and the process of institutional reform are extraordinarily conservative by nature. Thus, most reforms constitute the minimum possible response to a specific circumstance or condition; they seek neither to address future issues nor to redress their own negative consequences. Thus, the inert civil service bureaucracy.

Likewise, voting-rights reform ensured access and opened the political process, but often institutionalized deadlock and encouraged race-based politics. The liberalization of municipal incorporation rules made high-quality city services available to a broader segment of the population, but encouraged urban sprawl and political fragmentation within the metropolis.

To a great extent, the "dark side" of local government is embodied in its everyday conduct. The professionalization of local government administration has virtually ensured that local policy — whether good or bad — will be efficiently and effectively implemented. As the 20th century draws to a close, it is not so much the apparatus of government that requires "reinvention," as the processes of governance that demand the reformer's scrutiny.

Despite the staggering technological advances and substantive political and social reforms of the 20th century, the development, location, and range of potential uses assigned to available urban land remain the primary forces shaping the conduct of local government. Development interests either dominate or significantly influence government in most localities.

As indicated above, corruption no longer plagues local government, thanks to the political and civil service reforms of the progressive era. Nonetheless, isolated and celebrated cases of corruption in local government persist. Many cases of contemporary corruption, predictably, concern development. The traditional alignment of real estate and political interests was recently underscored in a suburban Maryland county where it came to light that incumbent county commissioners routinely solicited area developers for campaign contributions. For their generosity, the developers received tacit assurances that land-use and zoning questions would receive favorable consideration when brought before the county commission. Responding to charges of apparent impropriety, county commissioners pronounced their actions "business as usual" — no more corrupt than those of other local officials in communities with abundant inventories of undeveloped land.

Instances of classic depravity in office for personal gain, as opposed to maintaining incumbency, also, occasionally, come to light. In one New Jersey township, seven top municipal officials — three former mayors, a chief financial officer, a deputy treasurer, an auditor, and a town clerk — were recently indicted for conspiring to steal over $2 million from the city's coffers, either by paying themselves more than their authorized salaries or cashing checks to imaginary vendors. One of the former conspirators was reported to have gambled away some $500,000 of the township's money in Atlantic City casinos! The financial mischief spanning four mayoral administrations was uncovered only when a reform mayor took office and promptly noticed evidence of severe financial mismanagement.

Another recent example, in a larger northeastern city, surrounded a top municipal official's bid for US Senate. With campaign funds dwindling, the candidate sought a loan from an area bank to finance a last-minute, pre-primary media blitz. The loan was approved, but the senate campaign, which had been floundering for weeks, never picked up momentum. Months later, the official's bid for re-election to her municipal post was foiled when public records revealed that the bank had been awarded a lucrative contract to float a municipal bond issue, in an apparent quid pro quo for the earlier campaign loan.

Excepting egregious raids of municipal treasuries, the extent to which such transgressions place the public's interests in jeopardy, is arguable. If such practices are merely expressions of "business as usual," then they apparently do no great harm. But, neither do they do any good. Maintenance of the status quo implies that no progress is being made toward solving new and emerging public issues. What is certain is that when cases of official impropriety come to light in a prevailing climate of skepticism and public distrust, citizens will become increasingly discouraged with a governmental system that seems closed, unresponsive, and dismally ineffective. Local government has improved dramatically, over the past 50 years, but even when it works well, it is not perceived to fully meet citizens' needs. When local government works poorly, or when its reputation is tarnished, its failings are amplified ten-fold.

131

CHAPTER 10

HOW THE ELECTION PROCESS WORKS

by Mr. David Beiler
Senior Editor – Campaigns & Elections Magazine

GLOSSARY
for How The Election Process Works

Agrarian
1. Relating to or concerning the land and its ownership, cultivation, and tenure.
2. a. Relating to agricultural or rural matters. b. Intended to further agricultural interests.

Anarchist/Anarchism
1. An advocate or a participant in anarchism - the theory or doctrine that all forms of government are oppressive and undesirable and should be abolished.
2. Active resistance and terrorism against the state, as used by some anarchists.
3. Rejection of all forms of coercive control and authority

Ballot
1. A sheet of paper or a card used to cast or register a vote, especially a secret one.
2. The act, process, or method of voting, especially in secret.
3. A list of candidates running for office; a ticket.
4. The total of all votes cast in an election.
5. The right to vote; franchise.
6. A small ball once used to register a secret vote.

Campaign
1. An operation or series of operations energetically pursued to accomplish a purpose.

Caucus
1. A meeting of the local members of a political party especially to select delegates to a convention or register preferences for candidates running for office.
2. A closed meeting of party members within a legislative body to decide on questions of policy or leadership.
3. A group within a legislative or decision-making body seeking to represent a specific interest or influence a particular area of policy: a minority caucus.

Checkers Speech
1. In 1952, political critics accuse Gen. Eisenhower's running mate, Sen. Richard Nixon, of taking a "slush fund" of $18,000 from California businessmen. Nixon appears on television September 23 and denies that any of the money in question went for his personal use and adds, "I did get something, a gift after the nomination. It was a little cocker spaniel dog, black and white, spotted. Our little girl Tricia, 6, named it 'Checkers.' The kids, like all kids, love the dog. Regardless of what they say about it, we are going to keep it." The speech produces more than one million favorable letters and telegrams. Eisenhower wins 55 percent of the popular vote and 84 percent of the electoral votes.

Colonial Era
1. Of or relating to the colonial period in the United States (the time of the American colonies - just before and during the Revolution).

Contiguous
1. Sharing an edge or boundary; touching.
2. Neighboring; adjacent.
3. Connecting without a break.

Decennial
1. Occurring every ten years.

Delegate
1. A person authorized to act as representative for another; a deputy or an agent.
2. A representative to a conference or convention.
3. A member of a House of Delegates, the lower house of the Maryland, Virginia, or West Virginia legislature.
4. An elected or appointed representative of a U.S. territory in the House of Representatives who is entitled to speak but not vote.

Disenfranchised
1. To be deprived of a privilege, an immunity, or a right of citizenship, especially the right to vote.
2. To deprive of a privilege or franchise.

District
1. A division of an area, as for administrative purposes.

Egalitarian
1. Affirming, promoting, or characterized by belief in equal political, economic, social, and civil rights for all people.

Electoral College
1. A body of electors chosen to elect the President and Vice President of the United States.

Elitist
1. One who believes that certain persons or members of certain classes or groups deserve favored treatment by virtue of their perceived superiority, as in intellect, social status, or financial resources.

Factionalism
1. Preference to form into a cohesive group of persons, usually a contentious minority within a larger group, rather than interact with the majority.

Feifdom
1. The estate or domain of a feudal lord.
2. Something over which one dominant person or group exercises control.

Intelligentsia
1. The intellectual elite of a society.

Largesse
1. a. Liberality in bestowing gifts, especially in a lofty or condescending manner. b. Money or gifts bestowed.
2. Generosity of spirit or attitude.

Lobbying/Lobbyist
1. To try to, or one who tries to, influence the thinking of legislators or other public officials

Monopoly
1. a. A company or group having exclusive control over a commercial activity. b. A commodity or service so controlled.
2. Exclusive control by one group of the means of producing or selling a commodity or service.

Neo
1. New; recent.
2. New and different.

(glossary coninued on page 150)

HOW THE ELECTION PROCESS WORKS

Mr. David Beiler
Senior Editor – Campaigns & Elections Magazine

"Only a country that is rich and safe can afford to be a democracy, for democracy is the most expensive and nefarious kind of government ever heard of on earth."

— *H.L. Mencken*

PART I:
THE EVOLUTION

HOW WE GOT HERE

The method by which America selects its leaders is indeed a complex and treacherous tournament, unfolding on a field fraught with hidden pitfalls, steamy bogs, and slippery slopes. To understand how this hazardous game is played, we must first study its rules and practices and how they came to be.

No doubt you've read the "news" on most every editorial page or seen the "evidence" presented on innumerable TV news essays: Our democracy is in imminent peril, due to the shocking degeneration of our electoral process. Sound-bite TV coverage, poll-driven policy-making, special-interest shakedowns and campaigning by thirty-second commercials have supposedly reduced our leadership to a pack of ventriloquist dummies, manipulated by shadowy consultants whose only mission in life is to fatten their own wallets. Anyone with backbone, moral character, and at least half a brain, steers clear of the political arena, mindful that their private lives may well become a public spectacle if they dare enter.

Relax. Despite the high-tech trappings of politicking today, such hand-wringing is actually older than our venerable republic. "If a man solicits you earnestly for your vote," warned a pamphlet from colonial times, "avoid him; self-interest and sordid avarice lurk under his forced smiles, hearty shakes by the hand and deceitful...enquires after your wife and family." Neither George Will, Ralph Nader, or Ross Perot could have said it more succinctly.

Electioneering has always been viewed with some disgust in our culture, most particularly when viewed by the elite intelligentsia of pundits and social commentators. At the time of the American Revolution, the word "democracy" was usually employed as a disparaging term; men (and only men) with enough leisure time to follow affairs of state involved themselves in politics, and they tended to distrust the "rule of the mob." Our "founding fathers" placed numerous obstacles in the path of direct control of the government by the governed.

Over time, many of these impediments have gradually fallen away, though the squeamishness felt by the American elite in the face of our democratic process has never really dissipated.

IN THE BEGINNING

Our first elections, for the federal government's most important offices, the Senate and the Presidency, were the private preserve of state legislators. Governors and congressman were selected by popular vote, though in most states only owners of real estate were permitted to cast ballots. By unwritten convention, candidates were expected to "stand" for election, rather than run; any attempt to further their own cause was considered a breach of the dignity required to hold public office. Unless leaders were drafted into their positions of power, they were deemed unworthy.

This genteel system soon proved untenable. It worked well enough while the universally acclaimed, paternal figure of George Washington was around to lead the new nation, but as his retirement from the presidency approached in 1796, political divisions and rivalries gave rise to a more competitive approach.

Conservative elitists—who wished to preserve the status-quo republican system—banded behind Treasury Secretary Alexander Hamilton in support of Vice-President John Adams for the presidency. Liberal democrats, favoring decentralized government, more direct elections, and universal suffrage (though their "universe" was restricted to white male citizens), backed Secretary of State Thomas Jefferson.

Calling themselves "Federalists," the conservatives narrowly prevailed in this first competitive presidential contest, but they were as doomed as the dinosaurs. The expansion of the frontier, heavy immigration, and the higher birthrates of Jefferson's egalitarian farmer-class were all tipping the scales toward a more populist political system. With most of their their support confined to country squires and coastal merchants, the steadily outmanned Federalists never won another presidential election, and had all but passed from the scene by the War of 1812.

Andrew Jackson campaigning in 1832

The Jeffersonians (organized as the Democratic-Republican Party) succeeded in electing their hero to the presidency in 1800 and continued to control the executive branch for forty years. The decline of party competition led to something of a revival for closed politics known as the "Era of Good Feeling" (1808-1824). Democratization slowed, although individual liberties were expanded and state sovereignty continued to ride high. Competitions for the US House and state offices grew steadily more competitive, and a partisan press bloomed into full flourish.

THE RISE OF DEMOCRACY

Increased partisanship at the local level eventually led to renewed factionalism within the Democratic-Republican Party, a phenomenon that spilled out into a four-way brawl for the presidency in 1824 along regional lines. Frontier favorite Andrew Jackson won far more popular votes than any of the other candidates, but fell short of a majority in the Electoral College. As directed by the Constitution, the contest was decided in the House, where third-place finisher Henry Clay threw the election to John Quincy Adams, son of the old Federalist.

Infuriated by this "corrupt bargain" (Clay became Secretary of State in the Adams administration), Jackson and his followers spent the next four years campaigning for direct election and universal suffrage. By 1832, the system had broadened significantly, enabling Jackson to overpower the President and his neo-Federalists, even in the Electoral College. "Old Hickory" threw an inaugural party at the White House for anyone who wished to come; the place was nearly leveled by a buckskin army of drunken celebrants of democracy. The festivities foreshadowed the institution of a patronage "spoils" system by which Jackson rewarded his political allies with government jobs and prerogatives.

Abhorring such displays of mobocracy and vehemently opposed to the new President's policies toward Indians and

the banking system, anti-Jacksonites eventually coalesced into a new party, the Whigs. But the wily backwoodsman was a step ahead. Jackson wanted his trusted friend, Martin Van Buren, to succeed him in 1836, but feared he could not hold his rough-and-tumble following together for the urbane New Yorker. A supreme organizer who probably qualifies as being the first political "boss," Van Buren persuaded the President to formalize his support structure into a powerful mechanism that would select its candidate at a national gathering. The first modern political party, the Democrats, was born, as was the first presidential nominating convention.

Backed by the President and his own supreme skill at political horse trading, Van Buren won the nomination and defeated four Whig regional candidacies in the general election. But he seemed an anomaly, leading an alliance of rough-hewn commoners with his dandified manner and upper-class sensibilities. The Whigs decided to run their own Indian-fighting hero in 1840, General William Henry Harrison, and to do it with a rank excess in populist appeals that would make even Andy Jackson blush.

THE FIRST MEDIA CAMPAIGN

Harrison had made something of a military reputation in the War of 1812, but his real claim to fame came as the slayer of the notorious Indian chieftain Tecumseh, at the Battle of Tippecanoe. After Virginia patrician John Tyler was added to the ticket, America's first advertising slogan was born: "Tippecanoe and Tyler Too!"

Although the old warrior was born to one of Virginia's most elite families in an old manse, pioneering Whig image makers spun the myth that he was a frontiersman from the wilds of Indiana. Even his opponents were taken in. "Give [Harrison] a barrel of hard cider," a newspaper partial to Van Buren sniffed, "and my word for it, he will sit the remainder of his days in his log cabin." Harrison's precocious handlers jumped on this gaffe with glee, cranking out thousands of song-sheets that proclaimed:

> **They say that he lives in a cabin**
> **And that he drinks hard cider too.**
> **Well what if he does, I am certain**
> **He's the hero of Tippecanoe!**

Whigs held torchlight parades through hundreds of communities across the nation, often rolling a ten-foot leather ball emblazoned with partisan slogans. Barrels of free hard cider evoked hearty renditions of Tippecanoe jingles from rallies of up to 25,000 souls who partied for days. A campaign weekly (dubbed *The Log Cabin* and edited by a young journalist named Horace Greeley) reached a regular circulation of 80,000 - all the press could print. Elaborate hand-painted banners, ribbons, and even brass "log cabin" snuffboxes flooded the countryside in what Smithsonian curator Keith Melder has called "the first media campaign."

General William Henry Harrison's "hard cider" campaign of 1840

A concerted image campaign made use of the candidate's distant past as a rail-splitting woodsman, as legends hailing his honesty found expression in banners, song-sheets, and campaign newspaper stories. Buttons appeared for the first time: lapel pins with cloth or brass frames encasing a tin-type photo of the candidate.

Lincoln probably owed his election more to a vicious North/South split within the rival Democratic Party than to this slickly packaged image, but a new standard had been set forth for Presidential candidates. For the next five generations they would be expected to have either risen from humble beginnings, or, like the Roosevelts and John Kennedy, be committed to an ambitious agenda to assist the "little guy."

The bewildered Democrats were outdrunk, outsung, and eventually outvoted. President Van Buren was held up to such widespread ridicule that he found it necessary to partially disrobe at one gathering to disprove the rumor that he wore a corset. Despite his full disclosure, the President lost in a landslide and was heard to lament: "I have been washed from my high office in a tidal wave of apple juice." Organized ballyhoo had entered the electoral process, which soon became a favorite form of local entertainment. Buttons, banners, ribbons, and medals bearing the likenesses of various leaders proliferated, but Presidential candidates remained above it all. Not even Andrew Jackson had stooped to hitting the campaign trail; Harrison had delivered only a half-dozen speeches in his general neighborhood. The office was still supposed to seek the man.

"MEN OF THE PEOPLE"

The late-ballot presidential nomination of Abraham Lincoln by the Republican Party in 1860 was a curious choice. Lincoln had lost more elections than he had won in his checkered political career and had not succeeded at the polls for more than a decade. Although he had gained national notoriety in 1858 in a series of campaign debates with the renowned Sen. Stephen A. Douglas (D-IL), he had lost that race as well, and certainly would not be expected to carry his stump skills onto the *Presidential* campaign trail. Heaven forbid! That was just not done. It would demean the sacred office of George Washington, or so the conventional wisdom believed.

A basically modest man, Lincoln did indeed steer clear of the campaign hoopla raised on his behalf; Armies of Republican activists, called the "Wide-Awakes," marched in torchlight parades through hundreds of communities across the North, chanting slogans, singing partisan songs, and carrying replicas of the candidate's log cabin birthplace. Unlike Harrison, the humble roots of "Honest Abe" were genuine, and his handlers made the most of them to garner popular support.

THE "WHISTLESTOP" CAMPAIGN

In 1896, a fellow came along who embodied both the populist image and program: 36 year-old William Jennings Bryan, "The Silver-Tongued Nebraskan." A two-term congressman whose claim to fame was an unparalleled ability to move men with a booming eloquence, Bryan arrived at the 1896 Democratic National Convention as a part of a massive agrarian/labor revolt against the party's eastern establishment. Inspired by the Populist Party—which four years before had polled eight percent of the national vote and carried a few western states—these reform Democrats demanded the scrapping of the gold standard, a move calculated to cause inflation and relieve pressure on mortgages.

Speaking on behalf of a platform plank calling for a new monetary system, Bryan captivated the convention by railing against Wall Street:

> *"We shall answer their demands for a gold standard by saying to them: You shall not press down on the brow of labor this crown of thorns; you shall not crucify mankind upon a cross of gold!"*

Swept away in emotion, the delegates soon gave their nomination to the young orator, who became an instant legend.

With industrialist "Dollar Marc" Hanna raising three million dollars for GOP nominee William McKinley (the equivalent of more than $50 million today), a desperate Bryan threw campaign tradition off a fast-moving train. Traveling 18,000 miles to give 600 speeches before a total of five million people, the burly Nebraskan invented the "whistlestop" campaign. Pulling into a station, he would deliver a fire-breathing speech to the assembled crowd from the rear platform of his train, then chug to the next stop.

Theodore "Teddy" Roosevelt re-creates the "whistlestop campaign" in 1904

THE MECHANIZATION OF DEMOCRACY

The "robber barons" of monopoly were not the only great power in American politics at the turn of the century. The era of the big-city political machines was at its zenith, utilizing a system which ironically constricted democratic choices while providing practical, hands-on assistance to the masses.

As the Industrial Age took hold in America during the mid-1800s, it was inevitable that politics, too, would become mechanized. Areas of high population density were more easily organized into political fiefdoms, teeming as they were with recently naturalized immigrants ready to sell their votes for a job or a reliable source of food. Urban centers became so large (particularly in the northeast) that they could control whole state governments if they produced lopsided majorities for a particular faction.

The first to harness this great potential for power was Van Buren, who began his career as a clever coalition builder in upstate New York and cultivated ties with the "Tammany Hall" political fraternity of New York City. The future president amassed great power, but relied principally on a network of influential community leaders. Events overseas soon changed the character of political machines, however.

In 1848, a potato famine in Ireland and a series of failed revolutions across central Europe brought the first flood of immigrants to America's door. By the outbreak of the Civil War, 13 years later, they had become numerous enough to seize control of Tammany Hall, and with it, the municipal government of New York City. The leader of this suddenly powerful band of new arrivals was William Marcy Tweed, a Scots fireman with an artistic gift for wholesale fraud.

Under Tweed's direction, local government built a $250,000 county courthouse that cost $12.5 million - a 5,000% overrun. Among the purchases: $190 per spittoon (about $6,000 in today's currency), and $7,500 for thermometers. In Tweed's mind, politics was an industry whose profits were to be maximized for those who invested in the machine. He dismissed the electoral ambitions of one of his few honest acquaintances by advising, "Forget it. You'll make no money for yourself or anyone else." After a dozen-year reign during which he came to control all three branches of state government, Tweed went to jail for malfeasance (misconduct or wrongdoing), the victim of a pioneering publicity campaign spearheaded by political cartoonist, Thomas Nast.

In a desperate bid for survival, Tammany Hall turned to a respected reformer for leadership. As mayor, the accurately nicknamed "Honest John" Kelly made the machine work as a tireless dispenser of constituent service and limited graft to the minimum amount required to keep the gears of the machine greased. The system employed a pyramid power structure that rested on a network of precinct captains, people familiar with the individual voters of a given neighborhood, who were charged with solving reporting problems from the streets, doling out largesse, coordinating patronage, and making sure that those serviced fulfilled their bargains at the polling place.

The Republican publicity machine depicted Bryan's rabble-rousing tour as a traveling carnival and derided the Democrat as a raving anarchist. McKinley tried to remain aloof from the fray in the customary manner, but Bryan was making undeniable inroads with his personal contact. Finally, Hanna took the extraordinary step of bringing the electorate to the candidate. McKinley made some 300 speeches from his own front porch in Canton, Ohio, appearing before a total of 750,000 voters, all railed into town courtesy of Marc Hanna. (What do you say to *that* special-interest leverage, Jerry Brown?)

McKinley won comfortably in 1896, and ran for re-election four years later with Spanish-American War hero Teddy Roosevelt as his running mate. Republican bosses had hoisted TR onto the ticket as the only means of getting him out of the governorship of New York. When McKinley was assassinated, shortly into his second term, one of the bosses was heard to lament, "My God! Now that damn cowboy's in the White House!"

Energetic, audacious, athletic, a lover of the outdoors and a firm moral leader, Theodore Roosevelt may have projected the most vivid image of any candidate in American history. But he was not beyond groveling for special-interest cash to make sure that the image got projected to the masses. During his 1904 campaign for a second term, he literally went to his knees on the Oval Office carpet to appeal for money from a group of financiers headed by J.P. Morgan. Roosevelt got his money *and* his second term. The day before it began, he warned an aide: "Tomorrow, I walk into this office in my own right. Then—watch out for me!" Teddy II turned out to be a ferocious trust-buster, destroying the monopolies that had paid for his election.

Big-city political organizations, using the Kelly model, flourished, and by the time immigration hit an all-time high during the first decade of the 20th century, the large collection of urban bosses exercised a virtual veto over the presidential nominees of both major parties. From that point on, however, a long, slow decline set in, propelled by the slackening pace of immigration, and election reforms brought by the progressive era.

It may seem inconceivable to us now, but until this century very few American elections were conducted by secret ballot; voters had to show up at the polls and declare their preferences verbally, under the watchful eye of the precinct captain. Following a practice that had first taken hold in Australia, reformers succeeded in instituting anonymous voting virtually everywhere in the country, by the time women were given the franchise in 1919.

The "good-government" lobbies (derisively called "goo-goos" by the machine crowd) were less successful in their campaign to popularly elect party nominees. While the relatively boss-less South and West readily adopted party primaries—and even runoffs in one-party Dixie— the machine-dominated East and Midwest clung to nomination by party executive committee, or (in the case of major offices) convention. Other reforms of government organization—such as hiring by merit and higher auditing standards—gradually reduced machine patronage and graft. Hit squarely in the pocketbook, the bosses began to weave and stumble. The final knockout was delivered by broadcast media, which enabled candidates to bypass political organizations in delivering their personal messages to the voters.

DEMOCRACY OF THE AIR

The election of 1920 was truly a milestone in modern democracy. For the first time, women exercised the right to vote; also for the first time, voters learned of their collective decision through a broadcast medium. Radio had brought massive, instant communication to the political arena.

As radio began to exert its influence, the high nasal twang of Calvin Coolidge and the guttural New York rasp of Al Smith gave way to the inspiring elegant tones of Franklin Roosevelt and the motivating straight talk of Huey Long. Campaigners had begun to move into a one-on-one relationship with the voters.

That personalization of the electoral process was greatly accentuated with the arrival of television at mid-century. The first political TV commercials were produced in 1950 by the candidate himself, US Senator Bill Benton (D-CT). The most successful radio copy writer of the 1930's, Benton had gone on to develop Encyclopedia Britannica Films and Muzak in the 1940's. In 1949 he was appointed to the Senate by Connecticut Governor Chester Bowles, his former advertising partner.

Senator Bill Benton demonstrates his political innovation to President Truman

Intrigued by the power of television, Benton used the facilities of EB Films to make a series of 60-second documentaries about himself, and ran them on the state's lone TV station, as well as street-corner projection machines. When he used one of the machines to show his newfangled innovations to President Harry Truman, Benton was told to go out and shake 25,000 hands.

Political television spots remained an isolated novelty to most Americans until 1952, when the GOP presidential campaign of General Dwight Eisenhower introduced them to most of the country. A political novice, Eisenhower's first speeches were unbearably boring and his press conference performances were prone to gaffes. The General's alarmed handlers rectified the problem by limiting his public appearances and carrying the campaign with saturated levels of spot TV advertising.

One series of 20-second spots, called "Eisenhower Answers America," depicted the candidate folksily responding to questions from everyday people who appeared to be in the studio with him. In fact, Eisenhower's segments, in all 40 spots, were shot in a single day; the questioners were cast and filmed later. Finally, lifted from his marathon siege before the cameras, the General mopped his brow and muttered, "To think an old soldier would come to this."

It was a sentiment shared by Democratic nominee Adlai Stevenson, who mocked the Republican "soap flakes" campaign. The intellectual Illinois governor rejected spot ads for half-hour televised speeches, which he never seemed to finish before being cut off. Buried under a landslide of votes, Adlai returned to challenge "Ike" again four years later, a chastened man, chatting to the camera while holding a sack of groceries.

Stevenson had come a long way in appreciating the new medium. Introduced to his television adviser at the 1952 Convention, the Governor appeared to be puzzled. The poor consultant didn't hear from him for two days; then, the phone rang at midnight: "Could you please come up to my room and fix this thing" Stevenson's bewildered voice asked. "All I get is snow and static."

Senator John Kennedy and Vice President Richard Nixon in the first televised Presidential debate

By 1960, the tables had turned. Democrat John Kennedy had studied the Republicans' successful use of television ads and approved the use of montages, jingles, and dancing cartoon figures in his own ads. Stung by charges that the Eisenhower ad campaigns had been vacuous and manipulative, GOP nominee Richard Nixon went to the opposite extreme, insisting that all his ads consist of his speaking directly into the camera without a script. Such a strategy had paid big dividends with Nixon's 1952 "Checkers" speech, but the incident had given the candidate an exaggerated opinion of his communicative powers.

This fetish for appearing "real" rather than phony led Nixon to disaster during the first presidential debate ever televised. Arriving at the studio in the same light suit he had been wearing that day, Nixon blended into the background, while Kennedy's crisp dark suit cut a strong figure. Unshaven and, at first, refusing to be made up, Nixon relented to a compound called "Lazy Shave" to try to hide his stubble. As a result he appeared to be pale and drawn, while the made-up Kennedy seemed radiantly tanned and rested. Polling later showed that while radio listeners thought Nixon had won the debate, TV viewers judged the showdown heavily for Kennedy. The Republican had fallen behind and never quite caught up again.

The full power of political television was startlingly demonstrated in the presidential campaign of 1964 by the celebrated Madison Avenue ad firm of Doyle-Dane-Bernbach. Producing spot advertising for incumbent Lyndon Johnson, Doyle-Dane used a sophisticated mix of subtle scripting, dramatic visuals, and audience targeting to saddle challenger Barry Goldwater with the public image of a confrontational, unfeeling, itchy-fingered cowboy, ready to blow up the world in a nuclear showdown.

The most controversial and effective ad in the series depicted a small girl plucking petals from a daisy, her childish miscounting suddenly giving way to an ominous countdown over a loudspeaker. With the girl's face frozen in a frightful stare, the camera pulls in until the picture dissolves in her eye, as the count reaches zero. The screen then explodes into a mushroom cloud as Johnson's voice intones, "We must all love each other, or we must die." Considering Doyle-Dane had already alerted the public to Goldwater's seemingly casual attitude toward nuclear weapons (saying at one point that we could "lob one into the men's room of the Kremlin"), the inference was clear. So clear and so powerful, the ad aired only once; that was enough to make it a top TV news story for days; to have repeated it would have invited a backlash reaction from the electorate. As it was, Goldwater was buried under one of the largest presidential landslides ever.

ENTER: THE POLITICAL CONSULTANT

The enormous impact of the Johnson ad campaign followed on the heels of the great success Kennedy had achieved in 1960, with the first in-house campaign pollster, Lou Harris. Candidates suddenly recognized the value of professional assistance, and political consulting began to take shape as an industry.

Public-relations pros had been taking on candidates as clients since the 1930s, when the pioneering firm of Clem Whitaker and Leona Baxter used a series of newsreels to derail the frontrunning gubernatorial candidacy of socialist author Upton Sinclair, in California. But, now the political specialists arrived on the scene, leveraging their ability with modern technology, replacing the weakening party poohbahs as power brokers.

Among the early "communications giants" of the trade: Filmmaker **Charles Guggenheim** (Democrat), whose cinema verite style made his clients appear to be down-to-earth and in touch with the common people; strategist **David Garth** (bi-partisan), who favored a direct approach, having his candidates face the camera head-on and admit to their mistakes, and often opting for a scroll of the script as a visual; **Bob Goodman** (Republican), a producer of 30-second epics, replete with grand vistas, hordes of extras, and soaring music that he himself composed; recluse **Tony Schwartz** (Democrat), producer of the Daisy spot, who continued in politics after Doyle-Dane abandoned the field in 1968, becoming renown as a campaign doctor and brass-knuckle specialist; and the team of **Doug Bailey** and **John Deardourff** (moderate Republicans), whose five-minute mini-documentaries piled up warm-and-fuzzy goodwill for their clients.

Early pro campaign managers who directly usurped the role of the old party bosses: organizer/labor liaison **Matt Reese** (Democrat), a flexible co-opter of competing strategies, who once insisted "My greatest talent is having the taste to know what is good enough to steal;" strategist **Clif White** (conservative Republican), who masterminded the right-wing takeover of the Republican Party in 1964 with the first massive grassroots effort fueled by common ideology; generalist **Joe Napolitan** (Democrat), who exported American campaign techniques overseas, working in more than 20 countries and representing several chiefs of state; and candidate svengali **Stu Spencer** (Republican), who guided the transformation of Ronald Reagan from faded B-movie idol to president, and became the GOP's top West Coast tactician.

Pioneers in political numbers-crunching included the brilliant scientist **Richard Wirthlin** (Republican), another long-time Reagan hand, who developed complex computer models of multiple regression analysis that are able to accurately forecast the impact of a political decision on a future election; enfant terrible **Pat Caddell**, who, at the age of 22, helped George McGovern capture the 1972 Democratic presidential nomination with his almost mystically perceptive readings of voter disaffection; and theorist **Lance Tarrance** (Republican), a master at predicting the behavior of voter sub-groups and strategizing the building of ideological coalitions.

The famous Johnson "Daisy Ad"

And of course, the money men, the people whose hi-tech methods spawned economic independence from the bosses and organizations: Civil rights attorney **Morris Dees**, who raised several million dollars for McGovern with a single, nine-page fundraising letter; right wing avatar **Richard Viguerie** who established the financial underpinnings of the modern conservative movement by using direct mail to tap into a huge small-donor base for third-party presidential candidate George Wallace in 1968; and liberal money-maker **Roger Craver,** the first virtuoso at squeezing political money out of commercial mailing lists.

By the 1970's, having one or more of these thoroughbreds in your campaign stable often proved more valuable in establishing candidate viability than nabbing the endorsement of the local chief executive, party organization, or newspaper. Donors began opening up their wallets and reporters their notepads when a candidate spoke, based upon the reputation of their consultants. Television became the new political boss in every market; those who could dominate the airwaves and master the nuances of the tube's astounding communicative powers, became almost certain winners at the ballot box.

A REASSURANCE

Okay, so it's clear that election campaigns have always been fraught with cynical gamesmanship, manufactured images, and special interest war chests. Often they have turned on the most superficial of appearances. Does that mean that the current voter rebellion over the pay raises, check bouncing, perk padding, double talking, and influence peddling of our elected officials is doomed to come up empty? Not completely. History has also shown that once their mortality rate increases, public-office holders became amazingly receptive to the common voter. No, democracy isn't pretty; the shenanigans it breeds can make the product seem cheap and inefficient. But the process *will* cause government to reflect the will of the governed, as long as the governed make that will known. And besides, it can be fun.

PART II:
RULES & MECHANICS

CONTROLLING OUR DESTINY:
THE ACT OF VOTING

The means by which we select our leadership has evolved into a complex system that is, paradoxically, more democratic and more exclusive than at any other point in our history: More democratic in that the rules of procedure are now more open in terms of participation and public scrutiny; more exclusive in that the means of achieving success are increasingly becoming a trade secret. First we will outline the seemingly democratic rulebook of today's electoral process; then we will trace the arcane means by which elections are actually won in the real world of today.

American citizens can effect public policy through a variety of civic activities. By speaking out at local zoning or school board hearings, they can directly control and mold governmental policy. Displaying a political bumper sticker or simply tying a yellow ribbon around a tree are also meaningful vehicles for political expression. But the most important and effective political activity in America is the selection of government leaders through the ballot.

In the United States today, voting is a privilege granted to each law-abiding adult citizen who has lived in the same residence for at least 30 days and has registered his or her name, age, and address with local election authorities, but that was not always the case. At the birth of the nation, voting had been restricted to literate property owners who were of a specific race and sex, and in some states, religion was even a qualification. But as years passed, the groups of people who felt alienated by these qualifications made their grievances known, and these restrictions were eventually removed.

While knowing who to vote for—and why—often requires making difficult decisions, the physical action of voting is as easy as going to your local precinct (polling location), the address of which is recorded on your voter registration card. While registering to vote may have been subject to difficult or confusing procedures in the past, a recently enacted federal "motor voter" law promises to make the process much easier. Now you can simply check an additional box on your next motor vehicle license application, or tax filing, or fill out a voter registration form picked up at your local library.

In colonial times, most voting was done publicly by voice vote, and voters were often cheered or mocked as they indicated their preferences. By the mid-1800's, political parties began to pass out paper ballots for voters to fill out; but because each party had its own colored ballot and the ballot box was in public view, voters were still subject to the political pressure of powerful party organizations. But beginning in 1888, election reforms brought a new system of voting to America. Originating in Australia, the "secret" ballot tempered the amount of influence political organizations had in elections, allowing everyone to vote their conscience without repercussion. The new system called for ballots to be printed by non-partisan election officials at the public's expense, listing all qualifying candidates from all parties on the same ballot. These were then passed out only to registered voters at official polling places, with the actual marking of the ballot taking place in privacy.

Voice-Voting in 1854 as depicted by George Poingham's "The Verdict of the People"

The Australian ballot is still used for general elections today, with two variations: the *office group ballot*—where all qualifying candidates from all parties are represented, arranged by elective office; or the *party column ballot* (or "Indiana ballot"), where all candidates are represented, but arranged by party—often with the option of pulling a single lever for the selection of all of the party's candidates for all offices. (More on parties later.)

AN ELECTION FOR ALL OCCASIONS

Once you have registered to vote and have located your voting precinct, you are ready to participate in all forms of governmental elections:

★ **General Elections** are the voters' final selections as to who they want to direct the government. Besides selecting individual public officials, the general election process ultimately determines which political party will control the different levels and branches of government. General elections for federal offices are held on the first Tuesday following the first Monday in November, in even-numbered years. In each of these federal elections, the entire House of Representatives and one-third of the Senate is elected. Presidential elections are held every four years. General elections for state and local offices may be scheduled for different dates than federal general elections, but they usually occur on the same date.

In addition, proposals and special issues that require a public vote will often occur during a general election. The plethora of choices that can be piled into a general election has given rise to critics of the "bed-sheet ballot," who claim that too many choices make the voter's decisions more difficult. Others feel that a truly democratic government requires as many voter choices as practicable.

* **Primary Elections** allow each party's rank-and-file membership to select the candidates who will represent the party in the general election later in the year. Two-thirds of the states use the *closed primary* system, whereby only voters who have pre-registered as party members may participate. In most of these states, independent voters cannot participate in a primary; others allow them to temporarily join a party on their way to the voting booth. One-third of the states use the *open primary* system, whereby voters do not have to identify their party preference. In an open primary, registered voters may choose which party ballot they shall use, sometimes in the privacy of a voting booth. Alaska and Washington State have <u>totally</u> open primaries where voters may choose candidates for each elected office from any party, with all the candidates listed on a single ballot. Many voters prefer the more open primary elections because they offer more freedom of selection; while many party members prefer the closed primaries because they make candidates more responsible to their party's membership.

The states will only hold primaries for parties that automatically qualify for the general election ballot. Parties usually achieve this "official" status by polling a certain portion of the vote in the last election for governor or president— usually five percent. Independent candidates and nominees of minor parties must qualify through the petition process.

(A more comprehensive explanation of primaries will be provided below, when we take up the nominating process.)

* **Special Elections** are held whenever an issue must be decided or an office must be filled by the voters before the next primary or general election. The latter occurs when elected representatives die or resign their office, with most states requiring such an election be held between 30 and 120 days of the vacancy. Special elections may also be called to put referendum issues to a public vote.

DIRECT DEMOCRACY

A referendum is a method by which voters may approve or reject legislation that is being considered by their local or state government. Many state laws require the legislature to refer certain decisions to a referendum (such as changes to the state constitution), which are known as "mandatory referendums." In other instances, an "optional referendum" will be voluntarily presented by the legislature so the electorate can vote on a controversial issue that the legislators don't want to decide on their own.

Another type of ballot question found in about half the states is the *popular referendum* or *initiative,* where voters may repeal policies legislated by the government, or go over its head and pass new legislation of their own device.

A voting machine in use

Activists gain a place on the ballot for such direct democracy by gathering a minimum number of qualified signatures during a prescribed window of time. These requirements vary widely from state to state: In North Dakota, at least two percent of the state's registered voters must sign an initiative petition to place it on the ballot; Arizona requires at least ten percent. Some states have only indirect initiatives, where the minimum amount of signatures puts the proposed legislation to an immediate vote in the legislature; only if it fails, is the measure put to a public vote.

LIFE OF THE PARTIES

When someone registers to vote in most of the United States, they are asked to identify their political party, or their preference to remain independent of affiliation. A political party is a voluntary group of citizens who organize to try to win elections, control government, and influence public policy with some common coordination. One may join a political party either formally—by becoming a staff member or volunteer at the local party office—or informally, merely by expressing a party preference when registering to vote. While there have only been two major parties on the American political scene for the last 140 years—the Democrats and the Republicans—there are many minor "splinter" parties as well, including the Libertarians, New Allies, Patriots, Populists, and Socialist Workers. But because the vast majority of its elected officials are either Democrats or Republicans, the U.S. political system is commonly referred to as a "two-party system."

Dictatorial nations—such as Cuba or the People's Republic of China—have only one legally recognized political party, but they qualify as "no-party" systems because the lack of competition leaves the party organization little more than a board of directors for the government. Other "free" nations— such as Italy, Germany or Japan—have several competitive parties with equal political strength and are referred to as "multi-party systems." Such systems usually arise from parliamentary democracies, where a majority of the legislative branch forms most of the executive branch, facilitating the formation of coalition governments. Under such circumstances it is not all-important for one party to gain a majority, because a temporary alliance can be formed among several parties sharing common goals.

President Ronald Reagan creates a photo opportunity by re-creating the old Whistlestop Campaign

off a given candidate's slate in a presidential primary is usually somewhat proportional to his or her popular vote, though the precise formula varies from state to state.

The presidential primary process is a lengthy series of contests that lasts nearly four months. It's drawn-out format gives the candidates the opportunity to gain name recognition with the public and offers an opportunity for the ultimate winner of the nomination to define and refine their political message. As the stronger candidates gain public support (usually determined by campaign contributions and random polling), the weaker candidates will drop out of the race. This winnowing process has been extremely effective in reaching consensus nominees; the last presidential nomination actually determined at a major party convention was more than 40 years ago.

NOMINATING CANDIDATES

One of the major functions of a political party is to nominate members to represent it in races for elective office. Today, that is usually accomplished through primary elections, where registered members of the party (or, in some states, merely voters who ask for a particular party ballot at the polls) select a nominee from a list of candidates who have qualified for the ballot, either by paying a fee, collecting signatures on a petition, or both. Most southern states have a primary provision which calls for a runoff between the two top finishers if no one receives a majority in the primary. Although this system has been under attack in recent years by black activists who charge it is racially motivated, it in fact stems from the old days of one-party rule in Dixie, when the Republicans were so weak there that general elections were rendered meaningless. Using the primary runoff as a general election substitute lives on today in Louisiana, where everybody runs in a common primary race and the runoff slots are awarded to the two top vote-getters, regardless of party.

Several state parties hold a series of local caucuses among rank-and-file members, culminating in a state convention where candidates receive the party's endorsement if they achieve a certain percentage of the delegate vote. Party-endorsed candidates typically receive immediate financial and organizational assistance, even if they still face a primary. If a candidate loses at the state convention, most such systems will allow them to contest in a primary if they polled a significant portion of the delegate vote. Only in Virginia can a party select its statewide nominees by convention, with no recourse whatever to a primary.

Major party presidential nominations are won at national conventions, with more than two-thirds of the delegates having been selected through primaries, about a fifth through caucus/convention systems, and the remainder by virtue of the office they hold. The number of delegates selected

OTHER PARTY FUNCTIONS

Both state and national party conventions also concern themselves with the writing of a *platform*—a written statement of the official public-policy positions and political philosophy of the party. Although drafted by committees, each component or *plank* in the platform can be challenged on the floor of the full convention, if a substantial number of committee members wish to present an alternative or *minority report*. Very seldom are party members— or even party nominees—required to support the positions taken by the party platform, but these documents are a good indicator of where we might find the ideological heart and soul of these organizations.

The support that party organizations provide to their nominees for the general election campaign is often crucial to success. The sums of money they can contribute directly to their candidate's campaign committee are usually limited by law, but can be very substantial. In addition, parties can provide assistance in the form of: 1) expert advice; 2) "generic" advertising for the entire *ticket* (i.e., roster of candidates); and 3) "foot soldier" volunteers for both door-to-door canvassing and phone banking, whether the objective be fundraising, voter persuasion, "get-out-the-vote" (GOTV), or poll-watching on Election Day.

To expand their base and prospects of success, parties conduct voter-registration drives or political rallies, inviting potential voters to share fellowship, food, and entertainment while getting acquainted with the party's candidates. Most party organizations publish newsletters and/or produce cable TV shows to coordinate the activities of their activists and report on current public-policy issues. Such voter education provided by the parties will usually be quite biased and supportive of the party's positions, but nevertheless brings many important policy debates to the attention of the general public.

A prime funding source for such activities is "legal loophole" or "soft" money. First provided for by the Federal Election Campaign Act amendments of 1979, such party-dispensed funds are raised by the campaigns of the major party presidential nominees (who are themselves publicly financed and prohibited from raising money for their own campaigns). In 1988, for example, Bush and Dukakis were allotted $46 million each in public funds, earmarked for that purpose by a check-off on income tax forms. Supposedly that was all they could spend, but together they raised $47 million more in "soft" money, which was spent on state party affiliates for get-out-the-vote drives and other promotions where the race was close. That allowed Dukakis and Bush to spend more public funds on such items as television advertising than they otherwise would have been able to.

During his Presidential Campaign, Bill Clinton creates a photo opportunity by conversing with minority children

While contributions to a federal candidate's campaign committee are limited to $1,000 per election, "soft" money contributions are far less constricted. In 1988, both parties came up with a concept called "Team 100," in which individuals and corporations contributed $100,000 each. Common Cause says the Republican Team 100 was "a veritable Who's Who of American business," including 66 in the investment and banking community, 58 in real estate and construction, another 17 in the oil industry and 15 from agribusiness.

Among the contributors were many who had substantial matters pending with federal agencies, such as Frank Lorenzo, chairman of Eastern Airlines, which was then faced with a strike. Following his election, Bush rejected arbitration of the dispute, recommended by the National Mediation Board—the first time in the board's history a president had declined to take its advice. Eastern also later landed a $52 million government contract to provide air travel to federal workers.

PARTY POOPERS

Steadily increasing numbers of voters do not directly identify with a particular political party, even though they may register as members to avoid being disenfranchised during the primary round of elections. Such people consider themselves free from party obligation, and "vote for the man" (or woman) on a case-by-case basis. These "ticket-splitters" should not be confused with organized parties that use the word "independent" in their name—such as George Wallace's American Independent Party of a generation ago. According to Federal Election Commission data, the percentage of voters who identify themselves as independent of political parties has risen from approximately 19 percent in 1970, to over 35 percent in 1992. Much of this decline in party identification is due to a growing public sentiment that neither major political party is adequately keeping up with the changing times, or effectively representing the needs or views of the common people.

The most recent shake-ups of the two-party system came in 1980, when independent presidential candidate John Anderson drew seven percent of the popular vote; and again in 1992, when the independent candidacy of Ross Perot drew enough public support to make the presidential election a competitive three-way race, ultimately drawing nearly a fifth of the vote. While the two major parties are still effective at the polls and quite powerful, it appears that the growing movement toward independent politics may soon spawn a multi-party system.

OF SPECIAL INTEREST

Another reason for the decline in party membership may be found in the growing participation of pressure-group organizations. Many citizens feel that they can have a greater impact on government by supporting groups more particularly suited to their policy goals, whether they be motivated by ideology or self-interest. Such support is usually demonstrated through financial donations solicited by mail, but can also take the form of contacting government offices on cue or performing volunteer work. Since these special interest groups are not legal parties, they don't have ballot status in the electoral process. But their money and considerable influence with their adherents make them major forces, in both the crafting of public policy and the conduct of the electoral process.

In general, pressure groups fall into six broad categories: 1) *Public interest* groups that attempt to affect change by concentrating on a specific issue. For example, Common Cause focuses on government reform while Public Citizen focuses on the issues of consumer protection and abuse of power. 2) *Civil rights* groups such as the NAACP (National Association for the Advancement of Colored People) and NOW (National Organization of Women) address special needs associated with gender, age, and even national origin. 3) *Labor* groups such as the AFL-CIO represent the interests of common workers.

4) *Business* groups such as The Chamber of Commerce or the National Savings and Loan League push for policy favorable to corporate America. 5) *Professional* groups such as The National Education Association and the American Medical Association seek to influence issues that have a direct bearing on the trades of their members. 6) *Agricultural* issues are the area of farm groups such as the National Grange or the American Farm Bureau Federation, with some geared more toward the personal interests of the family farm, others the bottom line of large agribusinesses.

These pressure groups affect public policy in various ways: by lobbying in the halls of the legislature—wielding the influence of their money and membership as a carrot or stick—or through legal recourse, arguing their case in court (last year such groups were responsible for more than 60 percent of all cases brought before the Supreme Court). But such groups come to bear most effectively in the electoral process.

Once a pressure group officially endorses a candidate—either by a vote of its board, convention delegates, or rank-and-file membership via mail poll—it may provide money, volunteers or favorable publicity through its organs of communication. Federal law strictly regulates such activities with regard to federal elections, and most state laws emulate these same regulations, to some degree, in their state and local elections codes.

Pressure groups are required to conduct their federal election activities through officially registered organizations known as political action committees (PACs). Individuals are limited to a per PAC donation ceiling of $5,000 per year; the PACs themselves can give each candidate's campaign a maximum of $5,000 in both the primary and general elections. If a PAC elects to conduct an *independent expenditure campaign* (IEC) for or against a candidate in a particular race, there are no limits set on what they can spend. They must administer the IEC themselves, however, maintaining a total communications ban on the candidate campaigns involved.

Pressure groups have a natural inclination to focus only on their own parochial interests, usually involving a single issue. That degree of concentration of resources can often warp the perspective of those charged with crafting public policy, and the overall "common good" suffers. Lawmakers too often seem to sense: "I don't represent people; I represent votes. And if supporting one side of an issue will sway more net votes my way than my taking the other side, the public interest be damned."

ENTRENCHING THE PLAYING FIELD

The time, place, and manner of holding elections is generally prescribed by state law; but the U.S. Constitution requires that members of any legislative body (except the U.S. Senate) represent constituencies equivalent in population, to ensure equal representation for all citizens. There are currently 435 congressional districts; the number may be changed by a simple act of Congress, but it has not seen fit to do so in nearly a century. Following each decennial census, the number allotted each state is refigured according to the new population totals in a process known as *reapportionment*. All districts—state, local, and federal—

THE GERRY-MANDER!

must be redrawn every ten years, soon after the results of each U.S. Census are released. While election activity is overseen by each state's secretary of state, the state legislature is charged with the redrawing of districts. In some states, the governor may veto a redistricting plan, in others he has no direct influence.

While districts must be drawn with contiguous boundaries, the process often gets quite creative. Throughout history, the dominant party in each state has drawn these boundaries to maximize its own partisan advantage—a technique called *gerrymandering*, in honor of an early, accomplished practitioner, Gov. Elbridge Gerry of Massachusetts. After Gerry and his supporters had finished redrawing the state's districts to their own advantage in 1812, a painter visiting a local newspaper office saw a map of the strangely shaped configurations on the wall. He outlined a particularly imaginative district, penciled in a head, wings, and claws, and commented that it now looked like a salamander. "Better say a Gerrymander!" the editor replied, noting the Governor's hand in its creation. The newspaper published the embellished rendering under that title, and the name has stuck, as a term for manipulative redistricting.

Gerrymandering usually involves placing as many of the opposing party's members as possible in a minimum number of districts, while spreading the adherents of the ruling party out among the other districts in numbers sufficient to carry a majority. The result: huge, wasteful landslides for the minority party in a small number of districts; modest, efficient victories for the majority party in a large number of districts. The results of such shenanigans were amply demonstrated in California in 1984, when the statewide popular vote for Congress was evenly split between the parties, while the Democrats took a 27-18 (60 percent) majority of the congressional seats.

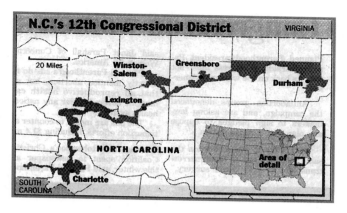

An old tactic used by majority parties to manipulate the vote was to draw districts without regard for population size. Following a remap in 1962, Michigan's largest congressional district contained over 800,000 people, while the smallest district contained fewer than 180,000 people. Finally, the Supreme Court ruled that such unequal representation was in violation of the constitutional principal of "one person-one vote," and that all districts must be virtually equal in population.

The Court has been reluctant to cage the partisan gerrymander, however, terming the process "a political thicket." Racially motivated gerrymandering had been held unconstitutional when it involved the attempted disenfranchisement of minorities, but 1984 amendments to the Voting Rights Act resulted in a wave of racial gerrymandering aimed at *increasing* minority representation following the 1990 census. The Court's preliminary ruling on this latest practice indicates it will be tolerated only if practiced in moderation. The case before it involved a North Carolina "median strip" district sprawled across the state along an interstate highway. The enclave was so narrow for so much of its course that a legislator who helped draw it—and later ran to represent it—boasted that "if you drive down that highway with both doors open, you'll kill half the constituents."

AND THE WINNER IS...

After an election when the polls close, election officials at each precinct count the votes and report their returns to either the city or county election board or commission. The city and county officials will then combine their returns and forward them to the state election board or commission, which is headed by the secretary of state. All of the state's regional returns are then totaled, and in a few days that state issues certificates of election to each of the winning candidates. Since newspaper, radio, and television reporters cover the elections very closely, they will be able to report the winners long before the certificates are issued.

In US presidential races, however, the voters do not directly elect the President. Whether or not citizens are qualified to choose a President was a hotly debated issue at the Constitutional Convention of 1787. Most delegates felt that voters lacked sufficient knowledge of the abilities and qualifications of the candidates to make an informed decision, leading many to believe that Congress should appoint the President. Opponents of this philosophy were quick to point

out that such a system would jeopardize executive independence. The compromise solution was the creation of the *Electoral College,* with each state being allotted the same number of presidential electors as its combined number of senators and representatives in Congress. (The District of Columbia—which has no voting representation in Congress—is allotted three electors.) Each presidential candidate on the general election ballot is listed with a slate of electors pledged to his or her candidacy. The slate of whichever candidate polls the most popular votes is then selected to represent the state, in the Electoral College.

The College never meets as a national body, but each state's slate of electors convenes in its respective state capitols about a month after the election and cast their ballots for President. By custom or state mandate—*not* Constitutional law—electors vote for the candidate to whom they were pledged at the time of the election. The sealed ballots are then sent to Washington where, in early January, the Vice President opens and counts the ballots before a joint session of Congress. To win, a candidate must receive at least a simple majority—270 electoral votes. If a majority does not exist,, the House of Representatives decides the winner. That has happened on two occasions, with Thomas Jefferson being chosen in 1800, and John Quincy Adams in 1824. In addition, Presidents Rutherford B. Hayes and Benjamin Harrison ran second in the national popular vote, but were elected by virtue of their majorities in the College.

Repeated attempts to change this controversial and unpopular system have failed, most recently in 1977-79, when President Jimmy Carter proposed legislation that would have selected presidents via the national popular vote. Such a change is difficult, as it requires a Constitutional amendment ratified by 38 states, and most small states—over-represented in the College by virtue of their equal number of senators—fear that scrapping the system would diminish their influence.

In all other American elections, if the winner prevails by a very slim margin—or if there is reason to believe that there have been serious irregularities in the balloting—a recount may be called for by the state election authority. In extreme cases where winning candidates stand accused of corrupting the election process, the courts or Congress may disqualify the winning candidate, or a special runoff election may be held.

Presuming all is on the up-and-up, the election winners will go on to claim victory before their jubilant, adoring supporters, while the runners-up sullenly deliver their concessions of defeat. If the often grueling campaign process has not been abused, the losing candidates will congratulate the winner, assuring their supporters that the victor is qualified for the job and deserves their cooperation. The winners, in turn, will laud their fallen opponents for a race well-run and helping to bring the issues before the public; then they will enjoy their victory celebration while they can, before preparing for the hard work of governing.

PART III:
THE REAL-WORLD

PRACTICE & REFORM

In the heyday of the old political machines, political campaigns commonly used tactics ranging from the aggressive-but-legal (e.g., networking resources and capital), to gray areas (promising favors and special treatment), to outright criminal activity (vote buying and intimidation). Such raw abuse of power is rare in these politically sophisticated times, but the onslaught of technological advance has brought a new set of moral challenges to the political arena. Reforming our electoral process remains a constant struggle after several generations of conflict—and it has sometimes brought unintended consequences. Today, public interest groups are fighting to broaden voting participation, tighten campaign finance scrutiny, promote meaningful campaign communications, and diminish the role of special interest groups in the election process. As a result, American voting systems are constantly changing—usually in the direction of increasing fairness.

Whether or not an individual exercises his or her political rights is strongly determined by political socialization—a process largely influenced by the family, though it is also a primary function of the public school system. For several generations, sources have been teaching Americans from an early age to honor a particular social value system—though increasingly those values are being impacted by friends, TV commercials, popular songs, and even comedic monologues.

Because of this socialization, virtually all Americans share very fundamental political beliefs, such as freedom of speech and use of the democratic process in determining the role of government. Such fundamental shared beliefs bring valuable stability to the American political system. The primary tenet of American political values was perhaps best expressed by Abraham Lincoln in the Gettysburg Address,

when he outlined the cause of liberty as "government of the people, by the people, and for the people."

But today, perhaps more strongly than at any time in the past, the American people sense that they have been disconnected from their elected leaders and representatives. Often it appears we are ruled by a government of the elite, or by morally bankrupt politicians who are backed by powerful special interests. As we have already seen, this perception is substantially accurate. How has the pure promise of American democracy come to this? What can we do to restore it?

At the core of the problem, according to keen observers on both sides of the political spectrum, are the modern corruptions of campaign finance and the administrative state. The latter refers to the often uncontrolled growth of government bureaucracy, which in turn is heavily influenced—and often fueled—by special interest groups. According to a 1991 report from the Heritage Foundation—a conservative think tank that heavily influenced the Reagan Administration—the mutual powers and dependencies of this "iron triangle.... create government by backroom deal making." The net effect on members of Congress, according to the report, is to lead them into using the system "to retain office, often regardless of their political views or actions, by acting and campaigning first and foremost as ombudsmen...and their ability to deliver pork." Heritage also notes that campaign spending and its rapidly escalating cost is a key element of the administrative-state syndrome.

STATESMEN FOR SALE

In response to the growing outcry over the corrupting influence of special-interest money in Washington, a variety of reforms have been proposed in Congress in recent years. One that succeeded was the elimination of honoraria (paid to congressmen for speeches and articles), enacted by the House while it simultaneously boosted its pay.

Table 1: TRENDS IN CONGRESSIONAL CAMPAIGN FINANCE

Cycle	Total Spending in '92 Dollars (millions)	PAC Money as % of Total	Winners' Portion of Money	# of Candidates	# of Successful Challengers
1982	$504	24%	70%	2,240	33
1984	$512	26%	75%	2,036	24
1986	$586	28%	76%	1,873	14
1988	$548	30%	80%	1,792	10
1990	$479	32%	81%	1,759	16
1992	$678	27%	71%	2,956	49
1994	$740	24%	54%	2,378	40

Such extraordinary figures, according to most observers, indicate that our political system may be driven by private money, effectively closing it to all but an elite, wealthy minority, or ones who can raise such campaign funds.

Campaign finance reform has been a tougher nut to crack, partly because most proposals would lessen incumbents' advantages, but mostly because each method of reform has its own partisan implications.

Republicans tended to be supportive of PACs during their first years of existence in the 1970's; but by the mid-1980's, Democrats had become adept at leveraging their committee control into big bucks from impacted industries. PAC money began to tilt toward the Democrats, and Republicans suddenly decided they should be done away with. Conversely, Democrats would like to limit spending on congressional races as —all things being relatively equal—Republicans usually has a fundraising advantage because of their closer business ties. But the Supreme Court has ruled that such limits are legal only when entered into voluntarily by the candidates. That requires the enticement of public matching money, which Republicans are dead-set against.

These partisan inclinations have made for some artful gamesmanship in recent years. In 1990, for example, the Democratic Congress loaded up a campaign finance bill with every popular reform imaginable—including a ban on PACs—most of which a majority of Democrats were actually against. They knew, however, that President Bush would have to veto the bill because of the presence of spending limits and public financing. As expected, Bush vetoed the heavily window-dressed bill and had to take the heat as the enemy of reform.

As federal politicians continued to resist cleaning up their campaign act, special interests strengthened their control over the process. From 1974 to 1982, money spent on congressional campaigns increased a whopping 94 percent in constant dollars (after accounting for inflation). Over the next eight years, real federal campaign spending began to flatten and then decline as the increasingly closed buddy system of Washington began to tighten its grip on the electoral process, choking off competition.

Looking at the revealing statistical trends in Table 1, we find plain evidence of a fascinating cause-and-effect interconnection: a rise in special interest influence over elections corresponding with declining candidate competition and increased incumbent security. Over the four campaign cycles from 1982 to 1988, the trends persisted: PAC share of campaign dollars, up; proportion of PAC money to winners, up; number of candidates, down; number of successful challengers, down.

Those trends continued in the 1990 cycle with an important exception: growing voter anger over the unresponsive elitism of Washington nudged six more incumbents out of office, despite a dearth of qualified competition; the number of challengers who had previously held elective office had declined by 52 percent since 1982. The flood of resentment began spilling over the levees in 1992, aided by redistricting. PAC shares of campaign contributions and winners declined sharply, candidacies zoomed 69 percent higher, and incumbent casualties more than tripled, even though 77 members of Congress had already shown themselves the door. Even campaign consultants had cause to celebrate, as the markedly increased competition pushed total campaign spending up 42 percent in constant dollars.

THE REVOLUTION RETURNS?

These encouraging developments appear to have continued into the 1994 cycle: PAC shares were down and retirements remained high, though candidacies have declined somewhat since the redrawing of the district lines. How is this sudden upheaval being accomplished? Will it continue? Will it succeed in rekindling government's responsiveness to the general population?

While polls indicated that public discontent was present at the time of the 1990 elections, there was very little organization present to conduct that energy. The previous elections had only confirmed the growing and nearly complete invincibility of incumbents: 98 percent had secured re-election to the House. In 1982, incumbents outspent the combined totals of all their challengers by more than 2:1; by 1990 the ratio was 11:3. Anyone with a lick of political sense could see it was foolish to take on those kinds of odds.

But by 1992, conditions were changing. Faced with the growing prevalence of term limits (pushed through by grassroots initiatives) legislators, city councilmen, and school board members began trying to kick themselves upstairs, taking on incumbents for higher office that they otherwise would not have dared challenge. Women's groups began raising money by the millions to crack the glass ceiling of power with candidates of their own. Ross Perot emerged to cajole incumbents into responsibly discussing the issues and to encourage the politically powerless to assert themselves in the electoral arena.

Lo and behold, the entertainment moguls running the television networks discovered there was actually an audience—a HUGE audience—for programs that brought the candidates and issues before the people in a readily understandable format. Presidential primary debates got surprisingly high ratings, Democratic nominee Bill Clinton revived his campaign by appearing on Arsenio Hall and MTV, and Perot swept his time period with "folksy professor" programs that co-starred a pointer and charts. When it was all over, turnout at the polls ran far ahead of projections, and the number of voters who said they had not learned enough to make an informed decision had been cut in half from 1988 (see Table 2).

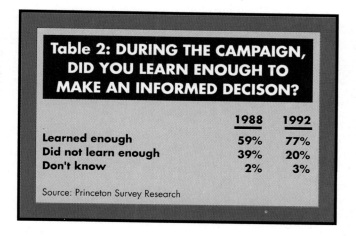

Table 2: DURING THE CAMPAIGN, DID YOU LEARN ENOUGH TO MAKE AN INFORMED DECISON?		
	1988	1992
Learned enough	59%	77%
Did not learn enough	39%	20%
Don't know	2%	3%
Source: Princeton Survey Research		

OVER THE RAINBOW

But has all the tumult really amounted to anything? Perhaps not as much as we might have expected. There has been some slight progress toward reducing the deficit, making the tax code more based on ability to pay, and reviving the economy; it appears we may even be getting more accessible and affordable health care before long. But there are strong indications that much of the huge congressional Class of '94—supposedly a phalanx of dedicated reformers—has already been corrupted to the ways of Washington (just as the huge congressional Class of '92 had been). Scores of them are pumping PACs for every dollar they can extort, dumping franked planeloads of self-serving propaganda at public expense, and helping the "old bull" leadership scuttle reforms in hopes of lucrative committee assignments.

One election cannot save the world, or even make it seem markedly better. Progress requires persistence. Victory demands vigilance. A functional democracy does not mean merely voting for someone who <u>says</u> he or she will represent the common interest; it's making sure the people in power actually <u>serve</u> the common interest. If they do not, bring new candidates along for the next election who will. Don't rely on whatever choice the elite clique of politicos might be willing to let you have. **Make your own choices!**

Unlike a scant four years ago, today's New Populism has plenty of infrastructure from which the common agenda can be pushed. **United We Stand, America** is pursuing an ambitious strategy of voter education, election reform, and deficit reduction. **The Concord Coalition** is holding the feet of Congress to the fire with aggressive lobbying in behalf of fiscal responsibility, while **Citizens Against Government Waste** exposes the most embarrassing and destructive practices of a mindless bureaucracy, left to its own devices.

Americans for Tax Reform is mounting initiative efforts in several states to institute a voter veto over state and local tax boosts. **U.S. Term Limits** is having great success bringing back the concept of the citizen legislature through the initiative process, while the **Term Limits Legal Institute** is helping to accomplish the same thing through the courts. **The Christian Coalition** has constructed an information network whereby millions of churchgoers are informed of candidates' positions on moral issues, while **People for the American Way** stand guard over civil liberties.

The Independence (a.k.a. **Patriot**) **Party** is fielding viable radical/centrist candidates across the country who promise to shake the Republicrat/good ole boy/elitist network to its roots. And there are always those old standbys for government reform, **Common Cause** and Ralph Nader's **Public Citizen.**

All of these groups are having a profound effect on our electoral process, as witnessed by the campaigns and returns of 1992 and 1994; but they will dry up and blow away without the support of citizens determined to reclaim their government. They are there to enable <u>you</u> to assert control, but they cannot do it for you.

That is up to you alone.

GLOSSARY
for How The Election Process Works
(continued)

Ombudsman
1. A man who investigates complaints, reports findings, and mediates fair settlements, especially between aggrieved parties such as consumers or students and an institution, an organization, or a company.
2. A government official, especially in Scandinavian countries, who investigates citizens' complaints against the government or its functionaries.

Partisan
1. A fervent, sometimes militant supporter or proponent of a party, cause, faction, person, or idea.
2. Devoted to or biased in support of a party, group, or cause: partisan politics.

Patronage
1. a. The power to distribute or appoint people to governmental or political positions. b. The act of distributing or appointing people to such positions. c. The positions so distributed or filled.

Political Machine
1. An organized group of people whose members are or appear to be under the control of one or more leaders; often a dominant political force or group, advocating reforms for the common people, but increasingly controlled by the privileged classes.

Populist/Populism
1. A supporter of the rights and power of the people.

Precinct
1. a. A subdivision or district of a city or town under the jurisdiction of or patrolled by a specific unit of its police force.
2. An election district of a city or town.

Progressive Era
1. As a result of the cumulative scientific, economic, and political changes which occured during the nineteenth century, it is considered to be a turning point in history, commonly referred to as "the progressive era."

Pundit
1. A source of opinion; a critic: a political pundit.
2. A learned person.

Robber Baron
1. One of the American industrial or financial magnates of the latter 19th century who became wealthy by unethical means, such as questionable stock-market operations and exploitation of labor.
2. A feudal lord who robbed travelers passing through his domain.

Special Interests
1. A person, a group, or an organization attempting to influence legislators in favor of one particular interest or issue.

Trusts
1. A combination of firms or corporations for the purpose of reducing competition and controlling prices throughout a business or an industry.

Untenable
1. Being such that defense or maintenance is impossible.

CHAPTER 11

WHAT A CITIZEN CAN DO

by Mr. Steve Max
Regional Director – Citizen Action

Citizen
Action

GLOSSARY
for What a Citizen Can Do

Athens
1. The capital and largest city of Greece, in the eastern part of the country near the Saronic Gulf. It was at the height of its cultural achievements and imperial power in the fifth century B.C. during the time of Pericles and is considered to be the birthplace of democracy.

Bill
1. A draft of a proposed law presented for approval to a legislative body.

Boycott
1. To act together in abstaining from using, buying, or dealing with a specific product, company, or group, as an expression of protest or disfavor or as a means of coercion.

Bureaucracy
1. Administration of a government chiefly through bureaus or departments staffed with nonelected officials.
2. The departments and their officials as a group.
3. Management or administration marked by diffusion of authority among numerous offices and adherence to inflexible rules of operation.
4. An administrative system in which the need or inclination to follow complex procedures impedes effective action: innovative ideas that get bogged down in red tape and bureaucracy.

Coalition
1. An alliance, especially a temporary one, of people, factions, parties, or nations.
2. A combination into one body; a union.

Criteria
1. A standard, rule, or test on which a judgment or decision can be based.

Industrial Revolution
1. The complex of radical socioeconomic changes that took place in the late 18th century, which are brought about when the extensive mechanization of production systems resulted in a shift from home-based hand manufacturing to large-scale factory production.

Monopoly
1. a. A company or group having exclusive control over a commercial activity. b. A commodity or service so controlled.
2. Exclusive control by one group of the means of producing or selling a commodity or service.

Plutocracy
1. Government by the wealthy.
2. A wealthy class that controls a government.
3. A government or state in which the wealthy rule.

Robber Baron
1. One of the American industrial or financial magnates of the latter 19th century who became wealthy by unethical means, such as questionable stock-market operations and exploitation of labor.
2. A feudal lord who robbed travelers passing through his domain.

Suffrage
1. a. The right or privilege of voting; the franchise. b. The exercise of such a right.

Trusts
1. A combination of firms or corporations for the purpose of reducing competition and controlling prices throughout a business or an industry.

Tumultuous
1. Characterized by tumult; noisy and disorderly: tumultuous applause.
2. Confusedly or violently agitated.

WHAT A CITIZEN CAN DO

Mr. Steve Max
Regional Director - Citizen Action

"The humblest citizen in all the land, when clad in the armor of a righteous cause, is mightier than all the hosts of error."
— *William Jennings Bryan*

This chapter is a straightforward, nuts-and-bolts outline of community organizing essentials. It is based on a long history that has been passed from one generation to the next. It is part of a tradition, drawing strength from the fact that even in the most difficult times, ordinary Americans have made a difference. We have won victories and improved our lives. Take for example, the experience of one woman, Florence Kelley, who dared to challenge the power of the Robber Barons, and won.

19th CENTURY
SPECIAL INTEREST GROUPS

Robber Barons, Barons Of Industry, Barons Of Wall Street. J.P. Morgan, Rockefeller, Carnegie, Frick, Mellon, their names look down on us from the walls of universities, museums and libraries. Even those Americans who aren't exactly sure what a baron is, have heard of these men and of their great wealth and power. The time during which they rose to the leadership of American industry, the 1880's and 1890's, is known as the Gilded Age, in part because the number of American millionaires rose by over 300%. Their credo was simple and summarized elegantly by John D. Rockefeller himself: "Do you know the only thing that gives me pleasure? It's to see my dividends coming in." As to strengthening democracy in public life, the view of the robber barons was equally straight-forward. One of the wealthy men of the period boasted:

"The class I represent cares nothing for politics...It matters not one iota what political party is in power or what President holds the reins of office. We are not politicians or public thinkers; we are the rich; we own America; we got it, God knows how, but we intend to keep it, if we can, by throwing all the tremendous weight of our support, our influence, our money, our purchased senators, our hungry congressmen, our public-speaking demagogues into the scale against any legislature, any political platform, any Presidential campaign that threatens the integrity of our estate..."

How did it come about that a handful of people could say, without exaggeration, that they "own America"? To put it simply, before the 1880's, business believed in competition, after the 1880's, business believed in trusts and monopolies. Trusts were formed to regulate supply and prices in every branch of industry. When Andrew Carnegie went into the steel business, raw materials, iron ore, coal, and coke were bought from separate suppliers, but Carnegie had a different plan. He purchased iron mines, coal mines, railroads, ships on the great lakes, rolling mills, and he brought every branch of the industry into one company. To be sure, it was great accomplishment that increased production and lowered costs. What came next was more questionable. By 1901, Carnegie merged his company with the other largest steel mills to form United States Steel. By 1929, this giant monopoly controlled half to three-quarters of all the iron ore deposits in America. Carnegie was only repeating the success story of John D. Rockefeller's Standard Oil Company. In exchange for contracts to move his large volume of oil, Rockefeller told the railroads to charge his competitors higher rates than he paid. With higher transportation costs, other companies were unable to sell oil, and he bought them up at bargain prices. By 1904, Standard Oil controlled 86% of the oil market. The process was repeated in the sugar industry, where one company gained control of 98% of American production. It happened in the coal and lead industries, in rubber, autos, electrical, railroad and many others. As the historians Charles and Mary Beard, summarized the situation, "The idea... was to deliver goods, of a standard quality, promptly to merchants and consumers, as ordered, while making desperate and unremitting efforts to kill off competitors and maintain prices at a level yielding enormous profits."

Worse than price gouging was the shameless and cruel treatment of the American worker. With so great a concentration of wealth and power, the Robber Barons were able to keep wages ridiculously low.

Famous 19th century cartoonist, Joseph Keppler, depicts the Robber Barons as the "Bosses of the Senate" in one of his most famous cartoons

In 1883, weekly wages averaged between $7.50 and $8.00 (about equal to $62.00 dollars today) and the workday was ten to fourteen hours, sometimes longer. In Chicago, which was typical of industrial cities, rents in workers' tenement houses averaged around 40% of monthly wages. Thomas O'Donnell, a spinner in Fall River, Massachusetts, described conditions this way:

> "I have a brother who has four children, besides his wife and himself. All he earns is $1.50 a day. He works at the iron works at Fall River. He only works about nine months out of twelve. There are generally three months of stoppage...and his wife and family have to be supported for a year out of the wages of nine months...It does not stand to reason that those children and he himself can have natural food and be naturally dressed."

Needless to say, the Robber Barons lived differently.

> "At a dinner, eaten on horseback, the favorite steed was fed flowers and champagne; to a small black and tan dog, wearing a diamond collar worth $15,000, a lavish banquet was tendered; at one function, the cigarettes were wrapped in hundred dollar bills; at another, fine black pearls were given to the diners in their oysters; at a third, an elaborate feast was served to boon companions in a mine, from which came the fortune of the host."

Then, weary of such limited diversions, the plutocracy contrived more freakish occasions — with monkeys seated between the guests, human goldfish swimming about in pools, chorus girls hopping out of pies...

The contrast between rich and poor in the age of the Robber Barons is all the more shocking when we recall that the poor were not on welfare, but working far longer hours than does the middle class today, and that the rich derived much of their income not from the labor of adults, but from that of children. This is where Florence Kelley enters the story. Born in 1859, the daughter of a radical Republican congressman, her earliest recollection, at the age of five, was that of Lincoln's assassination. She became one of a remarkable group of reformers that included Jane Addams, Lillian Wald, Grace and Edith Abbott, and Dr. Alice Hamilton. Among her many organizational involvements, she was General Secretary of the National Consumers' League, a founder of the National Association for the Advancement of Colored People and a vice-president of the National Woman Suffrage Association, but the abolition of child labor was her life long goal.

A 19th CENTURY ACTIVIST

As is often the case with organizing today, Florence Kelley began with researching the problem. In 1889, she wrote a pamphlet, *Our Toiling Children*, dealing with the link between compulsory education and child labor. She reported that 1,118,000 children between the ages of ten and fifteen were employed in "every branch of industry in which the application of machinery renders child labor available." This figure would have made child labor equal to about 6% of the work force. Actually, it was a serious undercount. The Census Bureau only provided figures for working children over the age of ten, but Florence Kelley's research of state records found textile workers as young as five, and tenement house workers as young as four.

The lack of data to even define the problem brought her to an approach which is useful to citizen activists today: organize to win information. She and her allies began writing letters to the newspapers on the need for a competent investigation of child labor. This and her pamphlet led to an invitation to speak to the national convention of chiefs and commissioners of labor statistics. Although she was unable to attend, the paper she sent was read to the convention. It began with a criticism of data-collection methods, which today's citizen activists should note. Her example was a New York City Board Of Health report showing that, in proportion to population, fewer deaths occurred in tenement houses than other houses, an important statistic because many children were employed doing piece work in tenements. Florence Kelley revealed that in the New York report, the category of "tenements" included not only disease ridden slum buildings, the usual definition, but all apartment houses, even the finest with full sanitary facilities. She called for collecting detailed figures on working children by age, as well as for more frequent reports. With five or ten year gaps in reporting, she complained, the public is led to believe that the problem is corrected or diminishing.

The response of the delegates was typical of what activists so often hear. Impossible! "Parents will not tell the exact ages of their children." "Labor bureaus are not authorized or equipped in funds to do the type of census enumeration necessary." "...to compare conditions existing in a certain number of establishments at different periods...would be unreliable and misleading" "...the factory inspector reports directly to the legislature ..."

While many delegates derided Florence Kelly's ideas, she impressed the key participant, United States Labor Commissioner, Carroll D. Wright. He agreed that "the subject of child labor is so important that...investigation should be made whenever it is possible."

{In our own times, a senior citizen organization in Chicago complained to the police that seniors were particular victims of crime, especially on the days when the Social Security checks came. The police responded that they had no records showing that seniors were victims any more than other age groups. When the seniors inspected the records for themselves, they found that what the police said was literally true. There were no such records because crime reports didn't list the victim's age. Before they won extra protection for seniors, the organization, first, had to convince the police to record ages}

While the controversy over statistics continued, Florence Kelley took another step common to modern day organizing: She worked to convince important organizations, unions, women's groups, and temperance leagues to take up the child labor issue. She proposed a boycott of products made with child labor.

During this time, Florence Kelley helped found the Working Women's Society of the City of New York. She wrote many articles on child labor for national magazines, and attended the first convention of the American Economics Association. The Working Women's Society drew up a bill that was introduced in the New York legislature. Among other measures, it sought to reduce the work day for children to eight hours. It failed to pass, but agitation for similar legislation continued for years afterward.

In 1891, Florence Kelley went from being an advocate and writer to a community worker. Moving to Chicago, she joined the staff of that famous settlement house, Hull House, under the leadership of Jane Addams.

She wrote to a friend, "that over a thousand people a week came to Hull House for every purpose, from literacy classes to clubs and recreation, debates, union organizing meetings and help with finding work. The staff involved itself with the issues of the community including housing and sanitary conditions."

A 19th CENTURY COALITION

Florence Kelley's contact with the growing Chicago labor movement gave her a new base for her work in opposition to child labor. When she arrived in Chicago, factory communities were still seething in the aftermath of the Haymarket (police) Riot and the nationwide Eight Hour Day movement. Only five years before, in 1886, 80,000 Chicago workers had struck for the shorter work day. On the evening of May first, after a massive parade, a peaceful rally was held in Chicago's Haymarket Square.

Children, as young as five years old, working in textile factories during the Industrial Revolution

As the rally was ending, 180 policemen, with clubs drawn, marched into the crowd. Suddenly a bomb was thrown into the ranks of the police. Eight leaders of Chicago's Eight Hour Day movement were arrested for the bombing, although only two had actually been present at the scene. In the absence of hard evidence, the state tried to prove that the labor leaders were part of a conspiracy to overthrow the government. Articles they had written were read in court, and books found in their homes were quoted. Not even the judge, who sentenced them to death, pretended that the defendants had thrown the bomb. Said Judge Joseph E. Gary: "The conviction has not gone on the ground that they did actually have any personal participation in the particular act...but the conviction proceeds upon the ground that they had, generally, by speech and print, advised large classes to commit murder..."

It was as if the bombing had been a signal for a crackdown on the eight-hour movement. Hundreds of Chicago workers were arrested, meeting halls, newspaper offices, and private homes were broken into and ransacked, without search warrants. Suspects were beaten and tortured by the police. At the direction of the Robber Barons, the crackdown spread to other cities, with union officers arrested in Milwaukee, Pittsburgh, and New York, among other places. To add to the ferment, in 1892, as Florence Kelly was preparing to raise her child labor campaign to the state level, the major labor organization of the time, the Knights Of Labor, had met in convention with the leading populist farm organizations to form the People's Party. This was a presidential year and People's Party slates were running locally as well as nationally. Florence Kelley picked an opportune time to propose that the State Bureau Of Labor Statistics make a formal investigation of sweat shops. Not only was her idea accepted, but she was named a Special Agent of the bureau to undertake the study. Meanwhile, she continued her speaking and organizing. "On Monday, I told 64 Congregational Ministers about our neighbors of the cloak trade," she wrote to a friend.

**Members of the Woman's Suffrage Movement
at the turn of the century**

To counter the People's Party, Illinois Democrats successfully nominated John Peter Altgeld for Governor in the 1892 election. Altgeld, a strong liberal friend of labor, supported the reforms that Florence Kelley advocated.

It was an increasingly tumultuous year. The Robber Barons had never hesitated to use local police, the state militia, and even the United States Army as a private legion of strike-breaking thugs. They also subsidized the Pinkerton Detective Agency, in reality a para-military, strike-breaking organization. In July, 300 Pinkerton agents and the national guard had been brought into Homestead, Pennsylvania to break a strike at Carnegie's steel mills. The United States Army was dispatched to Cour D'Alene, Idaho, to arrest 1,200 striking miners. In Buffalo, New York, 6,000 armed militia broke a strike of railroad switchmen, and this was just the tip of the iceberg.

A 19th CENTURY VICTORY!

Bowing to pressure for reform that was building around the country, Congress, in July of 1892, instructed Labor Commissioner Wright to make a national investigation of city slums. Remembering Florence Kelley, he sought her out to work on the preliminary study for Chicago. Then, in July of 1893, with the Altgeld victory still fresh, the Illinois Legislature appointed Florence Kelley and another Hull House resident to guide its own study of sweat shop conditions. The Illinois study led to a comprehensive reform bill. It created a state factory-inspection department. It set strict sanitation standards for home workshops, and most important, it set a work day limit of eight hours for women, girls, and children, with fourteen years as the minimum age at which children might be employed. As soon as the bill was introduced, Florence Kelley and the Hull House staff organized a massive campaign for its passage. Building on the community work and labor support they had done over the previous year, they enlisted trade unions, churches, benefit societies, social clubs, and dozens of individuals. Jane Addams and Florence Kelley spent their evenings speaking to organizations, and their days organizing lobbying visits to the state capital by the members of many organizations. The bill passed overwhelmingly, and the Robber Barons figured that it was unimportant, as factory legislation always went unenforced in Illinois.

But the Robber Barons hadn't taken into account that now the governor was John Peter Altgeld, elected with the support of working people's organizations. He appointed, as the first Chief Factory Inspector Of Illinois, Florence Kelley. A few months later she wrote to a friend:

"The papers are so savage in their onslaught on us that I think we must be doing fairly good work. We have had no prosecutions, yet, under the new law... but I am preparing for a long series of them to begin next week and continue for a month or more. Meanwhile, the large manufacturers are obeying promptly and the little employers are bumptious, just in proportion to the badness of their shops."

Florence Kelley battled on, spending the rest of her long life campaigning to improve working conditions and abolish child labor. Her later activity with the National Consumer League led to another approach, educating consumers to buy only goods that the League could certify had been produced under humane conditions. Florence Kelley died in 1932, only six years before the passage of the Fair Labor Standards Act that included a ban on child labor, under the age of sixteen. Her dream was now the law of the land. In spite of the enormous power of her opponents, she had won.

DIRECT ACTION ORGANIZING

Bringing about change isn't just a matter of having a good idea, and while a few people are lucky enough to be in the right place at the right time, the process is usually slow and painstaking. Most of the people who have succeeded didn't think through every step or work according to a plan, but after looking at many examples, certain patterns do start to emerge that make planning possible. The most successful issue campaigns go through similar stages, and some methods work better than others. The task of this chapter is to make that experience explicit, so that you can learn from it.

There are many different kinds of organizations; some provide direct services for people, others educate people about issues, do public interest research, or encourage cultural events. There are organizations that advocate on behalf of people or issues. All of these are important in their own right, but all are different from the kind of organizing that will be the subject of this chapter. The type of organizing described here is called Direct Action Organizing. Here is an example of the differences: Suppose that the benches in the park near your home are broken. If you, or your organization, go and repair the benches, that is a direct service. You are doing a service for people who use the park. If you go to City Hall to convince the parks commissioner to fix the benches, that is advocacy. You are advocating on behalf of the people who use the park. If you set up classes to teach bench repair, that is self-help. The neighborhood people fix the benches themselves. On the other hand, if you call a meeting of the people who use the park, and the people at the meeting decide what solution they think would work best, and then they pressure the parks department or the city council to implement their solution, that is direct action organizing.

The people who are directly affected by the problem organize and take action against someone with the power to give them what they want. Direct Action Organizing means organizing people to take action on their own behalf.

The point is not that one approach is better than the others. In fact, often many kinds of organizing are needed. In her lifetime Florence Kelley did all of these things and, often, several of them at once. Here, we are speaking only about Direct Action Organizing.

THE THREE FUNDAMENTAL PRINCIPLES OF DIRECT ACTION ORGANIZATIONS:

1.   Win Real Victories that Improve People's Lives

The primary purpose for any Direct Action Organization to exist is to achieve concrete improvements in people's lives. Therefore, organizations should be assembled for the purpose of winning victories that will facilitate such improvements.

2.   Make People Aware of Their Own Power

Another purpose for Direct Action Organizations is to make people aware that they are not powerless against the system, and that they *can* make a difference in their society.

3.   Alter the Relations of Power by Building Staffed, Permanent and Strong Organizations

A well staffed Direct Action Organization that has a strong membership forms a permanent institution in the community that can assure fair treatment of that community's citizens. Such an institution will, effectively, alter the relations of power between the people of a community and those in power, such as elected officials, government agencies, and corporations. When we say that we want to "alter the relations of power," we mean building organizations that the people who make decisions about our lives will always have to take into account. We always want them to say, "What will that organization do if we do x?" Changing laws can alter relations of power; so can electing people. It is just as important to build a permanent organization as it is to win the issue, because experience shows that what is won this year can be taken away next year, if the organization that won it disappears. In Direct Action Organizing, building an organization is always as important as winning a particular issue.

FORMING A DIRECT ACTION ORGANIZATION

When we engage in Direct Action Organizing, we organize a campaign to win a specific issue that is a specific solution to a problem. An issue campaign usually goes through the following series of stages:

1.   People Identify a Problem

Some people have the luxury of choosing the problem they want to help solve, and then framing an issue to solve it. For other people, the problem chooses you. Poverty chooses you. Discrimination chooses you. Toxic chemicals, leaching from a dump near your home, chose you.

For the purpose of this discussion, it doesn't matter whether you chose the problem, or the problem chose you, because, in either case, you must still choose the issue. You, or actually your organization, must still choose the solution that you are going to try to win.

2.   People Form a "Core Organization"

All groups start from a small "core group" of concerned individuals that make the decision to take action. Often, they start with a single person, who puts together a few friends who would like to help solve a specific problem. They decide when and where they will meet to develop their strategy, and get organized. At that point, the process of social change has officially begun.

3.   The "Core Organization" Turns the Problem into an issue

There is an important difference between a problem and an issue. Organizations deal with problems. For example, rising taxes, crime, unemployment, discrimination, or solid waste incinerators are all problems. The problem is the thing that is wrong. We don't organize on problems, we organize on issues. That's a crucial distinction. An issue is a specific solution, or part of the solution to a problem. Getting more funding for education is an issue. Defeating a tax increase is an issue. Passing a bottle bill is an issue. These are partial solutions to problems. Whether or not you can successfully organize to solve a problem depends on your skill in finding the right way to frame the issue, so as to get the broadest support. (Organizers call that "cutting the issue").

For example, before the recent Disabilities Act was passed, a woman in a small New England town had tried and failed to get a wheelchair ramp built at the public library. She could never find enough people who cared about the problem to make the town vote to spend the money. As a result, her husband and son would carry her wheelchair up the library stairs with her in it, and leave her for the afternoon. She consulted a professional organizer who asked, "Suppose the fire alarm went off, then what would happen?" "I would be stuck at the top of the stairs," said the woman. "Then," said the organizer, "go and tell the Fire Chief that there is an unsafe condition in the library that prevents people from getting out, and his equipment from getting in." The Chief agreed, and the town had to build the ramp. By cutting the issue of the ramp as one of getting <u>out</u> of the library, instead of getting <u>in</u> to the library, the woman broadened her support.

Another example is depicted at a campus of a state university, where several of the dormitory buildings were flooded as the result of botched maintenance work by the University. The Student Association could have cut the issue narrowly, and got nothing more than compensation for the damaged property of students in those particular dorms. Instead, they cut the issue more broadly. Involving students from all the dormitories, they established that livable dormitories were a student right. The university agreed to refund dormitory fees for such violations as no heat or hot water, electric outages, and other problems, in addition to flooding.

THE FOUR MOST IMPORTANT MISTAKES TO AVOID WHEN FORMING A DIRECT ACTION ORGANIZATION

Don't Start By Hiring A Lawyer

You may need one later, but this is a sure way to short circuit the process of getting lots of people involved and active. The group ends up doing little more than raising money to pay the lawyer, and the lawyer often discourages a more activist approach.

Don't Start By Drafting By-Laws

Only legally chartered corporations need by-laws right away, and even those can be minimal. There is a kind of person who loves discussing by-laws more than anything in the world. If they are attracted to your group, they will bore everyone else to death. Establish an active program first and keep the structure informal for six months

Don't Start By Holding Elections

The principle test of leadership is who can get the most people involved, not who can talk the best game. If you hold elections before you have activities, you will elect the best talkers.

Don't Start With A Huge Research Project

So many groups never get beyond the research stage. Yes, you do have to have the basic facts right, but that alone won't give you a victory and you aren't being graded on it.

DEVELOPING THE ORGANIZATION'S ISSUE

In general, Direct Action Organization meetings will be better attended and more interesting if they are used to make decisions, rather than presenting reports and updates. Group decision making works best when clear alternatives are presented. This is particularly true for larger organizations. It should be the job of the leadership, steering committee, or whoever plans the meetings, to frame the alternatives for each decision to be made. Of course, the members are free to reject the choice of alternatives and start over, but even doing that helps to clarify the problem and moves the group forward. The worst possible meetings are those where everyone sits around for a while until, finally, someone says "Well, what would you like to talk about?"

It should be the goal of every organization to spend as little time in meetings as possible, and as much time as possible out doing something. Meetings should be planned to last for an hour-and-a-half, two hours tops.

Don't start by putting up the list of criteria for a good issue. Instead, ask the members of your group what <u>they</u> think the criteria are. Put them up in the front of the room. Allow discussion of each suggestion (with time limits).

Many of the criteria presented here will emerge from the group, along with others that are specific to the local situation. If any major ones are omitted, you can add them.

Suggest that the group narrow its criteria list to not more than 15 or so, tops. After a large majority is happy with the criteria, list the alternatives among which the group must decide, and ask which best meet the criteria. The criteria take into account something that many of us don't normally consider: the impact of the issue on the organization we are building, in addition to the impact of the issue on the problem.

How do you decide on, or "cut," issues in order to make them understandable and significant to your constituents? Here is a check list of the criteria that an issue should meet:

1.   The Issue Must Be Worthwhile

For any Direct Action Organization to be successful, it must represent an issue that is of great public concern. To expect people to go out of their way and to get involved in your crusade, it must be a worthwhile cause. While the color of your community's curbing may be bothersome to you, it is questionable whether you would be able to get a substantial amount of support for that issue. Decide what the long and short term goals of your Direct Action Organization will be, talk to some people about them, and determine whether it is an issue that the majority of people will find worthwhile.

2.   The Issue Must Be Winnable

While virtually nothing is impossible, you do need to determine whether your goals can realistically be achieved. Is there such a thing as non-winnable issues? While there are some problems that seem to have no end, we can always try to break them down into winnable issues, even if the victory is small compared to the whole problem.

How do you know whether your issue is winnable or not? Experience! Who won it elsewhere? Have you a plan for winning? What will it cost the other side if you win? How many votes do you need to win in the legislature? How many dollars do you need for the campaign? Can you get them?

Remember, the decision maker whom we are trying to influence is always a person, never an office or elected body as a whole. You can't fight City Hall because its a building, but you can fight the mayor. Approaching your goal in such a fashion, will get the targeted person to react to your group. You'll either get what you want, or your group will have to go out and organize still larger numbers of people for a second round of the fight. Sometimes it takes several rounds before the fight is won. That is why we think of organizing as a whole campaign, not just as a series of one shot events. Once your group wins, it can go on to the next campaign. If not, it will need to regroup and come back with more power.

3.   The Issue Must Be Widely Felt

The larger the goal, the stronger an organization you will need to achieve it. An issue that is widely felt will draw the large number of supporters that it takes to win. Determine what your organizational strengths and weaknesses are. Who are your potential allies? Who has the power to give your group what it wants?

What tactics can your group use to apply its power and make it felt by those who can give you what you want. Can you involve large numbers of people?

4.   The Issue Must Be Deeply Felt

Some people must feel strongly enough about the issue to devote a lot of effort to it. What is widely and deeply felt changes over time. Sometimes there needs to be a period devoted to consciousness raising before an issue campaign can be won. Often we tie consciousness raising into an attempt to win a specific solution, so that we have a way to measure just how far consciousness has been raised. Example: Last year we only got 10 votes, this year we got 25.

5.   The Issue Must Be Easy To Understand

You need to put your issue to a simple test by asking the members of your group three simple questions: Can a leaflet explain the issue in one paragraph? Can your neighbor understand it? Can you explain it to a news reporter in fifteen seconds?

6.   The Issue Must Have A Clear Decision Maker

A decision maker is the person who can give you what you want. A decision maker is always a person, it is never an institution such as a board, an elected body, etc. We personalize the target because individual people are the weakest link in the power of any institution. Individuals have their own ambitions, dislikes, rivalries, and misdeeds that are separate from those of the institution of which they are a part.

The problems we face don't just happen. They happen because other people with power are making decisions about our lives. We need to find those people, name them, and make them accountable to us. That is why we don't say, "The Congress." We name them, and we look for individual ways of getting to them. They are strongest when we treat them as a united, faceless group. In addition, there is great truth in the statement, "All politics are local." If you think of a committee of the legislature as "The Committee," you make it state-wide instead of local, and give it more power. On the other hand, if you think of it as Committee Chairman Jones, who has to run for reelection in my neighborhood, you start to equalize the power relationship.

7.   The Issue Must Have A Clear Time Frame

An issue campaign is like a novel; it has a beginning, a middle and an end. With a good issue, the critical times in the campaign can be controlled so that they come when you can mobilize the most strength. If the vote is coming in mid August, it may not be the best issue for your organization, because people will be away.

8.   The Issue Must Be Non-Divisive

Look down the road a year or so and consider who you may need to be working with. Look for unifying issues. Avoid issues that divide people who should be working together. The goal is not to push the problem into someone else's neighborhood, or to pit the races, sexes, or generations against each other.

9.   The Issue Must Build Leadership

Most issues will build leadership if you frame them right and create visible roles for many people. An issue that must be won in court often fails to build leadership because the lawyer becomes the leader. Other people learn to depend on lawyers. An issue that results in getting one person added to a civic committee, who is then co-opted, doesn't build leadership. Setting up a citizen watchdog panel to observe that same committee would build leadership, and it would accomplish more than having one friend on the committee.

10.   The Issue Must Set You Up For The Next Issue

Choosing issues is like playing pool: each shot has to set you up for the next one. Make sure that the issue you choose will naturally lead to other related issues. In this way you build a permanent organization that can safeguard the accomplishments won by your efforts. Experience shows that what is won this year can be taken away next year, if the organization that won it disappears. In Direct Action Organizing, building an organization is always as important as winning a particular issue.

11.   The Issue Must Have A Pocketbook Angle

Issues that help people financially often have the greatest impact. Always try to translate the net impact of an issue in terms of how much money it will save the public, or how much "bang for the buck" it will produce. In our capitalist, free- market society, many things will become an issue of money.

12.   The Issue Must Be Able To Raise Money

A good reality check on any issue is whether people will give money to help win it.

13.   The Issue Must Be Consistent With Your Values
and Vision

People working to clean up Boston Harbor got a court ordered plan to pump insufficiently treated sewage out to where the tides will carry it into Cape Cod Bay. This solution to the problem is not consistent with the values upon which the campaign was begun, because the solution may cause as many environmental problems as the original problem did. It is important that your issue effectively deals with a problem, and doesn't merely sweep it under someone else's rug.

BUILDING THE ORGANIZATION'S MEMBERSHIP

In an ideal world, an organization is a group of like-minded people who come together to share in a common enterprise. In reality, an organization is a handful of highly motivated leaders who compete with other interests for the time and energy of a larger number of members. The members, in turn, attempt to mobilize much larger numbers of even less motivated supporters (or constituents) for the purpose of exercising power over reluctant policy makers. It is a wonder that this arrangement works at all, but it does.

People talk about building organization, but what exactly is meant by that? An organization has specific assets, and building it means increasing and improving them. The main organizational assets are:

A.	Leaders	E.	Skills
B.	Members	F.	Communications
C.	Supporters	G.	Information
D.	Allies	H.	Money

A.   Leaders

Leaders are the people who really want the group to work. For leaders to develop, there needs to be places for them in the organizational structure, such as heads of committees, heads of projects, organizer of specific events, etc. Setting up these structural niches may seem bureaucratic or cumbersome, but without them, the only way for leaders to arise is by strength of personality, and that reduces their numbers and leaves out some otherwise good people which, often, creates conflict with existing leaders.

B.   Members

Most members don't want to be leaders (unfortunately). They want to contribute a limited amount of time, without taking a great deal of responsibility. They want to know that their time is being used well and effectively. During the two or three hours a week that most members can give to an organization, they would usually rather be told what needs to be done than to spend the time discussing it. Meetings should be held only when there are major decisions to be made. The rest of the time, have work nights instead of meetings. Membership should be a formal status, in which people go through the procedure of joining and paying dues. They will value their membership more if this is done.

* There are two key concepts to membership building
* Constant Recruitment
* Entry Level Program

Constant recruitment means that almost every week the organization is doing something to recruit new members. This can be a table on a busy street or outside a mall, or holding your own events such as a block party, or film showing that attract large numbers. There are two rules for constant recruitment:

* People won't join unless you ask them.
* Recruit to an activity not to a meeting.

The first event that you ask people to come to should be an actual activity, not a planning meeting. Constant recruitment, therefore, requires constant events. This is a good thing. Entry level program means that you always have an activity for people to do that doesn't require a lot of experience. The problem with most organizations is that they deal with complicated issues. The leaders start to speak a special language that new people feel they can never learn, or successfully present, as to what the group is for. An entry level program includes distributing literature, keeping lists up to date, making turn-out phone calls, mailing newsletters, helping at information tables with a more experienced person, doing art work and making posters, going to demonstrations, etc. There needs to be something of this nature every few weeks. Remember, members are people who want to do something, and if you don't provide it, some other group will.

C.   Supporters

Supporters are individual people. Allies are organizations. There are two kinds of supporters, those whose names you have, and those whose names you don't have. Every group should keep a list of supporters who can be reached by phone and mail. In addition, there needs to be systems for getting the word out to the others. The goal is to constantly increase the size of the supporters list. Petition drives can accomplish this, as well as "send me more information" cards and coupons. At least once a year an event should be held for which you attempt to mobilize every possible supporter.

D.   Allies

Allies are another major organizational asset. The more allies you have, the stronger you become. The key to building alliances is not to get other groups to help you, and then having to return the favor; it is to show them how they can build their own membership and program by working along with you. Knowing how to do this is a special skill that older leaders must teach to new leaders.

E.   Skills

Many skills are needed in an organization, including leading meetings, public speaking, planning, organizing large events, writing, computerized publishing, fund raising, etc. Of course, it is really people, not the organization, who have the skills, but a strong organization will find ways of getting skilled members to teach others so that the skill is passed along within the organization from year to year. A clear division of labor within the group, helps to facilitate this. A committee structure is also helpful, even though people in smaller, less formal groups, often feel that they don't need one.

F.   Communications

Communications means the ability to get the word out quickly and often. Organizations need both internal and external communications systems. Internal systems include telephone trees and up-to-date mailing lists. External communications include literature distribution systems on street blocks or in apartment buildings, people who will speak for you at other neighborhood clubs and organizations, regular outdoor leafleting and tabling, contacts with media, and the ability to generate press events. Once these systems are in place, they need to be used regularly or they deteriorate.

To sum up this point on recruitment, there are four elements to getting people to come to some type of event:

1) General Publicity: posters, leaflets, ads, etc:
   These are important, but alone won't get people to come.

2) List Building:
   This is the process of constantly collecting the names of potential members and supporters. Make every activity an opportunity to pass around a sign-up list.

3) Personal Contact:
   Whether face to face or by phone, this is the process that will bring most of the people.
   The publicity reinforces the personal contact.

4) Exciting Program:
   Recruit to an activity. The best outreach is useless if the organization isn't doing anything.

G.   Information

Information is what gives your group the edge and ties in coalition partners and individual members. Information includes specific problems and issues, the status of legislation at the national and state level, what other organizations are achieving and what is happening locally. Part of the value of belonging to a larger organization, state wide or national, is the accessibility of information, as well as being able to have an impact on issues, beyond the community. A strong organization develops reliable sources of information and disseminates it to members.

H.   Money

"Whenever five or more are gathered together, pass the hat." This is the first rule of organizing. It means that fund raising must be built into everything you do. In America, more money is given to churches than any other kind of organization, partly because they ask for it once a week. Fundraising also makes an organization more democratic. If a few members put up most of the money, they come to think of it as their organization.

BUILDING COALITIONS

Building a coalition is one of the hardest parts of organizing. What's hard isn't getting groups to join, that is usually easy. The hard part is getting the coalition to work, and keeping the groups in it. Often we expect a coalition to function the way a group of friends does, but this is seldom the case.

Organizations in a coalition have institutional needs and self-interests that are different from the needs of individual people. To make coalitions work, we must identify these institutional needs and work to meet them. The job is sometimes complicated, because the people who represent groups in a coalition may not be experienced enough to articulate their institutional needs. They just know that something isn't going well, and they feel that their organization is getting weaker instead of stronger. Let's start with a definition:

Coalition: *A coalition is an organization of separate organizations that formally agree to work together. It is not an organization of individuals who are different from each other. It is not an organization of individuals who happen to belong to other organizations as well. Many groups that call themselves coalitions, aren't coalitions. A coalition is an organization of separate organizations.*

At least this is the way it is supposed to be. In real life, many coalitions are a mixture of individuals, representatives from organizations and people who happen to belong to organizations, but who weren't sent to the coalition by their group. The main difficulty with coalitions of this type is that the people in them have different needs and goals. For example, every organization knows that it must get some public recognition for its work if it is to recruit members, develop a base, and keep its funding. Individuals who are not faced with the problem of maintaining an organization often don't understand this, and consider the organizational representatives to be 'power hungry' or 'domineering' or 'only interested in getting the credit'. In a coalition where everyone is a formal organizational representative, they might be more competitive, but at least they understand each other's motives.

To further define coalitions: There are four basic types of relations between organizations, all of which are often referred to as coalitions. It helps to sort them out.

A.   Allies

Groups with which you work from time to time. You might attend some of their events to show support, and they yours, but you do not have a structural relationship with them and have not agreed to coordinate programs. Having an allied organization is not the same as being in a coalition.

B.   Networks

Useful for a regular exchange of information such as mailings, newsletters, and occasionally meetings. They don't entail working on joint projects, and are not coalitions and should not be expected to act like coalitions.

C.   Coalitions

Coalitions exist when groups enter into a formal agreement to work together toward a specific objective.

D.   Permanent Coalitions

Formed when groups decide that they want to work together on an ongoing basis in order to take on larger issues or work at the regional, state, or national level. Permanent coalitions can often raise money more successfully than smaller groups and can provide the benefits of full time staff, research, materials, and continuity.

GUIDELINES FOR SUCCESSFUL COALITION BUILDING

OK, your group knows what the problem is and what the issue is. It also knows that there are other organizations that are concerned. In order to increase your power and resources, and to win something you couldn't win alone, you decide to build a coalition. Here are tried and true guidelines for successful coalition building:

A.   Choose Unifying Issues

Avoid shopping lists. Often coalitions form to work on a specific issue. That is a relatively easy structure to organize, because those who aren't interested just don't join. When an organization is a permanent ongoing coalition that moves from issue to issue, then the choice of issue needs to be made more carefully. This is key. The issue needs to be one that is important to all groups in the coalition. It should not be the main issue of any one group. This avoids having some groups feel that they are being co-opted to work on someone else's issue.

Also, avoid coalitions based on groups agreeing to exchange help, "We'll help you to fight the tax increase if you help us ban fur coats." Organizations can rarely deliver their members to work on some other group's program, and no group feels that it gets enough out of the coalition. Coalitions in which groups put their issues on the table and try to work on all of them are called shopping-list coalitions.

B.   Understand and Respect Each Group's Self Interest

Every organization needs to:
- Gain new members.
- Raise money.
- Be seen as powerful by officials or politicians.
- Get publicity.
- Build relationships with other groups.
- Provide an exciting activity for its members.
- Build internal moral.
- Have a public role for its leaders.

These are good things to do. Experienced leaders can use a coalition to achieve them. Inexperienced leaders neglect them, and their groups dwindle. The coalition should help its members accomplish these things.

C.   Respect the Group's Internal Process

Every group has its own way of making decisions. Don't rush them. If you don't like the answer you got from the group's chair, don't go around the chair to someone else in the leadership. Don't get involved in another group's factionalism, or worse, cause it. Don't use the work of the coalition to draw the members of another group into your own group.

D.   Agree to Disagree.

Not everyone has to agree on everything. The coalition can only function within the areas of agreement.

E.   Play to the Center with Tactics

All groups should be comfortable with the tactics. There are sometimes advantages to encouraging the more militant groups to go off and do their thing independently.

F.   Recognize that Contributions Vary

A coalition should have a budget, even if everything is contributed. Some groups are better at research, others can turn out a large number of people, still others may have good community contacts. There is no one "right thing".

G.   Structure Decision Making Carefully

One-group-one-vote only works if the groups are of equal strength. The smaller groups should not be able to out-vote the larger, just because there are more of them. Individuals should not be able to out-vote organizations. It is often better to recognize that, in some coalitions, everyone is not equal. The program won't work if the strongest groups don't support it, and it is O.K. for marginal organizations and individuals to just sit out a particular activity in which they don't feel comfortable participating. The decision-making process is often smoother when the coalition is composed strictly of organizations that can make more or less the same level of contribution to the work.

The decision-making process should be clear from the outset. So should the ground rules. If this is a temporary coalition for a single event or fixed length of time, it should dissolve on schedule and not live on to be a rival of its own members. Call it a campaign instead of a coalition, and give it a time limiting name, such as "Campaign Clean-Up '93."

There is no such thing as the "democratic right" to join a coalition. You can allow in, and keep out, whichever groups you wish, including sectarians, disrupters, and crack-pots. Don't be guilt tripped.

H.   Urge Stable and Senior Representation at Meetings

The same people should represent a group at each coalition meeting, and they should be people with the power to commit the group or approve the coalition program. Otherwise, the coalition can't move without long delays.

I.   Distribute Credit Fairly

The coalition itself needs to get the larger share of publicity or credit. Otherwise, the whole isn't greater than the sum of the parts. Try to distribute the remainder of the credit or media attention or spokesperson positions among the individual members fairly, but with an eye to the contribution that each makes.

J.   If there is Staff, It Should Be Neutral

Problems develop when the coalition's staff is contributed to by members of the separate organizations of the coalition. If there is staff, they should be people with no other loyalties, whose main job is to build the coalition as a whole.

GUIDELINES FOR JOINING AND PARTICIPATING IN COALITIONS

Say another organization approaches you, as the leader of your group, to join a coalition. There are several things that your group must first assess before agreeing to do so. Here are some guidelines for joining and participating in coalitions.

1. Know What You Want To Get Out Of It

Of course you want to win on the issue, but you are also building an organization. How will participation in the coalition help do that? Will it:

* Expose you to more potential members?
* Allow you to win more significant victories?
* Share the burden of organizing large activities?
* Get you publicity?

Once a neighborhood organization was fighting the construction of an interstate highway. Under the law, if the highway plan was rejected, 80% of the federal share of the construction costs could be transferred to mass transit. Naturally, the neighborhood group was very interested when a city-wide coalition was formed to fight for better mass transit. Before joining, however, the neighborhood group set the following conditions.

a. Opposition to the highway is to be a major demand of the transit coalition.

b. The neighborhood organization was to be the only member of the coalition in its geographic area, so that everyone who wanted to work for better transit would have to join it.

c. The organization's leaders would be frequently used as spokespeople for the whole coalition.

d. The first major city-wide turnout event, a mass transit speak-out, would be held on the neighborhood group's turf.

This arrangement not only strengthened the neighborhood group, it also strengthened the city-wide coalition. The Transit Speak-Out drew over 900 people, half of them came as a direct result of the neighborhood group's efforts.

2. Maintain An Independent Program

A group that is only strong enough to do one thing at a time shouldn't join a coalition. If you have no program outside the coalition, you won't develop your own identity or membership. It may not seem to matter, but when the coalition goes, your group will go with it.

3. Evaluate Your Role Carefully

Is it really necessary for the leaders of your group to play a large role in the leadership and decision making of the coalition, or is it enough to get your members to show up for occasional coalition activities? The coalition can absorb all of your time and energy just as easily as your own organization can. If three-quarters of your effort doesn't go into building your own group, your members will be drawn into the activities of the coalition or be recruited away by other groups.

SUMMARY

In ancient Athens, the birthplace of democracy, government positions were drawn by lot. People served short terms in public office and returned to private life. The Greeks believed that every citizen was capable of doing any administrative job, and that, in those more simple times, no one could mess things up beyond repair. Of course they knew there were risks, but they thought that the risk of involving too many people in governing was less than the risk of involving too few.

Today, we need to regain the confidence in ourselves to say, once again, that everyday people know what's best. Citizens organizing on issues, great and small, is another way of participating in governing and of taking our country back from the special-interest descendants of the robber barons.

Portions of this material are based *Organizing For Social Change. A Manual For Activists In The '90s* By Kim Bobo, Jackie Kendall and Steve Max. The book is available from Seven Locks Press. 800 354-5348 P.O. Box 68. Arlington, VA. 22210

Steve Max is a Regional Director of Citizen Action, a national citizen organization with over 3.5 million members, working for economic and environmental justice through affiliates in thirty-one states. Steve is also the training director of the Midwest Academy, a national school for citizen organizers.

CHAPTER 12

THE 12 STEPS TO POLITICAL RECOVERY

by Mr. Kerry Power – VOTE USA Chairman

for Lead or Leave

GLOSSARY

for The 12 Steps to Political Recovery

Addict

1. To devote or give (oneself) habitually or compulsively: She was addicted to rock music.

Exponentially

1. Mathematics. a. Containing, involving, or expressed as an exponent (denoting the power to which that number, symbol, or expression is to be raised; also called power).

Ideology/Ideologies

1. The body of ideas reflecting the social needs and aspirations of an individual, a group, a class, or a culture.
2. A set of doctrines or beliefs that form the basis of a political, economic, or other system.

Incumbent

1. Currently holding a specified office: the incumbent mayor.

Insane

1. Of, exhibiting, or afflicted with insanity.
2. Very foolish; absurd

Patriot/Patriotism

1. One who loves, supports, and defends one's country and the principles upon which it stands.

Platform

1. A formal declaration of the principles on which a group, such as a political party, makes its appeal to the public.

Pork Barrel

1. A government project or appropriation that yields jobs or other benefits to a specific locale and patronage opportunities to its political representative.

Sanity

1. The quality or condition of being sane; soundness of mind.
2. Soundness of judgment or reason.

Social Awakening/Enlightenment

1. Social: Of or relating to society.
2. Awakening: To cause to wake up.
3. Enlightenment1: To acquire spiritual or intellectual insight: "Enlighten the people generally, and tyranny and oppression of body and mind will vanish like evil spirits at the dawn of day" (Thomas Jefferson).
4. Enlightenment2: A philosophical movement of the 18th century that emphasized the use of reason to scrutinize previously accepted doctrines and traditions and that brought about many humanitarian reforms.

Unmanageable

1. Difficult or impossible to manage.
2. Not submitting to discipline; unruly: an unmanageable child.
3. Difficult to keep under control or within limits: unmanageable traffic congestion; an unmanageable federal deficit.

Utopia

1. An ideally perfect place, especially in its social, political, and moral aspects.

THE 12 STEPS TO POLITICAL RECOVERY

Mr. Kerry Power – VOTE USA Chairman
for Lead or Leave

"Life affords no higher pleasure than that of surmounting difficulties, passing from one step of success to another, forming new wishes and seeing them gratified."

— *Samuel Johnson*

The whole idea of a political "self-help program" started in December of 1993 with a conversation between the Executive Director of Rock the Vote, Nicholas Butterworth, and myself. Our discussion about the program inevitably fell into a conversation about "the problem with America today." Bantering back and forth, Nicholas and I mused about the roles of government, business, and the public, quipping about the limited role of today's citizenry in our "democratic" system. When we started to consider the mental health of greed-crazed stock brokers who crashed the market with their computer scams, and the power-drunk bankers who gambled away their depositors money, the "addict" metaphor became a common theme.

Amused by the term, we went on to apply the "addict" concept to politicians, who throw the country deeper and deeper into debt in order to feed their "pork barrel" habits. We applied it to industrialists who will do anything to get their next quarterly "fix" of positive profit statements, even if it damages the economy in the long run. Then we applied it to the mainstream public, whose obsessive habits and compulsive shopping seems to calm them while their nation continues to fall apart from neglect.

While it was argued that there are literally millions of Americans who are very active in our democracy, we ultimately concurred that no matter how threatening problems such as crime, poverty, or government corruption become, the majority of Americans seem to remain in some kind of trance.

As a result, the US government "experts" preside over a five trillion dollar national debt, rising taxes, lowered wages, a 15% poverty rate, the highest crime rate in the industrialized world, the world's highest medical expenses, and the most expensive public education system in the world - without the benefit of the healthiest people or the best educated students.

In the face of these failures, all that the government "experts" need to do to keep the masses stimulated is to continue the old game of "good-cop, bad-cop" that has worked for over twenty years. This is a fun game where the Republicrats (part Republican, part Democrat, and mostly bureaucrat) blame the other political party for screwing things up, promising that their party will make everything right again, and ultimately adding more insults to the nation's injuries. And the majority of Americans have fallen for it for over twenty years, ceaselessly hoping that the next election will usher in a new group of "experts" that can devise "a more perfect union" that does not require public involvement.

After contemplating this type of compulsive, irresponsible, and self destructive behavior, Nicholas and I concluded that the "addict" metaphor is appropriate for America's government, industries, and people who have become accustomed to our culture of instant gratification, and its accompanied social decline. The structure of our proposed program became obvious, and we went on to create the line items of a 12-Step program for the politically challenged.

Finally, I drafted a rough outline of this 12-Step program and passed it on to Rob Nelson, cofounder of Lead or Leave. As coauthor of another political self-help book titled "Revolution X," Rob became the natural choice to help complete this chapter. Ultimately, I dedicated this chapter to Lead or Leave; not only because Rob's editing brought both clarity and conciseness to the text of the program, but also because Rob felt that these 12-Steps embody the purpose and goals of his organization.

The following program offers a simple set of suggestions for those who would like to become more informed about the issues, aware of the solutions, confident to motivate government actions, and the leader of a winning life-style. It offers a great way for the politically inactive citizen to awaken from their daze and become an active participant in his or her community; or for the community activist to get back to the basics of citizen participation.

In any case, the program that follows offers an easy way for you to *gradually* become a part of the solution at your own pace. Give each step careful consideration for at least a couple of days, as this will help you to acclimate yourself to the concepts offered. Don't rush to the next step until you have fully completed the step you are currently on. Work-sheets are offered at the end of the chapter which will help you with the completion of steps three and six. By the time you have successfully completed all twelve steps, you will find that you have become the model of a true American Patriot.

THE TWELVE STEPS TO POLITICAL RECOVERY

1. I admit that I am politically powerless alone, and that my government has become unmanageable.

2. I believe that a power greater than myself can restore my nation to sanity.

3. I make the decision to dedicate myself to the improvement of my nation.

4. I make a searching and fearless moral inventory of myself.

5. I resolve to overcome my shortcomings and improve myself continually.

6. I become more educated and active in my nation's political process.

7. I become more educated about the issues that affect my nation and myself.

8. I become more aware of the interconnections that relate each issue to all other issues.

9. I become more tolerant and understanding of people who dispute my opinions.

10. I find organized groups of concerned patriots and join in their efforts.

11. I work toward a meaningful goal and help to resolve conflicts within each group.

12. Having had a social awakening as a result of these steps, I promote my ideology to my government representatives, colleagues, friends and interested strangers, and practice these principles in all my affairs.

I admit that I am politically powerless alone, <u>and that my government has become unmanageable</u>

a) Individuals may contribute to a passing poll, vote for a candidate, or write a letter to a representative, but little meaningful change will occur, as long as individuals stay separated.

b) The first step, in the improvement of anything, is to admit that there is something wrong in the first place. Many people choose to live in denial of what's wrong, to avoid the work of fixing it. The three branches of government are in an ongoing conflict between each other and within themselves. The substantial replacement and retirement of incumbent politicians, as well as the speeches of our political leaders *themselves,* indicate that our government is out of control. With the ever increasing role of lobbyists, Political Action Committees, and private agendas, the governing process in the US, has become so bureaucratic and corrupted that it can be accurately described as "unmanageable."

I believe that a power greater than myself <u>can restore my nation to sanity</u>

a) There seems to be a serious lack of outrage about a national debt which could bankrupt the nation, a crime rate that is the highest in the industrialized world, a substandard public education system that is the most expensive in the world, and trade agreements that favor other nation's economies over our own. If the founding fathers of our great nation were alive today, they would probably be quite surprised at how willing people are to accept increased taxation without adequate benefit, widespread corruption in our institutions, and violent turmoil in our streets. It would seem that anyone who accepts these conditions as normal or tolerable, can be characterized as insane. When the government, media, and public embrace an "economic recovery" bill that doesn't solve the problem of government overspending, but merely reduces the amount that the US will *go further* into debt to $200 billion per year instead of $300 billion per year, with no mention of when or how we will ever try to pay off this crushing debt, it is mass insanity. Public acceptance of congressional pay raises during an economic recession, massive military police actions abroad while our domestic crime rate soars, and politicians who don't say what they mean *or* mean what they say, is mass insanity.

b) G.P. Morris once stated: "United we stand, divided we fall!" Morris recognized that all of the great advances in human history did not occur by accident, but by the combined efforts of many groups of people. There has never been an instance in history when social ills simply "worked themselves out." Individuals may be powerless against the forces that currently misguide the nation, but *groups* of individuals that are organized have always been effective at overcoming amazing obstacles and accomplishing major social changes. The American patriots of 1776, as an organized group, fought against an empire that had not lost a war in over 1,000 years – and won! Organized labor unions in the US raised the standard of living for working Americans. Organized groups have succeeded tremendously, through the years, in improving the nation by winning the battle for civil rights, consumers' rights, worker safety, environmental protection and voter registration, just to name a few. That's the power of an organization – a power greater than yourself.

I make the decision to dedicate myself to the improvement of my nation

a) Decide whether you've had enough, or whether you want to see if the situation can get worse. Then decide how much time, per week, you can spare to help improve the state of the nation. Then make a schedule of how that time will be allocated throughout the week. Then decide when you will start on your new program. Then schedule step four for that date, and the remaining steps on later dates. Commit this schedule to writing and save the document. Show it to your spouse or a friend. Tape it to your refrigerator as a reminder. The writing and sharing of this commitment will make it more real, and will make you accountable for its fulfillment. It is a commitment that is sure to bring you great rewards, in the form of improved self esteem, a more fulfilling lifestyle, and a better nation in which to live.

I make a searching and fearless moral inventory of myself

a) The best place for one to begin improving the nation is at home. Make a list of the qualities and talents that you have to offer to your family, your community, a patriotic group, or the government itself. List at least three items for each of the following questions:

1) What qualities do I possess that others can look up to and admire?

2) What have I done in the past that helped my community or nation?

3) What qualities do I possess that help me to help others?

4) What talents do I possess that I can teach to others?

5) In what ways am I a positive example of a good American?

b) Next, make a list of your shortcomings. Make a list of the ways that you are a part of the problem. List at least three items for each of the following questions:

1) In what ways am I selfish, putting my personal gain ahead of the welfare of my community or nation?

2) In what ways am I deficient in recycling my trash or conserving energy?

3) In what ways am I stubborn and closed minded to opinions that are contrary to my own?

4) In what ways am I not supporting the principles outlined in the US Constitution?

5) In what ways am I an unbecoming example of an unethical American?

c) If you have any difficulty in listing three items for each question, ask your friends or associates to help you. Other's perspectives will often present a more accurate depiction of your positive and negative attributes. This is the "fearless" part of the step that will help you to more precisely identify who you are, what you need to work on, and what people admire about you most.

I resolve to overcome my shortcomings and improve myself continually

a) Before you call for the entire nation to change for the better, you should resolve to set an example of what that change should look like. Then, others can see that you walk the same path that you talk about. After successfully compiling both lists compiled from the questions in step four , try to establish how you can apply your qualities and talents to overcome your shortcomings. Then, make a firm resolution to continuously overcome your shortcomings and become the best American patriot that you can possibly be.

I become more educated and active in my nation's political process

a) Since our government affects almost every aspect of our lives, it is very important that we know how our government functions, and how we can play our part. A full examination of this Democracy Owner's Manual is a great place to start. Get to know the history that formed our system of government and the US Constitution. Get to know how our government functions, how it compares to other governments, and how you can participate. Call your city or town hall and make sure that you are registered to vote. Find out what federal district, state district, and voting precinct you live in, as well as the address of your precinct voting place. Find out who your representatives are, and write down their names, addresses, and telephone numbers. Compile this information for your city or town representative, police chief, fire chief, and postmaster; your state governor, senator, representative, attorney general and secretary of state; your federal Senators, US Representative, and the President of the United States (forms are provided for this task, starting on page 175).

b) Find out when the next elections are scheduled for each of these offices, who is running, and what their platform positions are. Find out what additional ballot questions will be included in the next election, and what the opposing opinions are, regarding those questions. Become informed about the various political parties and the "platforms" that define what they stand for. Investigate which groups and committees are donating to which parties and candidates, as this may offer an additional perspective of what they really stand for. Decide which (if any) of these candidates or parties represents a reasonable match with your beliefs and your goals for the nation.

c) Write a letter to each of your local, state, and federal representatives, informing them that you have resolved to improve yourself and are dedicated to the improvement of the nation. Let them know that another citizen has become a patriot, is willing to help, and won't settle for second best.

I become more educated about the issues that affect my nation and myself

a) Once you've become a part of the political system, it's time to become more educated about the issues that affect us all. American essayist Norman Cousins once said that "in a democracy the individual enjoys not only the ultimate power but carries the ultimate responsibility." Learn as much as you can about the economy, the environment, education, poverty, crime, health care, foreign relations, personal freedoms, etc. It's a tall order, so don't expect to be able to learn all of this overnight. It is best approached as a program or hobby that can be pursued enjoyably at your own pace. As a start, subscribe to one of the major newspapers, and include some periodicals that offer different perspectives. Start keeping a scrapbook, so you can categorize the issues and keep your facts handy. Sometimes, a trip to the library can help to bring you up to date on a specific issue, and today's on-line computer services are fantastic sources of issues information.

b) Consider how these issues effect the nation and your personal life. Scrutinize your information sources to determine whether they are faultfinding or solution oriented. Consider the intent, significance, and potential consequences of any proposed solutions. Most importantly, decide where *you* stand on each issue, and which solutions *you* personally support. Without making such decisions, how can you truly decide which candidates you agree and disagree with? It has been said that "a person who stands for nothing will fall for anything"(anonymous) "Only the educated are free" (Epictetus), and "Our high respect for a well-read man is praise enough of literature" (Ralph Waldo Emerson).

I become more aware of the interconnections that relate each issue to all the other issues

a) Once you've become more educated about the issues, the next step is to approach a state of social enlightenment. Try to find a perspective that connects the seemingly unrelated issues together, where chaos is replaced by cognition and "it all makes sense" to you. Take education for example: A deficient educational system impacts the economy because uneducated people have difficulty finding employment, resulting in less production for the economy, more poverty, and more welfare costs. People living in poverty are more susceptible to disease and less able to pay for treatment, putting an increased burden on the health care system. Lack of education and increased poverty usually results in more crime. More crime endangers personal freedoms and puts further stress on the economy, due to increased police and prison costs and health care costs due to injuries. All of these reactions ultimately result in fewer resources for education itself. In this example, the educational system has either an immediate or secondary effect on health care, crime, the economy, personal freedoms, and itself. Ask yourself: how does education effect the environment or foreign relations? By seeking the answer to this question, you have taken the first step toward social enlightenment, and toward becoming aware of the interconnections that relate each issue to all the other issues.

I become more tolerant and understanding of people who dispute my opinions

a) Now that you're becoming more educated and aware, it's time to put your theories to the test. The most beneficial and stimulating part of being involved in politics is interacting with those who you don't agree with. A lot can be learned from a rational debate, if both parties seek to learn from it. If one of the debaters is more interested in "winning the argument" than searching for truth, things can get uncomfortable. Accusations, personal attacks, intimidation, generalizations, broad assumptions, and misinformation are effective devices for frustrating people into throwing their hands up and walking away. This is the difference between arguing and bickering. Webster's dictionary states that to argue is "to apply reason to a problem and persuade by talk," and to bicker is "to quarrel about valueless, insignificant facts or things." Therefore, reasonable debaters seek to reach a solution to a problem through reason and persuasive talk, with all participants willing to learn from others how their ideas may be flawed.

(see "The 12 Traditions of Intelligent Arguing" on page 174)

I find organized groups of concerned patriots and join in their efforts

a) Once you've become an active, educated and tolerant participant in the political process, you're ready to engage your beliefs and join with other concerned patriots to restore the nation to sanity. Check with your friends, neighbors, family and colleagues to find out what organizations are already in your area. Contact these organizations and find out when they meet, then go and observe their meetings. If you like what you see and hear, then join the group; if you don't like what you see and hear, keep looking for a group that you like. Check newspapers, magazines, and other publications for mention of political, advocacy, or "grass roots" groups that sound interesting. Public television, such as PBS and C-SPAN, is another good place to look for advocacy groups. If you still come up short, consider starting a group of your own. Simply figure out what you want your organization to accomplish, put a few people together who would like to help accomplish it, and decide when and where you will meet. Step eleven will take care of the rest.

I work toward a meaningful goal and help to resolve conflicts within each group

a) The most important thing for any organization to have is a clear goal. Mission statements, statements of purpose, policies and procedures, articles of incorporation or bylaws do not constitute a clear goal. The goal should be easily communicated, in such a way that it can complete either of the following sentences: "The ultimate goal of this organization is..." or "If a magic genie granted this organization a wish, it would be..." If your organization cannot complete these sentences, it doesn't have a meaningful goal or purpose. In that case, simply bring the organization's membership together and establish a clear and meaningful goal.

b) Once you've established the organization's goal, find your place in the organization where you can best apply your qualities and talents. If the ideal position for you is already taken, try to become an assistant to that person. Do your best to get along with all of the people in your organization, and put out an extra effort to understand and communicate with those who have difficult personalities. If you notice a conflict or a situation that makes people uncomfortable, try to mediate and settle the situation. Try your best to keep your organization working toward its goal, without getting sidetracked by trivial, superficial, or counterproductive activities.

c) Make sure that your organization has a well thought-out plan of action, and that it sticks to it. Try to avoid taking on more projects than the organization can handle. Stay focused and don't get discouraged. Social progress tends to move slowly, and it may seem as if your goal is a long way off, but we've already come a long way from the days of lords and serfs. With adequate effort and patience, we together can achieve a more virtuous society that truly provides "life, liberty and the pursuit of happiness" for all.

Having had a social awakening as a result of these steps, I promote my ideology to my government representatives, colleagues, friends, and interested strangers, and practice these principles in all my affairs

a) This final step is the most important part of political recovery, as it incorporates all of the other steps into a way of life, and encourages others to follow a similar path. By practicing in all of your affairs, the principles acquired through the previous eleven steps, you are doing your part and setting an example. Your "social awakening" should make you an upbeat and positive representative of the new, high-tech democracy; a person who is optimistic about the future, a promoter of solutions instead of complaints, participation instead of indifference, and empowerment instead of subjection.

b) Share your ideology with your elected representatives through letters, phone calls, and even personal interaction, when you get the opportunity. Since there is power in numbers, try to gain support from friends, colleagues, and interested strangers. The key here is to be sure that they are *interested* in making a difference, before beseeching them to get involved. Many times you're better off letting your actions speak louder than your words, imparting all the while how much fun you're having and how good you feel, knowing that you're part of the solution. Sooner or later they will show a genuine interest, and you can bring them to one of your organization's meetings, share some literature from various groups, or simply discuss the steps *you* took to become a true patriot. Before long, the people that might have been scared off, if you "came on too strong," will be enlightened, and start promoting *their* ideology to others. As this process continues, the number of true, active patriots will increase exponentially, resulting in a social, cultural and political revolution to take a nation in decline and make a virtual utopia.

The 12 Traditions of Intelligent Arguing

1. Name Your Topic

It is very common for an argument about issue "X" to migrate into a completely different argument about issue "Y," and then issue "Z." By this point, you've strayed so far away from the original topic that your lucky if you remember what it was. When an argument begins, verbally identify the proposed argument topic and gain agreement from your counterpart(s). If the conversation strays, rustle it back in! Then stick to the subject until it is resolved.

2. Have an Objective

While "winning the argument" may seem like a popular objective these days, it tends to be the least productive. The most sought-after objective in any worthwhile argument is a compromise with which all debaters agree. Another objective could be to merely enlighten others to a different perspective, without necessarily gaining any kind of immediate agreement (give them something to "chew on" so to speak). In any case, a secondary objective should always include the exercising of polite discourse, where the participants agree to disagree respectfully.

3. Be Willing to Learn

Try to stay open minded and seek new information and perspectives from those who don't agree with you. This is easy to accomplish if you're willing to accept that you're human, therefore not perfect, capable of being partially incorrect, or possibly even completely in error. Assuming this humble attitude puts you in a position to learn whether your current assumptions are correct or not; or better yet, to learn something new!

4. Be Patient and Polite

It's amazing how many adults never mastered this often taught lesson as children. If someone starts to say something that you think you've heard before, wait until they have finished before jumping in. They may have a new twist to an old theme that makes sense. But in any case, it is always helpful to show respect for those with whom you are arguing. Such modifications in your debating style will help to prevent you from appearing arrogant or antagonistic.

5. Be More Informative than Opinionated

Opinions are like noses - everybody's got a different one. Credible, verifiable information is what makes an argument worthwhile. Try to replace absolute statements with qualifying statements. For example, instead of saying "the world is flat and that is that!," try saying "I believe the world is flat," then explain why. Instead of saying "crime in the city is increasing," try saying "FBI statistics show that crime in the city is increasing," then explain by how much, within which groups, in a what time frame, etc.

6. Move Beyond Disputable Points

Make sure that everyone's "facts" have a reliable and verifiable source. If a participant of an argument doesn't believe that another person's "facts" are accurate, the argument can come to a swift halt. Unless you have the verification upon you, it is useless to continue the argument unless everyone agrees that the facts being presented are valid. Often it is beneficial to either move beyond this "point of contention" and debate other factors of the argument, or postpone the argument until everyone can research the stated facts, thus attaining a polite closure.

7. Try to Understand the Points of Others

Listen closely and carefully to the points and opinions that are being presented. Do your best to fully understand the reasoning of other's before arguing against them. If they say something that doesn't make sense to you, repeat it back to them in the form of a question, prompting them to explain their point in more detail. If that doesn't work, ask that they explain it in a different way, give examples, etc.

8. Make Your Points Understandable to Others

It can be frustrating when others don't understand your reasoning. Consider whether you are properly communicating your points. Try to rephrase your arguments using detailed examples, metaphors, anecdotes and illustrations.

9. Understand if Others Don't Grasp Your Points

If all else fails, consider that your opinion may be startling or difficult for someone to embrace immediately. At this point, all you can do is ask that they contemplate what you have said and gain agreement to debate the issue again at a later date. In the meantime you can contemplate a more effective way to communicate your opinion.

10. Keep Your Cool

Some arguments can become highly emotional, and the temptation to resort to name calling, accusations, or emotional outbursts can be quite compelling. When you're engaged in an argument, it is best not to raise your voice, wave your hands or lose your temper. If the discussion becomes heated in such a way, try stating, "I'm getting upset and I would appreciate a moment to compose myself." Then, take a moment to compose yourself. Often, a few deep breaths or thinking about a happy memory will bring you back into a calm, cool, and collected state.

11. Help Others to Keep Their Cool

You may find your counterparts resorting to bickering if their argument is flawed, but don't let it incite you into similar behavior. Simply remain calm, state that it is possible that you are wrong, and ask if it is possible that they are wrong. Then ask if everyone can resolve to stick to the facts, avoid insults, and regain a calm and respectful environment for your discussion.

12. End on a Happy Note

A successful argument will either end in a mutual resolution, or in a polite closure where the parties agree to disagree respectfully. When an argument ends in this way, the debaters may comfortably try to learn from each other again at a later date. With the proper application of respect, understanding and patience, mutual resolutions have been achieved in the Mid-East, South Africa, and even Washington DC.

Proclamation

I, _____, on this the _____ day of _____, hereby proclaim my admission, that I am politically powerless alone, that my nation has become unmanageable, and that I believe that a power greater than myself can restore my nation to sanity.

Resulting from this admission, I proclaim my decision to dedicate myself to the improvement of my nation, for no less than _____ hours per week, starting on the _____ day of _____, and adhering to this commitment until the goal of a more perfect union has been achieved.

Furthermore, I proclaim my dedication to master each of the 12 Steps to Political Recovery, in succession, and commit to the completion of step four, prior to the _____ day of _____.

I proudly sign my name to this proclamation, as evidence of my sincerity and commitment to this cause:

_____

MY VOTING INFORMATION

I Have Verified that I am Registered to Vote at My Local Voting Precinct

YES?

I Reside in Congressional District   #_____

I Reside in State Senate District   _____

I Reside in State Rep. District   _____

I Reside in Governor's Council District   _____

I Reside in Voting Precinct   #_____

The Address for My Precinct Voting Location is:

_____
Location Name

_____
Address

_____
City, State Zip

_____
Telephone and Facsimile #s

The Next Federal Elections will be   _____/_____/_____

The Next State Elections will be   _____/_____/_____

The Next Local Elections will be   _____/_____/_____

MY FEDERAL REPRESENTATIVES

The President and Vice President of the United States

_____
President

_____
Vice President

_____
Address

_____
City, State Zip

_____
Telephone and Facsimile #s

My Senior US Senator's Address in Washington, DC

_____
Senior US Senator

_____
Address

_____
City, State Zip

_____
Telephone and Facsimile #s

My Senior US Senator's Local Address

_____
Senior US Senator

_____
Address

_____
City, State Zip

_____
Telephone and Facsimile #s

My Junior US Senator's Address in Washington, DC

_____
Junior US Senator

_____
Address

_____
City, State   Zip

_____
Telephone and Facsimile #s

My Junior US Senator's Local Address

_____
Junior US Senator

_____
Address

_____
City, State   Zip

_____
Telephone and Facsimile #s

My US Representative's Address in Washington, DC

_____
US Representative

_____
Address

_____
City, State   Zip

_____
Telephone and Facsimile #s

My US Representative's Local Address

_____
US Representative

_____
Address

_____
City, State   Zip

_____
Telephone and Facsimile #s

MY STATE REPRESENTATIVES

The Governor and Lieutenant Governor of My State

_____

Governor

_____

Lieutenant Governor

_____

Address

_____

City, State Zip

_____

Telephone and Facsimile #s

My State Senator

_____

State Senator

_____

Address

_____

City, State Zip

_____

Telephone and Facsimile #s

My State Representative

_____

State Representative

_____

Address

_____

City, State Zip

_____

Telephone and Facsimile #s

My Governor's Council Representaive

_____
Governor's Council Representative

_____
Address

_____
City, State Zip

_____
Telephone and Facsimile #s

My State Attorney General

_____
State Attorney General

_____
Address

_____
City, State Zip

_____
Telephone and Facsimile #s

My Secretary of State

_____
Secretary of State

_____
Address

_____
City, State Zip

_____
Telephone and Facsimile #s

My State Treasurer

_____
State Treasurer

_____
Address

_____
City, State Zip

_____
Telephone and Facsimile #s

MY LOCAL REPRESENTATIVES

My City or Town Representatives

_____
Mayor or Chairperson   Local Rep #2

_____
Local Rep #3   Local Rep #4

_____
Local Rep #5   Local Rep #6

_____
Local Rep #7   Local Rep #8

_____
City or Town Hall Address

_____
City, State Zip

_____
Telephone and Facsimile #s

The Chief of Police

_____
Police Chief or Commissioner

_____
Address

_____
City, State Zip

_____
Telephone and Facsimile #s

The Fire Chief

_____
Fire Chief or Commissioner

_____
Address

_____
City, State Zip

_____
Telephone and Facsimile #s

MY LOCAL REPRESENTATIVES

My County Representatives

_____
Chairperson   County Rep #2

_____
County Rep #3   County Rep #4

_____
County Rep #5   County Rep #6

_____
County Rep #7   County Rep #8

_____
County Board of Commissioner's Address

_____
City, State Zip

_____
Telephone and Facsimile #s

School Board

_____
School Board Representatives

_____
Address

_____
City, State Zip

_____
Telephone and Facsimile #s

Postmaster

_____
Postmaster

_____
Address

_____
City, State Zip

_____
Telephone and Facsimile #s

INDEX

(bold page numbers indicate glossary definitions)

INDEX

(bold page numbers indicate glossary definitions)